# THE END
## OF
# MANHOOD

*Parables on Sex and Selfhood*

Revised Edition

# JOHN STOLTENBERG

London

First published 1993 as *The End of Manhood: A Book for Men of Conscience*
by Dutton, an imprint of New American Library

Revised edition published 2000 in the UK and the USA
by UCL Press
11 New Fetter Lane, London EC4P 4EE

The name of University College London (UCL) is a registered trade mark
used by UCL Press with the consent of the owner.

*UCL Press is an imprint of the Taylor & Francis Group*

© 1993, 2000 John Stoltenberg

The right of John Stoltenberg to be identified as the Author of this Work has
been asserted by him in accordance with the Copyright, Designs, and Patents
Act 1988

Typeset in Palatino
Printed and bound in Great Britain by
Biddles Ltd, Guildford and King's Lynn

*British Library Cataloguing in Publication Data*
A catalogue record for this book is available from the British Library

*Library of Congress Cataloging in Publication Data*
Stoltenberg, John.
The end of manhood : parables on sex and selfhood / John Stoltenberg — Rev. ed.
    p.    cm.
    1. Men—Psychology. 2. Masculinity (Psychology) 3. Feminism.
4. Sex role. I. Title
HQ1090.S76 1999
155.6′32—dc20                                                     99-1306

STET   1 85728 324 4
ISBN 1-85728-324-4 (hbk) ✓
ISBN 1-85728-325-2 (pbk)

# THE END OF MANHOOD

In this practical follow-up to *Refusing to Be a Man*, John Stoltenberg speaks to men—so that women can overhear—about how the social construction of manhood operates in ordinary relationships. Using a variety of stories and illustrations, he makes everyday sense of interpersonal conflicts and internal dilemmas that distress men's lives, and he shows how the same dynamics drive the behavior of gangs, race-hate groups, and other warring male factions. Readers will find here new perspectives on intimacy, gender, and violence and be pushed to re-examine their ideas of manhood and gender identity generally. Stoltenberg's new introduction sets the book in academic context, summarizing the game theory of gender that underlies his work.

**John Stoltenberg** is the radical feminist author of *Refusing to Be a Man: Essay on Sex and Justice* (rev. edn, London and New York: UCL Press, 2000) and *What Makes Pornography "Sexy"?* (Minneapolis, Minnesota: Milkweed Editions, 1994). He is cofounder of Men Against Pornography.

For Andrea,
who means courage

THE CORE OF ONE'S BEING
MUST LOVE JUSTICE MORE THAN MANHOOD.
—*Refusing to Be a Man*

# DISCONTENTS

# INTRODUCTION
# TO THE REVISED EDITION

Gender theory in the academy is sometimes like a private joke: You can "get it" if you are in on the jargon; but if you are not, you can't. Gender theory is rarely simply *told*. More often it is willfully obfuscated, propounded in sentences so packed with self-referential abstraction that they seem never to be *about* anything. Academic gender theory's relationship to people's real lives can seem as tenuous as its hold on recognizable human speech.

I do not believe this must be. I believe that a radical investigation of gender—a look at it by its roots—can be done with everyday language about everyday experience. This method not only makes more sense, it also more accurately reflects our social reality. We all first learned to find a suitable niche inside the gender system through narratives of real life: stories and dramas in which we were shown our part and how to play it. This learning was interactive, for as we played our part well or poorly, we were made ever more mindful of what bad things can happen to us if we do not do better. As we acted in accord with our own designated niche, so also we acted in our dealings with other people in accord with theirs. The prescripts of transactional conduct not only kept everyone who abided by them stationed somewhere in the gender system; these rules also gave the whole system its narrative meaning and force. To step outside the strictures of

gender—to opt out of its demands in confidence, not disgrace—
we do not need esoteric theory, some cerebral mumbo-jumbo, but
we do need to know how to reread those narratives of everyday
life.

At no time in history have so many humans felt such a gaping
discrepancy between the gender system that is given us and the
selves we long to be. At no time in history have so many yearned
for alternatives: ways to truly be oneself, without fear of failing at
fitting into one's gender niche, without being punished, without
being cast into exile. Especially among young people, pressing
new questions about the meaning of gender and one's bodily
experience of it have erupted in classrooms and chatrooms, in
music and poetry, in costume and adornment, in memory and
imagination, in sensation and sexuality. Some fine teachers have
conscientiously responded to students' questing with a host of
new courses, based in feminism, that take a political and historical
look at the lives of women. Such courses have functioned for
many students as an autobiographical correlative, or as a lens
through which to examine their own unease about the gender
setup. Other academicians, starting from the standpoint that gender is socially constructed (something feminists first figured out),
have developed complex new theoretical discourses that promise
if not answers at least rarefied ways of recasting the questions.
You may not ever actually *get* practical answers to whatever first
drew you to the study of gender theory, but by god you'll be
taught ways to ponder the perplexities so that you too can be as
prolix as the professionals who have tilled and fenced the field.
Regrettably, such obscurantism has often displaced feminism's
more concrete critique.

The seekers who flock to the academy today, as much to find
explanatory sanctuary from their gender dilemmas as to enjoy the
company of one another, have a myriad of inward questions—
about erotic desire and desirability; about the size, shape, and
look of their flesh; about their sexual rights and status, in both
intimacy and the body politic; about feeling at odds with a gender
ideal; about feeling one's niche does not fit. Frequently academic
gender theory helps these seekers frame their burning questions
inside "larger" issues with ever more gravity, and occasionally a
seeker finds satisfaction in the cogitation—perhaps even a career
path. But if one's soul or selfhood is parched and thirsty for a

solution to one's private disquiet in the gender setup, such cur-ricular approaches—deriving academic respectability in direct proportion to their opacity—can appear like the mirage of an oasis, promising to slake one's thirst just because they are the only watering hole around.

But academic credibility and radical inquiry are not necessar-ily compatible. Nor, for that matter, are complexity and personally applicable truth.

What I propose in *The End of Manhood* is a personal method-ology for a radical new look at gender. It begins with the notion that gender is an *ethical* construction. This starting point both refines and differs from the understanding, now widely accepted in the academy, that gender is socially constructed. Permit me to explain.

To say that gender is an ethical construction is to say that tracking all the familiar façades of gender as a social construct—so-called sexual identities, sexual orientations, body types, self-presentations or performativities, communication styles, and so forth—cannot disclose the dynamic transactional structure by which gender is constructed, just as a bookshelf full of dictionar-ies in different languages cannot explain what makes a sentence mean. As grammar makes sense of vocabulary, so too there is an underlying syntax that makes the surface markers of gender cohere and make sense. To say that gender is an ethical construc-tion is to say that what fundamentally grounds gender personally and socially as a hierarchical binary is a system of valuing con-duct, a codification of acts, which underpins all the trappings now recognized as gender expression. Once we parse the embedded value system in that conduct—once we learn to read the system-atic ethics that render gender meaningful in human affairs—we can grasp the "genome" of gender, the foundational scripts whereby gender comes to act, look, feel, and seem real.

Many people in the academy who are theorizing gender are conspicuously incurious about the systematic ethics that under-gird gender. Even academics who appear persuaded that gender is socially constructed resist interrogating gender as an ethical phenomenon. I have tried to understand why.

When gender as a late twentieth-century concept began to attract researchers, theorists, and scholars, their first project was to liberate it from ontology—to distinguish what we now know as gender from the panoply of corporeal and anatomical traits that have evolved in our species. Yes, there is metaphysical human matter, the reality of our anatomies, and there presumably always will be so long as *Homo sapiens* walks the earth: our brain pathways, neurological networks, hormones, gonads, genitals, and such. But thanks to an unprecedented inquiry undertaken largely within the academy and generously informed by the life experiences of people who do not neatly fit the categories "man" and "woman" (here I reluctantly use the medical establishment's terminology: intersexes, transsexuals, homosexuals, and so forth), we now know that all our metaphysical stuffness—including the "secondary" characteristics that we bracket off and call "sex," as if one's sex can be severed from, say, one's armpits or earlobes—is only relativistically germane to our epistemology of gender. We may *think* we know someone's gender when we see them— indeed we may at times think we know our own—but we cannot any longer presuppose that gender correlates with metaphysical stuffness in our species in any uniform, absolutist, either/or, one-to-one way. A few controversies continue to swarm around this historically unprecedented observation, typically in fundamentalist religious and partisan quarters, but there is now a credible consensus in academia that categories of "sex" have as little scientific validity as do categories of "race." Put another way: A gender identity and ideology such as "man" has, just like a racial identity and ideology such as "Aryan," no metaphysical foundation. It is a social construction. It gets made up. It is collective make-believe.

If gender is not essentially based in metaphysics because, as the academy generally concedes, it is not essentially any *thing*, what then *is* gender? To a growing extent, especially in such new discourses as postmodernism and its offshoot queer theory, the answer that has attracted the most professorial attention, the most student seekers, and the most book contracts is the notion that gender is, at bottom, an *esthetic* construction. When you come right down to it, according to this thought fashion, gender is merely a matter of putting in an appearance. It is performance. It is signs and signifiers with no intrinsic substance. It is some drag, dress-up, or other camouflage that creates the visual and tactile impression of gender specificity, averts confusion in others, and fends off the discomfort of ambiguity in oneself. It is an art form, a body art, exercised and fed or starved, sculpted by scalpels, adjusted by drugs, and accessorized. It is fantasy, sex object, fetish. It is subversion of the normative, normalization of the subversive. *Naturally* gender is not real, the pomos exclaim. But by god let it be good looking.

Whether at the experimental fringes, where gender expression is play-acting whoever and whatever one wants to be, or at the ground zero of orthodoxy, where conventions of costume and mien impart to each generation the masque of "man and wife," the public and private face of gender is, at first glance, an esthetic. And exactly like beauty—that elusive distillate which classical estheticists eulogized and sought—it is in the eye of the beholder.

To be fair, the notion that gender is fundamentally esthetic is a reasonable inference in an era defined as never before by the camera. The image and the technology-mediated gaze have irrevocably altered our species's epistemology of gender. We all see through viewfinders now; and we are all on view, in someone else's sight. Fewer and fewer people escape self-consciousness about whether they appear adequately gendered, especially in youth. Exposed film stock, videotape, snapshots, half-tone printing, lit-up pixels—these are not only what matters; they *are* the matter that makes *gender* matter; they are the last residue of metaphysical stuffness that reliably encodes and reveals to us the esthetic paradigms "masculinity" and "femininity." In real life, we resemble or conform to these gender standards well or poorly, and we are more or less bothered by our greater or lesser remove from them. But according to the dominant esthetic, now stamped like a diktat across capitalist cultures, representations are *always* better renderings of gender than anyone's flesh-and-blood body can possibly be. Little wonder that today so many academics are pursuing the study of gender as an esthetic construction. And little wonder that so many young seekers, ill-at-ease with both the gender schema and their own morphology in it, are also enthralled by that pursuit. They grew up, after all, bombarded by idealized images of gender that at some level they all know and fear will never be reflected back to them when they stand naked before a mirror.

The investigation into the *ethics* that construct gender is a far less popular and placating pursuit. Partly, I suspect, this is because doing so would seem dead-ended and dispiriting rather than enlightening, fun, and useful. Certainly, once one begins to look at the values in the conduct by which gender is constructed, inescapable questions of politics and power arise, and in mainstream culture, where male supremacy is god (and vice versa), such questions are unwelcome. Political inquiries are fine so long as they are about governments, nations, wars, trade, elections, and such, goes the Zeitgeist, but political inquiry into the gender system—into what really happens to women in it, for instance—is an unpleasantness to avoid thinking about and a discourse to be discouraged. Especially in the academy, where radical feminism is to career as the pox is to complexion, there is little institutional incentive to interrogate the moral values in conduct as it reifies gender—behavior that is recognizable as, say, "acting like a man." Wide-ranging analysis of gender as an ethical construction would require a sort of academic freedom that almost nowhere exists: an intellectual climate in which when the subject is gender there are not penalties for speaking the truth to power, and where a cohort of thinkers have not been cowed into changing the subject. Ethics is necessarily about acts and consequences—what happens to whom is one way of knowing what the values in any act are. But there seems now a consensus in the academy, perhaps because so much is already known tacitly about the consequences of gendering behavior, that on this perturbing topic no more shall be known.

Approaching gender as appearance rather than act, a matter of esthetics rather than ethics, therefore has academic appeal. But it also avoids understanding how conduct lends force to the gendered meaning of appearance. Our reverence for, or attraction to, various gender-coding images is not what is transmitted through media. The images and representations travel that way, but not how we feel about them, not how they make us feel, and not what they mean to us viscerally. Such subjective significances—perhaps as variant from person to person as our signature irises—arose historically, biographically, interactionally, narratively. The meanings and feelings that the esthetics of gender have for us are among the consequences of actions that are done to us and actions that we do to others.

My approach to gender theory in *The End of Manhood* identifies and demonstrates one particular transactional dynamic that is central to understanding and experiencing how gender is socially constructed. I imagine other such dynamics are likely to be discovered, other ways by which a specific ethics, recognizable in a variety of acts, makes the binary gender schema seem real. But because the ethical dynamic I explore here has what seems to me an extraordinary explanatory reach—from everyday domestic disputes to racial animosities to international power plays—I suspect it would be helpful to explain a few things about my method first.

The book is written very simply, about everyday life; the gender theory is embedded, unannounced. As I wrote each successive chapter, as if staging scenes in a gathering drama, I accumulated a list of words that I forbade myself to use: "patriarchy," "male dominance," and "sexism," for example. Any time I was tempted to fall back on such an abstraction, I tried to say what I meant in a more immediate and graphic way: a story, a fable, a diagram, a rhyme. I considered no literary genre off limits (except academ-ese), because though ethics by definition is about human inter-action, *perceiving* ethics is never a linear mental event. A mental picture of the ethics in interaction occurs to us as we attend to something that happens. It is recognizable in acts, but it is more than a matter of assessing a particular act as "right" or "wrong" or "good" or "bad." Instead, because the same act can be right/good in one ethical system and wrong/bad in another, perceiving ethics involves a metaquestion: "Right or wrong, good or bad, according to *which* ethics, according to *which* system of valuing conduct?" An act that transgresses one ethics can be the apotheosis of another. And an act that is completely congruous within one sys-tem of valuing conduct can be an outrage outside it. In order to contemplate in this sense the ethics of acts, including our own, we need first to perceive other people in action—as if we were specta-tors in the "seeing place" that was the ancient Greek theater. We need to attend to other actors, what they do, and what their doing does. Next we need to perceive ourselves in our own narratives. We need to attend to our acts from that inner point of view we first adopted as spectators to interhuman interaction. To communicate a theory of gender as an ethical construction, therefore, I chose a method that is dramatic (rather than, say, linear, argumentative, or documentary), because I believe it is the method that most closely resembles the way in which we learn of ethics in life.

The book is written in a form that is both modeled on and a send-up of a "self-help book," and its gender theory proceeds by problematizing "manhood." I wrote aware that this apparently "single-sex" tactic flies in the face of certain conventional wisdom, according to which the meaning of gender may be found, on the one hand, in the social construction of "men" and, equivalently on the other, in the social construction of "women"—as if the gender binary were a two-party government or bicameral parliament. I do not believe that this bifurcated and purportedly parallel form of inquiry accurately gets at the ways that gender is constructed ethically, for it evades the values in the conduct by which the meaning of manhood overdetermines whatever meaning people—women primarily but also many with male anatomy—have in a host of subordinate categories and classes. The construction of manhood as an identity, as I show, results from a particular transactional dynamic: one that requires *proving* manhood according to a distinctive ethic. Among the consequences of that ethic is the social construction of the identity "woman" as well as other categories indexed by genetic traits, creed, strength and size, and such. Put another way, the ethics undergirding the social proof of manhood produces the identities of "men" and "women" both. Further, the exact same ethics that produces the paradigmatic identities "man"/"woman" produces the identities "white"/"colored," "normal"/"homo," "Aryan"/"kike," "healthy"/"crip," and so on.

What distinguishes the ethics that constructs manhood is a particular if/then drama, a sort of game theory, which I reiterate, examine, and apply throughout *The End of Manhood*. For anyone raised "to be a man," the rules of the game go like this: *If* someone impugns or threatens your manhood and challenges you to prove it, *then* you have two choices: (1) to rise to the challenge or (2) not to (an option that necessarily risks confirming the challenger's imputation that your manhood is absent or defective). *If* you choose to rise to the challenge, *then* there are (apparently) two possible outcomes: either (1) you will prove your manhood is greater (by some act that disparages/dominates/damages your challenger) or (2) your manhood will be proved lesser (by dint of your having been disparaged/dominated/damaged in some conflict or combat from which the challenger emerges victorious, however scathed). Note that this is a familiar, recognizable, and

coherent system of ethics in which the set of acts that prove manhood is valorized and the set of acts that concede inferiority of
manhood is deplored. Within this behavioral code (which all
combatants for manhood necessarily subscribe to) and within the
context of a manhood contest (which all aspirants to manhood
must episodically engage in), any act that disparages/
dominates/damages someone else is "good" and "right" (meaning: "utilitarian, warranted, justifiable"). There are no exceptions,
no nettlesome gray areas, for this ethics is rigorous, internally
consistent, and evident throughout so-called civilization. Note
also that this gender ethics bears a striking resemblance to the
code by which male mammals of many other species vie for rut
rights—think rams battering and stags cracking antlers in the
woods.

To my surprise, in writing *The End of Manhood* I chanced upon
what may be a human evolution of the mammalian code by which
male dominance is acted out literally and seasonally—a distinctly
human elaboration of it. What I discovered is that in the human
species there is actually a *third* possible outcome to a male-
dominance contest, an option lower mammals rarely employ. It
goes like this: *If* one party challenges another to prove "manhood," *then* both challenger and challengee have the option of
engaging *together* in an act that proves their manhood mutually.
They may gang up to *jointly* disparage/dominate/damage *some
third party*; someone over and against whom they can collabora-
tively demonstrate the superiority of their manhood; someone,
for instance, anatomically female. In the human species, the systematic ethics of manhood-proving not only permits conduct
pursuant to this third option; this ethics fosters it.

How did this species-specific systematic ethics arise among
our forebears? The question is impossible to answer, of course, but
an intriguing hypothesis presents itself. In evolutionary biology
and paleoanthropology, it is an uncontroversial given that the
absence of estrus is among the features that distinguish our
mammalian species. But unlike other humanoid traits that can be
explained as evolutionary variations on a higher-primate theme
(large brain size, upright gait on two feet, and such), our species's
peculiar lack of estrus is a puzzler. Among other mammals,
females have zero tolerance for copulation except at particular,
cyclical times, when they physically advertise that they are

ovulating, and males are notably hardwired to know what time
that is and isn't. No such biorhythm organizes *Homo sapiens'* etiquette of penetrative sex—our species, basically, does not have
one. During a female's fertile years, there is approximately a time
of the month when conception can occur, but it neither tracks nor
trumpets the time for fucking. Some scientists speculate that
humanoid females once had an ovulatory signal but lost it over
time. Others believe the reverse: that primates' ancestors grad-
ually developed such a signal but that prehumans never had one.
No tissue remains to tell the tale. The only hard evidence is bones,
and they demonstrate that way back in humans' lineage, sexual
dimorphism was extreme: females then were less than two thirds
as large as males (whereas today, females and males are, on average, much closer in size). Moreover, the cranium was relatively
puny. Over eons, as the human brain ballooned, the female pelvis
became too small to give birth to the size of skull required for it
(which is why babies today are born with unfinished brains—it is
our evolutionary tradeoff for bipedalism). But back then, judging
from skeletal sources, hominid infants exited the womb far more
prepared to perambulate, which means that their period of
postnatal dependency was much shorter than now (hence, presumably, mamas did not need papas past the point of conception). The strong implication, by analogy to the behavior of
primates who are our near relatives, is that in those days there
was male–male battle, literal and bloody, for coital access to
females.

In contemplating the systematic ethics of manhood-proving as
identified and articulated in *The End of Manhood,* I thought to trace
it backward to the beginning of perceptibly human life. Speculat-
ing rather wildly, I admit, I guessed that the absence of estrus in
the human species, in evolutionary terms, made male–male combat for rut rights an enormous waste of energy—for if the coveted
window of opportunity for copulation can be opened all year
round, males had more need of unlocking *it* than of locking horns
with one another. Following upon that speculation came
another—that ganging up to perform penile, penetrative sex with
females held for males a classic sociobiological advantage: When
prehumans roamed the mists of prehistory, before there was
group living or tribal life, bonding together to fuck females not
only *increased* males' odds of getting their genes into progeny

(which, according to evolutionary biologists, is the big bingo) but—much more to the point—*decreased* their risk of being injured, perhaps mortally, by other perfervid males. From these *ad hoc* male alliances could well have emerged marauding packs, and the status that then obtained *among* members of the pack could have become, over time, that which was at stake whenever challenged by any *other* pack—fertile males who were also in solidarity over and against females in order to avert bloodshed among themselves. In an early flash of human intelligence, it could have dawned on the roving males that what worked so efficaciously with females (ganging together to inseminate) worked resourcefully against rival packs (ganging together to terminate); well enough, at any rate, to inspire (at least among survivors of such run-ins) the drama called war. This bellicose saga must have unfolded on the very cusp between primate and human, prior to the invention of the distinctly human concept of ownership of land and of other people's bodies, after which it would have become reproductively advantageous not to gang-bang females but to keep them as private chattel, necessitating policies against poaching. There would then have arisen such chiefdoms, patresfamilias, clans, and dynasties as are nowadays familiar to anthropologists and archeologists. But from earliest times, all such social configurations remained modeled on the game theory that is the ethics of the humanoid male bond: Defeat your challenger, be defeated by your challenger, or team up to disparage/dominate/damage some third party. According to this unpretty but plausible hypothesis, the cradle of civilization was gang rape.

Such speculation about our social origins—alluringly alluding to our material stuffness, including our species's reproductive anatomy (the very metaphysical fallacy that has now convincingly been exposed by those who recognize gender as a social construction) cannot by itself help us understand, solve, or evolve out of our contemporary gender dilemma. If ever this male-bonding based system of manhood-proving had a material foundation, that time was long, long ago. The system has persisted beyond the circumstances in which it arose. Today, as I dramatize in *The End of Manhood*, this male-bonding system of ethics is being driven by a historically unprecedented gender panic, the inward anxiety felt by more and more persons around the globe that one may not be fitting into one's specified gender niche convincingly—the achingly unanswerable question, for instance, "What is a real man?" (Not incidentally, this burgeoning gender anxiety is also driving a thriving consumer market in goods and services that promise the impression of authentic genderedness— the metaphysical fallacy again, now retooled for profit.) As belief in the material foundations of manhood withers, as more and more discern that manhood is a mirage and "there's no *there* there," focus has understandably shifted to the esthetics that mark out masculine and feminine, lest manhood evaporate or perish. The trouble is, the esthetics of gender do not go very far as evidentiary proof. They are not, as lawyers like to say, dispositive. Putting on the proper attire, crossing one's legs a certain way, assuming a gender-specific affect, owning a particular automobile or sound system—all such grooming tips and buying guides, no matter how rigorously one obeys them, cannot convincingly prove one has one gender not some other. Clothes do not make the man. The ethics of acts do: the cult of the pack and its behavioral code.

*The End of Manhood* is premised on the belief that that code must now be abandoned for the sake of our species's survival, and that to that end, there is enormous practical value in unencrypting the system of ethics by which human males are yet conditioned to try to resolve an irresolvable gender panic. "Conditioning," although among the words I assiduously avoided in writing this book, is a key concept here, as it is more generally in gender studies, where social learning is emphasized as much as, or more than, humans' biological heritage. But because *The End of Manhood* looks at gender as an ethical construction, it connects "nature" and "nurture" in a brand-new way: It offers a physically graphic explanation of how the ethics of manhood-proving become sensorially resonant in a human body born male. Through narrative example, it shows how that code can biographically be inscribed on the eroticism of an anatomically male body, such that sexual sensation and this system of ethics can seem virtually indistinguishable. Step by step, *The End of Manhood* viscerally sorts out the ethics of manhood from the ethics of self-hood, so that subjective sexual feelings need not be bound to domination.

The game theory of the proof of manhood, seen as a transaction with a distinctive ethics in which right/good and wrong/bad share a uniform utility, does several things that other theories of gender do not. It presents a unified way of interpreting what happens to anyone who has ever been disparaged/dominated/damaged—which is very probably everyone. Other ways of approaching gender tend, by bifurcating the classes "men" and "women," to explain what "men" do to "men" or what "men" do to "women" (and sometimes what "women" do to "men" and what "women" do to "women") as if these notions of gender specificity were metaphysically separable spheres and as if whatever "oppressions" happen to "women," on the one hand, or to some "men," on the other, are somehow contrastable because the spheres are ultimately divisible. While acknowledging that the spheres "men" and "women" bear some relationship, such liberal approaches cannot positively identify what that relationship actually is.

The radical approach to gender employed in *The End of Manhood* demonstrates dynamically and transactionally how whatever "men" do to "women" is intrinsically related to what "men" do to "men," and vice versa; it forges a tangible and verifiable structural link. It reveals in everyday detail how and why, for instance, men's violence against women is inextricably located in and driven by men's violence against other men. It shows why almost no one escapes the ravages of the ethics of manhood-proving. It makes such questions as "Which sex is more powerless?" moot. But, most important, this radical approach to gender opens space for dissidents—conscientious objectors to a hegemonic, anachronistic ethics—in a way that would be utterly inconceivable under rubrics of gender as an esthetic construction or as a metaphysical artifact. *The End of Manhood* calls that oppositional space "selfhood." My book *Refusing to Be a Man,*\* the philosophical precursor and companion volume to *The End of Manhood*, calls that space "moral identity." Various philosophical and spiritual traditions have called that space the "self," the "person," the "soul," and such. The notion of that space is not new. The longing to inhabit it confidently and fully is among the deepest cravings of our age. But as *The End of Manhood* helps readers realize, through

---

\* *Refusing to Be a Man: Essays on Sex and Justice* (revised edition, London and New York: UCL Press, 2000).

narrative details of daily life, conformity to the myth of gender binarism—in particular to the mandates of manhood—is inevitably an impediment to one's sure stance in that space. Anxiety about whether one conforms esthetically or metaphysically to the mythology of gender binarism has no esthetic or metaphysical resolution. Only in acts with consequences to others is manhood made flesh, and so long as manhood is believed to be worth proving, and the game worth playing, the code of the pack will determine who wins and who loses.

The question "Who am I?" has taken on a perplexing new edge: It has now been hijacked and transformed into the question "What is my gender?" For those, for instance, who have been raised "to be a man," the identity question "Who am I?" cannot sensibly be broached without insistent whispers in the next breath: "Am I man enough?" "Is my manhood real?" "Do I seem like a real man to you?" The identity question and gender anxiety have become twinned, sutured together; where one goes, the other follows. Even as gender has lost its material moorings, we cling to it lest we drown; we fear we will be no one if we do not stand surely to one side of a demarcation that has all the permanence of a line etched in sand already damp from surf.

The theory of gender as an ethical construction is writ small and large. It illuminates transactions between parents and children, among lovers and friends; it exposes the commonality in what happens whenever any agglomeration contests manhood—for instance gay-bashing gangs and race-hate groups; it applies also nation to nation, to affairs of state, to any time, any assemblage—in a pact together, having mutually disparaged/dominated/damaged others—jockeys for power over any other assemblage. But most pragmatically, this theory of gender makes sense not only in the head. It translates easily to real life.

I wrote in hope that one could reread the narratives of one's life in terms of the ancient ethics of manhood-proving (as I did myself while writing) and thereby see one's way toward living by a different ethics entirely (as I myself continue to try to do). *The End of Manhood*'s vision of the ethics of selfhood ("loving justice") is by no means original; the language used to speak of it is, but the humane aspiration expressed has been around a long time ("Love your neighbor as yourself," "I–Thou," and more). The moral breakthrough here, if there is one, is a demonstration that gender stands in the way of humanity's insistent longing for sharable and safe space. We are social creatures, after all. But we are yet on the brink of knowing how to be together. May this book help.

John Stoltenberg
Brooklyn, New York
October 1998

# PROLOG

*The Strange Case of Dr Jekyll and Mr Hyde* is often invoked, in everyday chat, to explain why men suddenly seem to change personalities. This eerie nineteenth-century tale has crossed over from literature into life, becoming an apt metaphor for men's apparent switch of behavioral identities—as if mysteriously—from one moment to the next.

Robert Louis Stevenson wrote the story—about a man "committed to a profound duplicity of life"—in 1885, when he was thirty-five. In it, Dr. Henry Jekyll, an upstanding physician in Victorian England, becomes from time to time a deformed, sadistic murderer, Edward Hyde. The doctor concocts a bubbly potion that at first reverts him to his more humane self. But eventually the drug's effectiveness wanes, and Hyde, the horrific double, claims Jekyll more and more of the time. In an anguished letter composed while "losing hold of my original and better self, and becoming slowly incorporated with my second and worse," Dr. Jekyll tries to comprehend this terrifying split, "this incoherency of my life": "Both sides of me were in dead earnest; I was no more myself when I laid aside restraint and plunged in shame; I was no more myself when I laboured, in the eye of day, at the furtherance of knowledge or the relief of sorrow and suffering." Applying his full intellect and moral intelligence, he attempts to grasp the meaning of his dilemma the only way he knows how: "I thus drew steadily nearer to that truth by whose partial discovery I have been doomed to such a dreadful shipwreck: that man is not truly one, but truly two. I say two, because the state of my own knowledge does not pass beyond that point."

This explanation rings somewhat hollow today, even though Dr. Jekyll and Mr. Hyde have become an everyday figure of speech for a man who seems split in two. In more than a century since the story's first publication, its central metaphor seems to have spoken more and more vividly to the sometimes profound contradictions that can be observed in men's behavioral identities. Yet the story's religiously inspired premise—"the duality of man's nature," "good" versus "evil"—no longer accounts for such contradictions sufficiently. Whether we seek a personal understanding from within (because, for instance, we live life *as* such a man) or whether we seek a useful explanation from without (because, for instance, we live *with* such a man) the story of Dr. Jekyll and Mr. Hyde works better as truism than as practical insight. Despite something vaguely recognizable about these now cartoonish alter egos, we cannot learn from them what we need to understand most—and the everyday experience of duplicity in men's behavior still prompts haunting questions without credible answers.

Why, for instance, does an ostensibly "honorable" man do something that betrays? Why does an apparently "honest" man do something deceitful? Why does a generally "kind" man do something that wounds? Why does a reputably "caring" and "decent" man commit an act so steeped in contempt that it is as if someone else had done it, for he himself could not possibly?

Those of us raised to be men must ask such questions of ourselves if we are to be at all honest with ourselves. And all of us must ask such questions about the men we observe and the men we know—perhaps especially the men whom we believe we know most intimately.

Sometimes a man will defend the discordant behavior. Challenged to acknowledge some injury that his act resulted in, he denies any wrongdoing, he recognizes nothing out of character in his doing it, and he may even displace responsibility for the act, laying the blame for it with someone else. This dodge comes as a shock. How can he possibly be so committed to it? Doesn't he experience his displacement of responsibility as a wedge that splits his own self—a wedge that he hammers in further with each and every evasion?

Sometimes, perhaps after a grueling interchange, a man will finally concede that "he wasn't himself," and he may express a perplexed sort of remorse, admitting a deflected sort of responsibility by not comprehending "what came over him." He will acknowledge that the egregious act was "out of character" but profess to have no clue as to what on earth "made him do it." Then, if he can successfully ensnare his challenger's fascination in this moral mystery, he will summon the conundrum the way one might cite a handy escape clause to get out of a contractual obligation: So you see, he'll say, I can't really be held accountable; I didn't really have any idea what I was doing; I certainly didn't intend whatever bad happened; I can't really have done what I didn't really mean—

Just who *is* this "I"?

I myself have been astonished to realize I have done something to someone that I would never "in conscience" do, much less recommend. I have been puzzled, too, as much by my own moral inconsistency as by my quite adroit ways of dodging responsibility for my own behavior. And I have occasionally despaired, as much at the seeming inability of other men to grasp and remember even the simplest issues of interpersonal conscience as at my own demonstrated lapses, my own forgetting to remember.

Why, I have wondered, are "good" men sometimes so completely unreliable morally? Why do we sometimes act as if we have lost our values moorings, lost sight of our beacon convictions, lost hold of our sense of self? What is going on in us? Why do we evidence such wanton behavioral swings—such unpredictable splits in who we are?

Sometimes, if we are honest, it seems as if we too may have exhausted our personal supply of Dr. Jekyll's restorative elixir— and we too are doomed to be overcome by the persona of our own private Hyde. Sometimes, in the torpor that seems always to accompany such introspective musing, such self-involved self-reflection, there seems to be no alternative. Perhaps, we consider, it is in our "nature" after all—as "men"—to be utterly split in two. Perhaps it is a fate peculiar to our "sex": never to be able to truly say "I" with any constancy, with any consistency, with any integrated conviction whatsoever—and therefore never able to address anyone else as "you" with any honesty in our mind or with any continuity in our heart.

✧

This book is written in the firm belief that our humanity—our authentic selfhood—can be honored and understood only through loving justice.

This book's main theme is that all we know and recognize as "manhood"—the personal, behavioral identity that is committed to gender, committed to "being the man there"—cannot possibly coexist with authentic and passionate and integrated selfhood.

This book is thoroughly informed by the radical feminist critique of gender—information that Robert Louis Stevenson could not of course have known but probably the most astute and personally useful set of ideas I have been exposed to in my lifetime.

This book therefore rejects the widespread notion that "manhood" can be somehow revised and redeemed—the contemporary project variously described as "reconstructing," "reinventing," "remythologizing," "revisioning," and re-whatevering gendered personal identity so as to bring its hapless adherents back into the human fold. That project is utterly futile, and we all have to give it up, as this book will carefully explain.

My heretical hope is that as more male human beings understand the fundamental dichotomy between manhood and selfhood—and learn in our everyday relationships to apply the practical lessons of that insight—there will be among us all more and more loving justice, and more and more of us will say "I" and "you" as if we each are equally real.

This book is written for people who believe it really matters right now that some humans raised to be a man learn how to live as men of conscience. Learning how to live as a man of conscience goes beyond one's reading, one's opinions, one's charitable contributions, one's community service, and so forth. Learning to live as a man of conscience is also about the personal, the private—one's full range of choices in everyday relationships—one's decisions about *what to do*, whether major or moment-to-moment.

This book is written as if such a life is possible. And this book is written as if all our lives depend on it.

✧

Justice between people is perhaps the most important connection people can have. Sex too is important. But sex and justice have been ripped apart. In many people's experience, a sharp edge seems to have sliced between the possibility of experiencing our full humanness, including our sexual humanness, and our fundamental need for fairness and complete respect together.

We need fairness and respect as much as we need food, air, shelter. No one is an organism in a void.

For anyone who cares passionately about reconnecting sex and justice in our world, these are difficult times. We live in a world where human sexuality and humane justice hardly ever happen at the same place and the same time. If you have ever experienced them both at once, you have been lucky. Very lucky indeed. When sex and justice are ripped apart, human beings are sometimes hurt so bad they don't even know what hurt them. If an event like that has ever happened to you or to someone you love, you especially know why this book is written in urgency; you especially know firsthand why there need to be people in the world ready now to create loving justice between as many human beings as humanly possible.

*The End of Manhood: Parables on Sex and Selfhood* is the practical sequel to my first book, *Refusing to Be a Man: Essays on Sex and Justice*. The two books are complementary, though they are quite distinct. *Refusing to Be a Man*, which originated as speeches written and delivered between my thirtieth and forty-fifth years, is somewhat more earnest, more about public policy and activism than the personal. *The End of Manhood*, conceived and written between my forty-sixth and forty-eighth years, is explicitly about the interpersonal—what happens between us—and more about issues of sexuality and identity. Whereas *Refusing to Be a Man* is more philosophical, *The End of Manhood* is more informal and experiential. Structured like a sequenced meditation, *The End of Manhood* comprises diverse voices (from erudite to earthy) and types of text (by turns antic and analytic), but always practical, here-and-now. I had fun writing it, and I decided to let the fun show.

But I could not possibly have written *The End of Manhood* before I had worked through the liberation theory that I articulated in *Refusing to Be a Man,* both in terms of its profound implications for my own self-understanding and in terms of its broad political implications for social change and activism. When I decided to write this practical sequel to *Refusing to Be a Man,* I found its beginning in a single sentence from that book, now the epigraph to this one: "The core of one's being must love justice more than manhood." In those words I found the genesis of this book's passion and also a kind of koan—an encrypted, enigmatic message—the full meaning of which I could only realize in my own life through the writing of this book. Writing *The End of Manhood* thus became a deliberate personal and political choice to apply the liberation theory articulated in *Refusing* in everyday human interaction—to apprehend what we mean when we think and say "I," and what we mean when we regard one another as "you." I am a different "I" for having written it. I hope some similar transformation awaits those who read it.

---

**lov·ing jus·tice** (*luhv*-ing *juhs*-tiss) *n.* **1.** An act of intense desire for, and attraction toward, fairness. **2.** That quality of fairness which exhibits love as well: *As a society of sovereign selves, we desperately need loving justice.* **—Idioms. to love (someone) justly.** *v.* To have an intense emotional attachment to someone's human selfhood, such that fairness never disappears. **to love justice.** *v.* To have an intense emotional attachment to the principle of fairness between human selves: *For any precious one of us to become fully human, some of us must learn to love justice more than we love manhood.*

# AN AUTHOR'S NOTE
# TO WOMEN READERS

This book is written to men—but so that women can overhear every word.

Throughout the book I address readers as "you"—meaning someone raised to be a man, not to be a woman. I talk directly to such readers who may have already tried very hard to embody abstract manhood, zealously believing that the ideal *can* be embodied, inwardly fearful that *not* to seem a real-enough man is to risk being deemed a worthless nobody. I offer practical and personal advice about how to become one's own best self. And I explain the ethical essence of "manhood": whenever any human tries to act like a real-enough man, his action must have negating consequences for someone else or the act does not work.

I intend this book to be of use to everyone who has ever experienced such consequences, which is, of course, nearly everybody. Therefore I hope very much that this book will be read and evaluated by women.

There is much information here that may interest a woman who is (or would like to be) in a relationship with a "man of conscience"—whether he is her son, her brother, her father, her friend or lover. I talk about what you can tell about a man by how he apologizes (Chapter Two), how he pays attention to children (Chapter Six), how he makes love (Chapters Twelve and

Nineteen), and why other men may seem more important to the man you love than you are (Chapter Five). I explain the secret social truces among men that cannot occur unless someone female or less manly is put down (Chapter One).

Growing up to be a real-enough man means having a lifelong problem with the manhood standard, as this book plainly acknowledges. And this book explains *what men can do about it.* Nowhere in this book do I try to explain or interpret "womanhood," or what it means to be raised to be a woman; many fine feminist books already do that. Nor do I say anything about what women should or should not do. Unlike many other books and articles that counsel a woman how to mend what's broken between herself and a man in her life, this book says unequivocally that you cannot fix it. You cannot change him—*he* has to change *himself.* The choice to live as a "man of conscience" is always his, in each moment, every day.

I must alert you that some parts of *The End of Manhood* may not be as relevant or recognizable to you as they could be to a reader whose life history has been as a man. This book is written to men in terms that will be emotionally familiar; therefore many references are specific to the culture that only exists whenever seekers after manhood meet or compete. This social zone intimidates *many* humans, whether they appear to qualify in it as "real men" or not. This book discloses many things within this separate sphere that men are never really encouraged to understand—and that women are not supposed to know about at all.

# ✧ 1 ✧

## HOW CAN I BE LESS AFRAID
## OF OTHER MEN?

All humans who grow up to be a man are raised to pass tests of loyalty to manhood. These tests can be routine ones; these tests can be episodically treacherous. However great or small, these tests have one thing in common: they cancel out some loyalty to selfhood that the human being might have felt before.

This may have happened to you in one of the most common tests of your loyalty: when you are confronted by another man who intimidates or scares you.

In the moment of the confrontation—when another man's threat rears up, when his opportunity to hurt or humiliate you becomes clear to you both—no amount of mental or physical preparedness seems to prevent your falling for the test and somehow attempting to prove your loyalty to manhood. Naturally you wish to save your neck. But more important, you wish to pass the test of your loyalty to manhood, which another man may have impugned. At the flash point of confrontation, it is unlikely that your mind has time to reflect on the fact that this test of your loyalty to manhood also tests your *dis*loyalty to selfhood. But consider these next ten points—and consider them as if you are but a heartbeat away from some escalation in such a confrontation. Perhaps you will find yourself recalling an event from your life, a specific moment in which you were faced with another man's anger and potential to hurt you.

## Ten Things to Remember When You're Faced With Another Man Who Intimidates or Scares You

**1.** You learned to fear other men very early, when you were a child. So did he. You both had to figure out how to be more threatening than threatened.

**2.** What you are getting from him now—in this edgy encounter—is how he's acting like a man so you won't suspect it's all just an act for him.

**3.** One of the main reasons you're frightened is that his behavior makes you feel he suspects that you haven't got your manhood act together as well as he has.

**4.** He seems to be testing you, challenging you, passing a judgment on your manhood. He wants *you* to be afraid of *his* manhood because then *he* won't have to be afraid of *yours*.

**5.** Though he is trying not to be afraid of *your* manhood, he is trying to stop feeling another fear as well: his fear you'll find out that he's just acting at manhood himself.

**6.** He is trying to confuse you into thinking that he *is* his manhood act. He does not want you to suspect he isn't who he seems.

**7.** You do not want him to suspect that you are not who you seem either. You may in fact be afraid or ashamed that your manhood act is inadequate, or even bogus, especially compared with his.

**8.** He can succeed at making you think that he *is* his manhood act only if you believe that you can be yours too.

**9.** For him to succeed, it doesn't really matter whether he is better at his manhood act than you. It only really matters whether you both agree that the manhood act is important—and whether you both believe that if you don't have a convincing manhood act, you don't have a life.

**10.** If, however, you personally don't believe that the manhood act is important at all—if you don't pretend to *be* yours, if you don't pretend to be *synonymous* with your manhood act, and if in fact you honestly don't *care* how he or anyone else judges your manhood act because your manhood act is nowhere near who you are or would like to be—then you are in a position of inner strength. You already know this game is not worth playing. You already know you have a life—an authentic selfhood—that is not your manhood act. So you cannot be so easily frightened by someone else's.

No one growing up to be a man gets taught how to think that fast—or with that much self-possession—in such a confrontation. No one growing up to be a man learns to read and comprehend what's going on in terms that will help stabilize oneself, center oneself, remind oneself completely that one can remain loyal to human selfhood—one does not *have* to fall for such intimidating tests of manhood. Quite the contrary, almost everyone growing up to be a man learns to respond to such loyalty tests as if by "reflex"—spontaneously, "involuntarily," without thinking at all. And what happens next? Generally, someone challenged to pass the test of loyalty to manhood tries to do so by acting like a man in response. Immediately, that's when actual human reflexes mix in with the manhood act, and the combination is potent: it can lead to certain combustion.

## Three Things That Usually Happen If, When You Feel Threatened by Another Man, You Act Like a Man Back

1. Your fight-or-flight reflex kicks in. You breathe hard, your heart pounds, your muscles clench, your eyes glare. Your body comes equipped with many involuntary ways of responding to fear, hazard, and peril—and these are all quite useful in situations where you have to defend your life or someone else's. These reflexes are built in for human survival. But defending your gender is not the same thing as having to defend your life—and just because he thinks it's the same doesn't mean you have to. Humans raised to be a man learn to perceive another man's fight-or-flight reflex as if it's his manhood act—because this involuntary reflex ap-

parently boosts anger to a "more manly" dimension, and it quickly intensifies threatening gestures and inflections and facial expressions. You have probably learned to interpret the conspicuous signs of this reflex as a warning: DANGEROUS MANHOOD ACT IN OPERATION. You may not have learned to interpret the effects of this reflex as indicating that someone is defending his gender as if it's his life. You may not have learned to sort out *your own* reflex reactions in this regard. The more you do, the more adept you'll be in reading other men's.

**2.** Once both humans' fight-or-flight reflexes have kicked in, and once both of you take this challenge to your manhood seriously, the confrontation becomes a contest. Once you disclose that you are willing to defend your gender as if it's your life, then you are ineluctably locked in a kind of combat and predictably . . .

**3.** It escalates, in one way or another, to one degree or another: shouting and gesticulating, insults and humiliations, swearing and threats, maybe shoving and hitting, maybe knives and guns, maybe missiles and warheads. It's a sliding scale. And a very slippery slope.

There are two kinds of reflexes going on here: one that really is instinctive—the reflexes of our autonomic nervous system—and one that we had to learn—our "gender defender" behavior. They are not the same reflexes, though they may sometimes feel alike because they seem to kick in simultaneously. But they're actually quite different and they can be sorted out. The inborn reflexes cannot be modified. The learned ones—fortunately—can be.

Sorting out the difference between these inborn reflexes and these learned reflexes begins with sorting out the dramatic structure of a typical confrontation when one feels that one's gender is being endangered (as distinct from one's human life). For instance, there is a classic dramatic plot line that occurs virtually every time two humans raised to be a man—flush with fight-or-flight fury—decide to lock horns, go *mano a mano*, "step outside," or do whatnot in order to pass the manhood test. The plot is so familiar, it would be utterly boring if not for the emotional investment so many men have in it—and if not for the high stakes for various offstage human beings whose fate may hang on the outcome of the duel at downstage center. This is how the drama goes when you're a featured player in it:

## The Three (and Only Three) Possible Resolutions When You and Another Man Are in Combat Defending the Manhood Act

**1. You lose.** He manages to humiliate you or he manages to hurt you in such a way that he comes off more manly.

**2. He loses.** You manage to humiliate or hurt him in such a way that he will have learned not to mess with you.

**3. You both agree to put down or pick on someone else.** You end up in a truce, a tacit treaty that must have a third party—someone you both agree has a relatively inferior manhood act or someone who is simply female. With (and only with) that third party for contrast, you both become comfortable enough to concede that your mutual manhood acts pass muster.

The sellout of selfhood begins exactly here, in this truce, this pact between men trying to prove to each other that they are loyal to manhood. Once this agreement is struck—once someone offstage has been betrayed or disparaged in order that the curtain will ring down on two former combatants taking a bow arm in arm—something has drastically altered in the character of each human who played out the manhood act in order to convince another player. Once the would-be duel becomes this particular deal—once this gender bond between "men" is forged at the expense of someone else who is "less manly"—each human's loyalty to selfhood has been abandoned, for the sake of loyalty to manhood. Therein lies an age-old and everyday tragedy. It is the story we must find the courage to rewrite with our lives.

## Why Does the Manhood Act Exist, Anyway?

Some random speculations (maybe true, maybe false) about the origin of the specious—the manhood act we fear:

- ❑ Maybe there was a time when the manhood act had evolutionary and survival validity.
- ❑ Maybe there was a time when the manhood act served to make male *Homo sapiens* willing to be suicidally dispensable and go to war in defense of the tribe.
- ❑ Maybe there was a time when the manhood act served to dupe males into taking idiotic risks in order to hunt down vicious beasts for food.
- ❑ Maybe there was a time when the manhood act was driven by DNA, so as to get spermatozoa to as many ova as possible, so as to keep everyone fruitful, lest there not be enough fucks and therefore not enough folks.
- ❑ Maybe there was a time when only mothers ruled; therefore they favored their daughters, the future mothers; and so petulant sons rose up in revolt, becoming predatory fathers.
- ❑ Maybe there was a time when the manhood act got divine authorization, through made-up rituals and mysteries (kept in the custody of certain males who were not themselves especially good at the manhood act but who were clever enough to protect themselves by clothing themselves in priesthood or shamanism and mouthing myths for the gullible of manhood's grandeur and wrath).
- ❑ Maybe there was a time when the manhood act just felt good—like a high, like an adrenaline rush—at least until you got killed at it, and then you didn't feel anything, so what the heck.

Whenever that time was—if ever that time was—it certainly is not now. The manhood act has become obsolescent. The manhood act has become an impediment to human harmony—perhaps even hazardous to our species' health. The more seriously anyone takes the manhood act, the more dangerous it becomes. Yet we cling to it still.

Sometimes, if you look really, really closely at a human raised to be a man, you can detect quick glimpses of an actual human being behind his manhood act. Now and then, in instants, you can sometimes recognize when someone inside a manhood act lets it drop, or lets it slip, or quivers or blinks or shivers or tears up because the mask doesn't fit and the pose is quite impossible. You see it mostly in boy children, when they are being scared out of their wits into wearing the mask of manhood. Then, as such traumatized children grow into tense young men, you tend to see it less and less, and sometimes one will go years or decades without letting you see so much as a peek, and then sometimes his human-beingness peeps through again only when he is old or seriously ill or facing death. Sometimes love lets his human-beingness show through, intermittently, until it flees for refuge behind the mask of manhood. As a deer caught in speeding headlights freezes in stark terror, the human being behind a manhood act cannot withstand a knowing and caring gaze for long.

Sometimes a human raised to be a man never risks perceiving the human being behind another's manhood act. It seems to take too much courage to let your own human-beingness show through. This becomes another agreement between men—not to relate to one another's selfhood, not to relate from one's own—but only from behind a precarious mask of masculinity.

Sometimes it's very hard to tell whether there's a human being left inside at all.

### Ten Ways You Can Fake It If You Fear Your Manhood Act Is Shaky

Believe in a very butch god.
Start a war.
Rape someone.
Lynch or gas someone.
Force someone to have a baby.
Whack off to a picture of someone being hurt.
Whack off inside someone you're hurting.
Hit or have sex with a child.

Leave a mess.
Laugh at a guy's joke.

Everyone raised to be a man fears his manhood act is shaky at some time or another. We "bargain" with that fear; we promise not to do awful things to fake it—things you do when you're just *insecure*. Such pathetic ways of proving manhood just go to show that a man's got an unresolved need to prove it, we say to ourselves; and all he really needs is a good relationship or a good job or some counseling or something else to perk him up.

Yet the fear of other men's judgment never goes away. The premonition lingers that something will still need proving somehow, now and then, at times when least expected. We harbor doubts that we don't really have our manhood act together. We make choices to avoid situations where our so-so manhood act might be vulnerable to ridicule. We try to remember our "gender successes" from one to the next. Yet try as we might to maintain within us a constant sense of being a real-enough man, we feel challenged at times to *prove* it—especially in confrontations with other, all-too-real men.

Learning to honor one's loyalty to selfhood will mean learning to accept that one's manhood act is shaky, *and that's OK*. That's not as simple as it sounds, but these ten points can help clarify what matters more:

## Ten Things to Remember If You *Know* Your Manhood Act Is Shaky but You Suspect That's OK— Because You'd Really Rather Act Out of Your Selfhood Instead

   1. Other men have only as much power to judge you as you give them. If you don't give them the power to judge *who you are*, they don't have it.

   2. All men grow up learning to fear other men's judgment of their manhood act.

   3. All men grow up learning to mistake their manhood act for *themselves*.

**4.** Some men learn to figure out the difference. You can be one of them. That means life as a man of conscience.

**5.** Some men will never learn the difference between their manhood act and themselves—even though their lives and the lives of other people depend on it. You can try to reach and teach such men if you want. But some of them are really tough cases. Shouldering *their* problem with manhood may become too much *your* problem with manhood. For whatever reason, they are intractably committed to their manhood act and to doing things to fake it that hurt other human beings terribly. So you may have to give up on them. There's only so much you can do, and life is short.

**6.** Your consciousness of your human-beingness does not depend on any common denominator of consciousness among all the other men out there who are also living behind the mask of manhood. Your freedom to let down your own mask does not depend on how many other men have already done so or how many other men will.

**7.** One of the main reasons the manhood mask stays stuck is because you think you're the only one who sometimes longs to take it off. You're not at all. But you might be led to think that a roomful of masks nodding their approval will give you the permission you need before you really can. You don't need their permission. Their seeming permission to take off your manhood mask is also their power to judge you. You don't need either. To let down your own manhood act, all you need is the courage of your own human-beingness, and the conviction of your own selfhood.

**8.** You may think that if you decide to live as a man of conscience you'll be alone. But you can't *be* a man of conscience alone, all by yourself, in isolation, outside of relation. The other people in your life—all the people of all their various races, ages, sizes, genders, and cultures, all of their unique and precious human-beingnesses, in all of their various connections to you—*they* will all be with you because for a change *you* will be with them.

**9.** Still, it isn't always easy to be a man of conscience.

**10.** The core of one's being must love justice more than manhood.

THE WAY TO BE LESS AFRAID OF OTHER MEN
IS TO BE LESS AFRAID OF ABANDONING THE MANHOOD ACT—
AND MORE LOYAL TO EVERYONE'S SELFHOOD.

## ✧ 2 ✧

# HOW CAN I BE
# CLOSER TO PEOPLE—
# IN FRIENDSHIP AND IN LOVE?

The insistent testing of our loyalty to manhood can eventually become a curse on our most intimate relationships. The "real man" standard so taunts and goads us that we end up believing no one would want to be our friend, and no one could possibly love us, if we don't measure up to it.

No one seems to know for certain what this "real man" standard *is,* and some men's striving for it goes so over-the-top that they become caricatures of hypermasculinity. But such bits of information offer small consolation. At some point nearly every human raised to be a man is smitten with the feeling that if only he made the grade as a real-enough man, he would not feel so acutely alone.

The learned shame of a shaky manhood act becomes the impetus and incubus we bring to every personal relationship, so that we seek friends and lovers who will really, truly appreciate us—as a real, true man. We expect their congratulatory perception of our manhood to heal the impacted pain of it. But there is always an unforeseen problem—the very manhood act we embrace is inimical to intimacy and trust. And so long as we keep up the manhood act, we miss the point of being human:

▶ **Loyalty to the manhood act means living with the constant fear of revealing one's own real self.** The manhood act is a mask you wear to keep you safe from other masked men, to keep you safe from their judgment on how well you have your manhood act together, and to keep you safe from getting hurt by them. It means comparing manhood acts all the time—looking out and watching your back, calculating when you can top someone else's and when yours is more likely to be topped. It means having one's most important emotional and relational decisions controlled by fear of other men.

▶ **Really connecting with someone else is not possible from inside the manhood act.** The whole point of loyalty to manhood is to present your manhood act as who you are. So if in your most intimate relationships you keep believing in other masked men's power to judge and hurt you if you let the act drop, you'll wear your fear of other men's judgment like a suit of armor. And the chances that you'll then connect with someone as your real self—to someone *else's* real self—are zilch.

We often experience the dichotomy between manhood and selfhood in our daily lives—but without knowing quite how or why. Lacking words to comprehend the contradiction, we suddenly stumble upon it when we feel blocked about revealing ourselves in a close relationship, for instance, or when we emotionally withdraw from intimacy without any apparent reason.

Faced with the damning dilemma of other men's judgment on their manhood act, many humans raised to be a man long for an interpersonal solution in the form of a loving, caring relationship. But inevitably—if the relationship is driven by the need to have one's manhood act personally appreciated in private, in relative safety, seemingly far from the judgment of other men—things start to go wrong:

▶ **If you expect a friend or lover to personally validate your manhood act, you cannot also expect to lose your fear of revealing your real self.** If you need the relationship primarily to have your manhood act affirmed—if that's essentially what the emotional relationship is for you—then the other person in it will be real to you only to the extent that they go gaga over your mask. That means the other person isn't real to you at all. That means you still wear your fear. That means you have not dropped your loyalty to the mask. That means you're not yet real either.

▶ **There are probably many people in your life who would prefer to recognize your real self for a change—you included.** Not everyone you meet is a masked man, after all. Not everyone defies you to keep your real self concealed or else. Just because revealing your real self would freak out a lot of masked men doesn't mean it would freak out everyone who might matter to you. *Or do masked men always matter more? Does their judgment power always supersede yours?*

The decision to give up loyalty to the manhood act is not easy to live out. But it is not difficult to make—for the sake of the people in your life who would prefer to know you as your real self, and for the sake of the self you would prefer to be. Disloyalty to masked men's judgment does not seem so impossible if seen as allegiance to the people you matter to and the people who matter to you.

We've each got only this one life on earth. The jockeying for credibility between two or more manhood acts has, throughout history, meant conquest, betrayal, and violence for billions of human beings—whether third parties to a temporary truce or ongoing losers in a permanent war. This insanity can only cease when one by one we each learn the commitment and the skills to disempower the manhood act by laying to rest our subservience to it. Then, amazingly, an extraordinary interpersonal potential becomes possible:

▶ **You never feel more real than when someone else is completely real to you.** This recognition tends to come as a complete surprise to those of us dunned and bribed into donning the mask of manhood. We grow up learning by rote and by rite that we are *less than nobody* if we haven't got our manhood act together. To be real is to be "a real man"—and the punishment and humiliation if you fail are a familiar memory to us all. But what counts as "success"? What passes for feeling *real to yourself* if your *credibility to others* always depends on wearing the manhood mask just right? You don't wear the manhood mask *to feel real*—only to be *judged* as real (as a real-enough man). You never actually *get* to feel real except when other masked men bestow their approval on your manhood act. That's a rush, that's a high, and you can easily mistake it for self-confidence and self-esteem—the transient certainty that you are a real man among real men. The problem is, if you depend on other masked men for your sense of self, you can never be sure who you really are apart from their approval, which is *very* conditional. If you blow it, if you don't qualify, they can make you feel *less than nobody*.

▶ **When you act toward others as if *they are as real as you*, you come to feel as real *as a human being can be*.** Instead of thinking about your sense of self as whatever results when other masked men judge you, think about your sense of self as that which results *when you completely regard someone else as completely real*. That's exactly the opposite of how one gets to feel real doing the manhood act. That's looking at your reality the other way around. That's looking at your reality as *what happens when someone else is real to you*—not as a function of what happens when you are judged manly enough by other masked men. To be a man of conscience means learning to experience from this *other* perspective—from another human's point of view—our fullest, deepest reality in regarding the whole reality of others. It feels so different you'd think it was magic. But it's not. It's simply deciding to live as a man of conscience.

The way to experience this interpersonal potential is not spiritual or poetical or mythological. The way to interpersonal selfhood is not even an allegorical "journey" or "path"—it's just practical, everyday attention to the matter of justice in one's interpersonal relating. A man of conscience is someone who pays such attention—a human raised to be a man who has decided to love justice more than manhood.

But practical, everyday justice is not always clear-cut and self-evident. And because it always happens (*when* it happens) *between* people, there is always someone else whose reality counts as much as one's own. Therefore no man of conscience can regard himself as an island of heightened consciousness, enlightened and insular, self-righteously in touch with "the truth." On the contrary—realizing that selfhood is always experienced, by definition, in relation to the complete reality of other selves—he tries to keep in mind the point of being *only* human:

▶ **You can't assume you'll act as a man of conscience all the time even if you decide to.** Certainly no one who really knows you well can assume that. So you have no grounds to assume it either. Living as a man of conscience is always one day at a time, one moment at a time—each encounter at a time, each decision at a time.

▶ **Even if you decide to live as a man of conscience, you will probably fuck up.** That's just a fact.

▶ **Having decided to live as a man of conscience, you may realize when you fucked up before anyone else does.** The person in your life whose selfhood you disregarded— and who matters to you—may or may not be the first to know what you just did.

▶ **Then again, you may *not* be the first to know when you did something that disregarded someone else's selfhood.** So your fuck-up may need to be brought to your attention—maybe by the person whose selfhood you disregarded, maybe by someone else who was paying more careful attention than you.

▶ **Deciding to live as a man of conscience is not a once-and-for-all-time event.** One decides in each decision one makes; one re-chooses loyalty to loving justice in each and every choice.

✦

## What Should a Man of Conscience Do When He Fucks Up?

In general, there are two different ways to disregard the selfhood of someone else, particularly someone you are close to:

**1. You can do something that disregards someone else's selfhood although *you didn't mean to*** (because you *had intended* to be living as a man of conscience but you fucked up).
*Or . . .*
**2. You can do something that disregards someone else's selfhood *because you meant to*** (perhaps because you somehow *had* to cancel out someone's selfhood, as if to guarantee the credibility of your manhood act).

In general, these two different ways of fucking up don't make a great deal of difference to the person whose selfhood was disregarded. To that other person, the issue is not whether you *meant* to hurt them; the issue is that you denied their humanity. Whether slightly or big-time, they got put down by you somehow—and their problem is dealing with what you did to them, not how to help you feel better about having done it. So if you are trying to live as a man of conscience, and you are trying to pay attention to the reality of other selves, here's what you might feel you had to do next:

- **Figure out exactly what you did.** (Don't leap to "why"; first get clear about "what" and "to whom.") Hear what you did, from the person you did it to. Or, figure it out yourself based on the next best available information. *Then . . .*

- **Acknowledge that you know what you did.** With particulars, not generalities. Make sure the person who was hurt knows you understand what you did as exactly as you can.

(This helps the hurt person not feel crazy and utterly detached from you. This helps you reach out to restore a human connection with another real human being.) *Then* . . .

- **Apologize.** Without qualification. Without rationalization. With your whole self behind your words. As if you are talking to someone who matters to you—no matter how well you know them, but *especially* if you know them well. *Then* . . .

- **Make amends.** Whatever and however you can. To make good for what you took away from the other person, to re-recognize their human right to be someone, to restore them to themself—and to restore you to yourself.

If, on the other hand, you are paying most of your attention to keeping your manhood act intact, here are some of the things you would probably feel you had better do next:

- **Dismiss or minimize the hurt.** Try to ignore whatever someone says who is trying to tell you that you hurt them. Try to make them think they're crazy to feel so bent out of shape over nothing.

- **Have sudden and complete amnesia.** Try to convince them you can't remember anything resembling whatever they're talking about concerning your alleged behavior.

- **Reverse "who did what to whom."** Switch around who got hurt. Claim *you're* really the injured party, and it's the *other person* who did the harm.

- **Undermine the other person more.** Try to make them think there's really something wrong with them, and there always has been, and you've been keeping a tally, and now's the time to let them have it.

- **Make an apology you don't mean**—a shallow and insincere generality with just enough content to keep the other person quiet for the time being.

- **Make a promise with no intention of keeping it**—a promise not to do whatever it was ever again, a promise not to hurt the person that way ever again—a shallow and insincere generality with just enough content to keep the other person quiet for the time being.

The contradiction between selfhood and manhood often reveals itself in daily life in such contrary interactions. In the first example, the problem is viewed as one of practical, inter-personal justice—between two particular human selves—and the reaction is to restore the selfhood that has been slighted by making sure the wrong is righted. In the second example—where the self who has been aggrieved is then written out of history—the reaction might be characterized as a one-way, end-run gender defense.

One's manhood seems real when treating someone else as less real. One's selfhood becomes real when honoring the reality of others.

You are not your manhood act. You are *who chooses what you do*. You become who makes each choice.

Living as a man of conscience means recognizing that one's connections to the whole, fully real selfhood of other human beings get *disconnected* when you hurt someone, when you disregard their selfhood. What you have to do next always has to begin with re-recognizing that other person's reality. To begin someplace else is to commit yourself to disconnection.

THE WAY TO BE CLOSE TO SOMEONE,
SELFHOOD TO SELFHOOD,
BEGINS WITH A COMMITMENT
TO LOVING JUSTICE.

## ✧ 3 ✧

# WHY CAN'T WE TELL OUR TRUTHS AS MEN, MAN TO MAN?

This book is not a man-to-man book, a men-only lowdown on the search for deep manhood. Its subject matter is completely different—selfhood—and so is its unconventional form. This book is intentionally not written "to ordinary men as men." This book is not even written like an ordinary book. It fundamentally questions the authority of other men's judgment in our lives. And in so doing, it breaks all the rules.

## Four Good Reasons This Is Not a Book for Men Only

1. **I have a very strong personal preference.** As a reader, I feel quite uncomfortable reading books that are written as if men can be honest only when women can't hear. Such books seem addressed to men *as if the most important communication that can happen must happen someplace far away from women.* In form and content, such books argue that men can only tell their deepest truths to one another if women aren't listening, or as if women can't possibly understand, or if women can't be there, or as

if women don't matter, or as if women are a basic reason that men have trouble relating in the first place.

My own experience contradicts this view—so I get the creeps reading such books. My own experience suggests to me that when someone raised to be a man declares that a woman cannot or must not hear what he's about to say, he is in effect deciding that he intends to speak only those words that are legitimate coming from a manhood mask. He has already decided his words are to be heard and evaluated solely by other men *as men,* so he has in effect already decided to speak only those words that other manhood masks could nod their head to.

Personally, such gender-defender communication makes me tune out. I don't accept that only other manhood masks are the standard for what I dare speak. I've had plenty of experience looking at the manhood mask from the *outside*—I've seen it on other men and I've learned to tailor my behavior accordingly so as to withstand the critical judgment that I have learned to predict. I know that I will never be able to look at my *own* mask from the *inside* if I cannot safely take it off *completely* and hold it up to view. And I have no personal reason to believe it is any *safer* to do this only in the company of others who also wear the mask—other men who have in effect decided to keep it *on* by keeping women *away.*

I know there are men who anticipate that women would be very angry to hear them speak the truth about what they may have done—particularly if it concerns behavior directed toward a woman. Not unreasonably, such men feel safer speaking frankly and candidly when they are only among other men. Already feeling some remorse for their misdeed, they have no need to further aggrieve any woman by regaling her with it. Thus they may expect that men's hearing will better help them to disclose their attitudes and actions so that they may come to some useful understanding, and this expectation may be both realistic and responsible.

Yet I know there are men who feel that they simply can never speak their truth with women present, because they feel unsafe as if by definition. There are men who feel completely unsafe whether in groups of women and men or "alone" in groups of women. I do not doubt that *is* their truth. But I do doubt the meaning of "safety" when, for someone raised to be a man, its precondition is gender exclusivity.

In general I believe that to exclude women's lives from communication about manhood and selfhood creates a false sense of safety. For anyone raised to be a man, the maneuver conspicuously resembles what masked men always do when they are defending their manhood by forging a bond: to agree not to top each other, they establish a truce, in contrast to some third party—a designated outsider, someone left out or put down.

I always hated it as a child whenever I was at risk of being that outsider—the butt of a bond between two masked men. So why should I feel better off today participating in a truce that could not exist without someone *else* as outsider?

If I self-consciously exclude someone "not a man" or "not a real-enough man"—and if I collude with others to do so—what rules must I obey to keep company with my fellow excluders? What must I do or not do, say or not say, so that they won't cast *me* out?

If participating in any ostracism makes me feel "better" about myself, more "free" to speak "my truth," how does my *dependence on that truce* determine *what my truth must be*?

How can we speak meaningfully of human selfhood if some selves (ours) matter *more* and some selves (women's) matter *less*? Do we not thus lock ourselves out of selfhood and enter lockstep into manhood? Do we not consign our lives to the manhood act any time we choose to speak only that which other masked men will nod their head to? Too much of what we must divulge is how and why we've scared the shit out of each other into wearing manhood masks in the first place. So I have come to this simple conclusion . . .

2. **To tell our truth, we must decode our truce.** We must honestly diagnose what has been "scary" about other men's judgment on our lives, *and* we must rigorously analyze our complicity in the exclusions and derisions committed to feel "safe" in other men's company. There is absolutely no way to get to our truth if we maintain our loyalty to such a truce.

   In other words, the form of our communication to understand and solve the problem cannot replicate the structure of the problem.

   This is especially true if the problem includes our memories of being scared by other men into being scary to others. I've never met a man who doesn't have such memories. I've never met a man who doesn't carry them anxiously somewhere, embedded in his behavior. I can even recall some of the people whom I've been scary to—people I put down so that I would feel I had my mask on right. So how can we expect to *get* anywhere—how can we understand our long-buried fears and what we do daily to flee them—if we start off by climbing into a rickety mythic tree house with a sign that says GIRLS KEEP OUT? Even if we can arrange to reach a "boy-boy" truce among ourselves—feeling relatively safe with one another far away from "the girls"—how will we ever really face the fears of loss of self that drove us to this tree house in the first place?

3. **The manhood problem is everyone's, even if everyone doesn't have the same problem.** We all must confront whatever it is that makes communication between people raised to be a man difficult, or stressful, or less than truthful, or hostile, or threatening and predictive of violence—to one another or to a third party. Whatever it is that gives rise to threats and standoffs and various

temperamental outbursts between people raised to be a man—whatever it is that makes people raised to be a man fundamentally terrified of revealing to one another who's behind their masks—whatever that drama is, whatever that dilemma is, it has consequences and implications for everybody, not just for humans raised to be a man. Everyone is affected when manhood masks clash or trash, collide or collude. So whatever can be learned from telling our truth, we must let everyone in on it. Everyone, somehow, has a stake in that knowledge. Everyone's well-being ultimately depends on it.

4.  **Sometimes it's a useful exercise for men to talk about men as "they."** Men get used to talking about women as "they" and men as "we." But that use of pronouns can't always be counted on to express all the experiences and feelings of someone growing up trying to act convincingly like a man. Very often such a human being has experiences, or memories, or feelings (grief, terror, isolation, and so forth) that can only be accurately expressed, if at all, in a sentence where "they" means *men*—not only *other* men but *men*.

    This is more than a subtle, semantic point. Many humans raised to be a man have stories to tell, and memories to reclaim, from a time when hurt and pain were administered by *men*. To say, if true, "I was hurt by *men*" may send yet another quake of hurt and pain heaving through one's chest—a surge of recollected anguish *at feeling cast out from the company of men.* To say, if true, "I was abused by *men*" may trigger tears not only because of the abuse itself but also because one's own social gender and human identity have come to seem inextricably linked, such that either one must *identify with one's abusers* or else one feels like less than nobody. To name *men* as perpetrators of one's pain, if true, can pitch a human raised to be a man into all the ambivalence and emotional imbalance of an identity upheaval. And that's not necessarily a bad thing. Because speaking the name of *men* in the third person can help in naming oneself a man of conscience.

Actually, for some people raised to be a man, it has become all but impossible to say "they" and mean "men"—because to do so risks replaying all one's hurts and fears of being shamed and humiliated. For others raised to be a man, however, saying "they" and meaning "men" is a useful way to *name* those hurts and fears— and learn to understand them.

THE TRUTH ABOUT MANHOOD
MAY NOT BE SAYABLE AS A MAN.

# ✦ 4 ✦

# HOW DO WE KNOW WHAT MANHOOD REALLY *IS*?

Often we're at a loss to know what manhood is all about, so we grope for answers wherever we suppose we can find them—in myths, in holy writ, in rude jokes, on toilet stalls. Many tales have been told to inspire us to manhood, to reveal its true nature, to allay our doubts about its existence, to help us remember where we lost it, to help us remember next time to put it back where it belongs. Many yarns have been spun about exemplars of manhood, heroic and stoic, cocksure and strong. Understandably, such gonzo bombast may underwhelm. Regrettably, not all such educative epics may be to your taste. So here's one that's certifiably tongue-in-cheek.

## The Wondrous Fable of a Young Man's Search for Manhood

This is the story of a child named Tom.

All the time that Tom was growing up, he noticed something that made him feel terribly uneasy and queasy inside: He noticed he always felt *compared* to other boys and to older men. And he noticed he always felt that some of them had *more* of something that he was supposed to have. And he didn't have *enough* of it, whatever it was.

It wasn't exactly strength, and it wasn't exactly size, and it wasn't exactly money, and it wasn't exactly age, and it wasn't exactly toughness, and it wasn't exactly anger— although certainly everyone who seemed to have *enough* of this something (*whatever* it was) seemed to Tom to be stronger, bigger, richer, older, tougher, and angrier.

Tom was never sure what this mysterious something was. Was it some *stuff*? Did it come installed in your *body* somewhere? *Where*?

Or was it in *what you did*? or *how you did things*?

Or was it in how everyone acted toward you when you acted that way?

Or was it in how you treated people?

Or was it in how everyone else treated you?

Tom could not be certain. Tom's questions only led to more questions.

"What *is* it with this stuff?" Tom wondered thoughtfully. "And how do you get enough of it, anyway?"

So Tom kept on the lookout for clues. Tom checked out everyone he met who seemed to have it—to see who really had it, to see who seemed to have more of it (and who seemed to have less), to see who seemed to have really a lot (maybe more than enough—maybe enough to share?), to see how they got it, and to see how Tom could get enough too.

Tom turned into a very smart sleuth.

As years went by, and as Tom grew older, he kept doing his detective thing—which had started out as a hobby but now took up more and more of his time. He paid close attention to whoever seemed to have this stuff and he began asking clever questions of everyone he met who seemed to have it. Two of the cleverer questions Tom asked always got very surprising answers. One was:

"Do you ever feel compared to someone else who has more of this stuff?"

And the other was:

"Do you ever feel someone out there has more of it than you will ever possibly have?"

What was surprising about the answers to those two

questions was that all the answers were "yes." Always. Without exception. No matter what different answers Tom got to the other clever questions he asked, he always got "yes" to those two.

Over a period of many, many years, Tom met and talked to many, many people who seemed to have this ineffable stuff—and every one of them told Tom they felt compared to someone else who had more of the stuff, and every one of them said they felt there was someone out there who had more than they themselves could ever possibly hope to have.

Tom—who had now taken to wearing a trench coat— became a full-time dick. He pursued his questioning, and his quest, through many lands, through many generations, and always he got the same answer, in words more or less the same: "Someone else has more of this stuff than I do. I'm afraid I will always have less stuff than they do. Try as I might, my stuff will always be compared to theirs unfavorably."

So Tom had an idea. He tried asking, "*Who* has more stuff than you do? *Who exactly?* Could you please tell me their *names*?"

To Tom's surprise, everyone he asked had at least one name to provide. And some people had quite a few. Some people gave Tom the names of their fathers, big brothers, uncles, stepfathers. Some people gave Tom the names of playmates from childhood—and popularly merchandized action figures. Some people gave Tom names of neighborhood bullies, gang leaders, coaches, high school sports stars, fraternity brothers. Some people gave Tom names of bosses, higher-ranking military officers, higher-ranking fellow prisoners, professional athletes, movie stars, CEOs.

Tom also found he got a lot of names that fell into a big category he first called "miscellaneous" because he couldn't make any sense of it. Then he realized what it was about and called the category "wished-for chums." It was for those who you once wanted very much to befriend you but they wouldn't have anything to do with you because you had insufficient stuff.

Tom persevered. "Who has more stuff than you?" he asked insouciantly. "Who exactly?"

As Tom logged the answers, he swiftly accumulated lists and lists of names. The lists became long and complex, so Tom got himself a computer to keep track. He got himself one of those superpowerful supercomputers. He also got himself a gigantic grant to hire interviewers. His worldwide field-research staff was soon enormous.

"Who has more stuff than you? Who exactly?" And Tom's supercomputer crunched all the data and traced all the contacts and cross-tabulated all the referrals and cross-indexed all the nicknames and finally plotted and printed out the results.

The printout was a maze, a diagram actually, approximately in the shape of a pyramid, showing the names of everyone alive who had grown up to be a man, whom they felt unfavorably compared with, who they felt had more stuff, and who *those people* felt had more stuff, and so on and so on all the way to the pinnacle.

At the peak of the pyramid was a single name: The one man more men felt unfavorably compared with than absolutely any other, statistically speaking. The one man whose name had never shown up when interviewers asked, "Who has *less* stuff than you?" The one man whose name only showed up in answer to the question "Who has *more* stuff than you?"

Tom stared at that name for a long, long time. For a trembling moment, Tom felt a cosmic feeling sweep through him, a premonition that he might be close to the end of his quest—for the man whose name appeared at the apex of the pyramid had not yet been interviewed. Somehow he had been overlooked.

So Tom went back to the supercomputer and keyboarded in a query:

DOSSIER?

And here's what the supercomputer screen shot back:

NAME:    Deep Bob
ADDRESS: A bosky bog

AGE:        Ancient
SEX:        What, are you kidding?

"So this is the ultimate man's man," thought Tom marvelingly. "A man among men—a man among *all* men! The fullest flowering of manhood known to man!

"He's got so much stuff he never has to prove it and it's never *ever* in doubt!

"He's the all-time greatest. The big enchilada."

Needless to say, Tom rushed off to that bosky bog forthwith.

There were hanging vines overhead, rank and scummy ponds all around, fungi and tree rot underfoot. It looked like the set from a Hollywood science-fiction film. It was.

"Deep Bob?" Tom called out imploringly. "Deep Bob?"

A nearby pond burbled.

"Deep Bob? Where *are* you? It's *me*—Tom!"

The murky surface of the swamp seemed to swell.

"I have some questions to ask you, if you don't mind? Clever questions? I won't be but a minute?" Tom felt a shiver. Tom also felt himself asking statements of fact.

Tom cringed—and had a momentary flashback to his mother. He recalled her musical voice, inflected just this way: she would voice statements as questions, no matter what their factual basis. Tom had always hated that. Tom swore he'd never do that, ever, himself. He vowed he'd never talk like his mother that way, he'd never let deference show that way, he'd always *ask* his questions and *state* his statements, and that was that. He had a right to say what he meant, dammit. And now here he was in the bosky bog about to meet Deep Bob—and sounding just like his mother! Intimidated, deferential, insubstantial, seeming to be nobody. The shame of it all! The humiliation!

Just then a massive hairy creature rose up out of the goo, slime sheeting down its matted fur. Tom felt a dank wind blow, and he wrapped himself inside his trench coat for warmth, shuddering with awe and angst.

The massive hairy creature loomed larger and larger. Its eyes glared, its tongue lolled, its throat cleared, and it roared.

Tom could not believe his eyes.

"I *know* you—" stammered Tom, clearing his own throat, lowering his voice somewhat, making a statement on his own authority. "I *know* you from somewhere—!"

The hairy swampthing roared some more.

"Aren't you—?" Tom sputtered, for now he really did have a question to ask. "Aren't you—?"

The Bob Beast growled at Tom even louder.

"Aren't you—*the tooth fairy*?"

"Yes," admitted the swampthing, suddenly sniveling from the cold and sheepish. "I only do this part-time."

That story has a punch line, which goes as follows: "Either Deep Bob exists, or else manhood doesn't." So it's probably not the sort of story that would clear up anyone's confusion on the subject. And it's certainly not the sort of story that gets tucked away in the collective unconscious of all seekers after deep manhood.

Actually, out of our confusion, we often compose manhood stories of our own, out of our own lives, writing little legends now and then about our gender to remind us "who we are." These stories are sometimes modeled after other stories that we've been told or that were acted out before our eyes. But each has an original, personal touch. And because it seems our lot in life to make up our manhood as we go along, when we make up such distinctive stories, they stay with us remarkably well— even when we have completely forgotten what really originally happened.

This is one such personal episode, first acted out many years ago and only recently recollected.

## The True Story of a Young Boy's Search for Manhood

This is the story of a child named John.

If John had been interviewed by Tom (see above), his name would have been entered in Tom's imaginary computer, and on the pyramidic printout, John's name would be nearer to the base than to the apex—especially when he was young, when he was called Johnny, but also into puberty, his teens, and his twenties.

John grew up experiencing a great gulf between who he felt he was and the masculinity he perceived in other men. John grew up feeling that there were always other boys who had more masculinity than he did, even at the earliest age he could remember. There were older boys, bigger boys, meaner boys; there were stronger boys, more athletic boys, more muscular boys, tougher boys. Everywhere John looked, there were boys who were more "all boy." And that's not counting the adult men in John's family, especially his gruff, pipe-smoking paternal grandfather, a man whom Johnny loved dearly, except when he embarrassed Johnny by remarking on what broad shoulders he thought young Johnny had grown, and what a tough football player he thought Johnny would become someday—and except now and then when he frightened Johnny by goading him into fistfights with an older, far more street-tough boy cousin, a prospect Johnny dreaded and dodged however he could.

Early on, Johnny got the idea that there was such a thing as rock-hard, fail-safe masculinity—the real stuff, the right stuff—perhaps whatever it was that Johnny's paternal grandfather expected him to have. And it was Johnny's job in life to have it—to have as much as he could muster.

But he never felt he had enough.

Inside, he felt he was just passing. Even if he was convincing to those around him—playmates, family members, schoolmates, teachers—he wasn't completely convincing to himself. He wasn't constantly certain he had enough. He was always afraid he'd be found out, discovered in his ruse. And then he'd be rejected by the boyfriends he wanted most to be liked by.

There were some older, meaner boys in the neighborhood who used to threaten Johnny and his boyfriends. Johnny especially seemed to be picked on and teased by those older boys. They would throw rocks at him and call him names. Once, they got him alone and they beat him up and stuffed him into a dirt tunnel they'd dug in a vacant lot and trapped him there and he cried his heart out with terror and pain.

But the boyfriends Johnny hung out with weren't mean

like that. There were three of them, all about Johnny's age, and they often played together. Johnny enjoyed and valued their companionship.

Throughout his early years, Johnny did a lot of things to act convincingly like a real boy with his boyfriends, because he wanted them to like him and accept him and because he was scared of seeming a girl. None of those things Johnny did stands out as vividly today as the things he did to his sister.

Johnny had a sister two years younger. Johnny's boyfriends liked her. Johnny's boyfriends liked to play with her too. None of Johnny's boyfriends had a sister their age, so she was special to them, and they accepted her as one of the kids in the neighborhood they sometimes played with.

But by the age of five, Johnny had begun to tease and taunt his sister cruelly. Johnny began to make fun of her in private and also in front of his boyfriends. Johnny made crayon drawings of her face and nailed them to trees in neighborhood backyards, cartoons of her with her name scrawled on them, caricatures that reduced her to tears and sent her wailing to their mother for comfort. "Don't let Johnny get your goat," was generally the extent of their mother's counsel. But Johnny had discovered that he *could*, and he could get away with it, and so for the next several years, he habitually tormented his little sister—beating up on her repeatedly in private—so Johnny could believe he was a real boy, so Johnny would not feel like a girl, so his boyfriends would believe he was one of them, so his boyfriends would like and accept him, and so Johnny could like and accept himself.

Johnny had figured out this strategy of sibling battery by the time he was six.

⋰                                    ✧

I know this story is true, because Johnny's behavior was mine. Although the behavior ended many years ago (and violence is now abhorrent to me), I have no doubt today that in some significant sense my behavior then *gendered* me—and probably my sister too.

I remembered this story with some difficulty, with some assistance from my sister. At first my story had significant gaps. I recalled my behavior toward her during our childhoods generally, but my sister brought crucial details of it to my attention in a conversation about a year and a half ago. When I recently showed her a version I had written, she alerted me to the fact that my telling of the story was still less than truthful. Understanding more fully the effects of what I did to her those many years ago, I revised it, trying to narrate more accurately the part about my violence, which she continues to recall far more clearly than I, but which I do not doubt I did.

The one who is making up the manhood has to forget a lot that goes into the legend of one's gender. The people whom one hurt along the way—the people one paid less attention to because one was paying more attention to one's quest for manhood—may eventually become but distant voices or may never be heard from again. That way the legend continues.

To make up one's own story of manhood is easy. The key is in what to leave out. What you especially need to forget is your violation of someone's selfhood. Then what you get to remember is the validation of your manhood.

TO KNOW WE REALLY HAVE MANHOOD,
WHATEVER THAT CAN MEAN,
WE HAVE TO DENY SOMEONE ELSE'S SELFHOOD—
OVER AND OVER AGAIN.

# ✧ 5 ✧

## HOW CAN WE HAVE BETTER RELATIONSHIPS WITH THE WOMEN IN OUR LIVES?

Deep Bob is not much of an oracle when it comes to interpersonal relationships between men and women. As a fantasy projection of ideal manhood, he may lift your sights and set a nifty standard if you're seeking a personal identity that's securely—if solipsistically—concentrated in gender. You may find yourself believing in, praying to, imitating, worshiping, or channeling a Deep Bob figure all your own if you believe his character would suit you.

Yet no matter how devoutly you revere your Deep Bob as the apotheosis of manhood, no matter how deeply he speaks to you, no matter how much you start to resemble him a bit yourself—you've got to admit that Deep Bob has a severe limitation: He does not provide much guidance for what goes wrong in ordinary affectional relationships between a man and a woman. Deep Bob—himself a fantasy projection—is not really cut out to exemplify how to be you in an interpersonal relationship with someone you love who is not *also* a fantasy projection. For one thing, the guy seems to live all alone in a swamp.

So we had best look elsewhere to understand what goes wrong in the everyday slough of despond between one partner in a relationship who was raised to be a man and another would-be partner who was raised to love and live with one.

Most people raised to be a man find it very difficult to be consistently present in an actual, real-life relationship with a woman. The fact is, *there is a reason* that someone raised to be a man has so much difficulty being in a personal relationship with someone raised to be a woman, and most people don't have a clue what that reason really is.

The reason is basic to the structure of manhood, and the reason is quite simple: *He* can't focus on being with *her* because he is mentally so busy with so many *other hims.* He is measuring himself against other men. He is comparing his manhood with theirs. He is valuing their judgment on his manhood more than he values her. He is valuing their judgment on his manhood more than he values his own self. His mental circuits are so overloaded defending his manhood act to other men that he can't even *perceive* her. Of course he has also lost sight of himself.

Problems in interpersonal relations between men and women often express and reflect hidden dynamics among men. These hidden dynamics may be between a man and men he has known or between a man and men he imagines. The dynamics are hidden because they take place "outside of the relationship"—which means outside of the woman's range of perception. But also, the dynamics are hidden because they are going on inside a man's head in ways that he has decided to keep from her—and therefore from himself.

These mental tape loops are the direct result of what happens whenever men challenge each other's manhood act. Recall any typical contest between two men, for instance, where one precipitated the spat by impugning the sufficiency of the other's so-called manhood. Literally or figuratively, the gauntlet has been thrown down, the challenge matched, and a conflict looms. In any such face-off, there can be three (and only three) resolutions:

1.   **The first man loses**—he is somehow humiliated or hurt by the second.
2.   **The second man loses**—he is somehow humiliated or hurt by the first.
3.   **They both agree to put down or pick on someone else.** The two men end up in a subtle social truce, a tacit treaty that must have a third party—someone they both

agree has a relatively inferior manhood act or someone who is simply female. With (and only with) that third party for contrast, they both can become comfortable enough to concede that their mutual manhood acts pass muster.

Loving justice between a man and a woman does not stand a chance when other men's manhood matters more. When a man has decided to love manhood more than justice, there are predictable consequences in all his relationships with women. When a man remains loyal to other men's judgment on his manhood, any woman he relates to is set up to be a potential "third party" in some truce he may need to transact with another man, in order to pass in that other man's eyes as having an adequate manhood act. Any woman who believes she is his "partner" may actually be a sitting duck for some put-down or betrayal that he may "inadvertently" or "unpredictably" commit owing to his prior allegiance to other men's manhood.

Learning to live as a man of conscience is a matter of learning how to recognize those dynamics and deciding to keep the effects of those dynamics out of the way of your life. Few men are alert to these secret dynamics—and fewer still have decided to keep the effects of these dynamics from impinging on their romantic attachments. Learning to live as a man of conscience means deciding that your loyalty to the people whom you love is *always* more important than whatever lingering loyalty you may sometimes feel to other men's judgment on your manhood.

The following chart illustrates the stark contrast between these divided loyalties.

The voice in the column on the left (Column A) represents the stream-of-consciousness of someone who is struggling toward action that will make clear to the woman he loves that she matters more to him than what other men may think of his manhood. The voice in the column on the right (Column B) represents what might be called a stream-of-*un*consciousness—someone shrugging off loyalty to his partner in favor of allegiance to the gender judgment of other men.

What you hear in your own mind may sound at times more like one voice than the other—or you may hear them debate.

## Some Typical Situations in Intimate Relations Between a Man and a Woman— And How Someone Raised to Be a Man Will Tend to React Mentally . . .

| A<br>. . . If Their Relationship Matters More Than Other Men | B<br>. . . If Other Men Matter More Than the Relationship |
|---|---|
| "There's a serious disagreement between us, and we have to talk it through further to understand each other fully. Maybe she's right. Maybe I'm right. Maybe neither of us is, exactly. But there's no way we can know without really talking and listening." | "There's a serious disagreement between us, and I have to show her who's boss. If I don't, other men will think she has authority over me, and I will lose rank with them. So I must pull rank with her. I must make her agree with me." |
| "She did something that made me very angry, but before I do anything else, I need to be careful to establish that she and I both have the same understanding about what it was she did—so I don't go off over nothing. Then, I need to check whether my feeling is actually anger. Maybe it's hurt. Maybe it's panic. Maybe I just had a flashback to someone who made me feel invisible once. If I can only remember to take time to be truthful here, perhaps I'd know I need to express an assortment of feelings—and it would be a cheat on myself and perhaps reckless toward her if I were to simply clump them all together under 'anger' and blow my stack. Whatever went wrong between us won't be helped if I rant and rage as if she's of no account to me. There won't be any *us* then." | "She did something that made me very angry, and she knows better than to make me angry because she knows just how I get. I explode. Instantly, I seize the right to rage just like other men. I feel their fury throbbing through me, their anger channeling through me, their implicit threat of violence deflected toward a woman, not targeted at me. Feeling other men's wrath at a woman saves me from my worst fear: when I feel angry at a woman I feel like other men feel— and I am spared other men's wrath at me. (Besides, I can pick on her or attack her and she won't physically hurt me back the way a man can.)" |

**"I did something that made her very angry,** and if I can only manage to get past all this defensiveness I'm feeling in the face of her angry accusation, I may be able to hear what she's telling me about what she felt when I did it, and I may be able to hear in her anger her pain and disappointment that I let her down. If I pay attention, I may then recognize her anger as anguished incomprehension because she thought I was someone who would never do that to her. And then I will have to figure out for myself what it means that I did do it: I indeed behaved as if I was someone she didn't think I was. Acknowledging my duplicity—both to her and to myself—is going to be tough. But can I honestly live with myself if I go on acting split like that? Or do I need to make apologies and amends right here and now and try to set myself right in the eyes of us both?"

**"I did something that made her very angry,** and I don't give a damn. She can complain all she wants, I don't care. If she wants to fuss and fume at me, so what? I'll tune her out. I'll ignore her. Act like she's nobody to me. She'll get over it. Besides, how could I hold up my head among my buddies if it got around that I was pussy-whipped? Do you think I could go out with the guys and have a good time if they thought I cared more about what *she* thinks of me than I do about them? A man's got to keep up his standing in the eyes of other men, and sometimes a man's got to do what a man's got to do. Making a woman angry at you, then making her swallow it—*that* really shows who's the man around here."

**"I broke a promise to her and she doesn't know.** So now I've got to tell her. I owe her that much at least. And I can't stand being in a position where I'm lying to her. It makes me feel like I'm lying to myself, like I'm a complete phony and our relationship is a sham. It's going to be difficult admitting I broke the promise I made—but not as difficult as it will be to sustain a lie. Ugh, I hate it when I mess up like this. But there's no point in disconnecting from her further. She matters to me. For me to lie would mean she doesn't matter to me at all. So it's time to tell her the truth. But it won't be easy."

**"I broke a promise to her and she doesn't know.** Everything will be OK if she doesn't find out. She *made* me promise, anyway. I just went along to avoid an argument. A promise is a promise, of course, but only if it's a real one—only if you really make a deal with someone of substance, where it's like you come to the bargaining table and make a sort of contract and you give your good name. Like between two buddies. Now, *that's* a promise. That's where you expect both parties to keep their word. But between a man and a woman? Not nearly as important. It's just an emotional thing."

## About Column B

When a man is alone with a woman, there may actually be various other men present—figuratively speaking—in his mind. He may carry with him vivid memories of individual masked men, he may remember their names, he may recall a particular humiliation he experienced in their eyes. Or he may imagine what they would say or think about him, because he knows well enough how masked men judge manhood, so he can predict with a high degree of accuracy what condemnation may befall him—especially if he regards the woman he is relating to as more real than the manhood of the men in his mind.

How else does a man know he's "the man there," after all? Only other men are the final arbiters of that. And if you fail their judgment, you are nobody at all. The surest way to mollify their judgment: treat a woman as nobody instead.

Even if a man manages his behavior so as not to express the full force of these mental pacts with other men, his actions may seem conflicted, not quite convincing, not done with credible conviction. His mental allegiance to the terms of a manhood treaty may prevent his being fully present in even his apparently "decent" behavior toward a woman. She may vaguely sense this emotional dissonance, this absence or ambivalence. He may too—but not recognize its source in the hidden dynamics between men that are structurally indispensable for there to be manhood.

Sometimes these dynamics are not hidden at all, of course. They become blatant frequently, as when a man makes a joke at a woman's expense in order to entertain male colleagues, or when a man shows off to other men his sexual orientation by leering at a woman's body.

But even when these dynamics remain hidden within a man's mind, they are not subtle, and they are not nuances. They are key to the social codification of manhood. Each time they are replayed, they prompt the behavior that underpins belief in the personal possibility of being a real man.

## About Column A

Before you decide what to do when something goes wrong between you and a woman you say you love, you have to decide which belief you want to make true. Two opposing beliefs are vying for your complete attention: the belief in the possibility of loving justice (Column A) and the belief in the ultimate existence of Deep Bob (Column B). Those beliefs cannot both be believed and acted upon at the same time. At critical junctures, those beliefs are not compatible, and you have to decide between them. Day-to-day relations between someone raised to be a man and someone raised to be a woman are chock-full of such critical junctures.

As mere mortal human beings we don't usually think of ourselves as having the power to decide what's "true." But humans do it all the time—and we have been doing it as a species throughout all recorded time. We pick a belief because we *want* it to be true even though we may not necessarily know for a *fact* that it's true; we may have no real *evidence* that it's true. But we want it to be true because we hunger for it to be true. Something deep in us longs for it. Or something more powerful than ourselves seems to draw us near to it. Or we are taught a tradition that offers no alternative. Then lo and behold: when we believe in the abstract value we want to be true, and when we act as if it's true, that helps *make* it true.

Manhood works that way. So does justice. They're both abstract ideals. We humble human beings, as it turns out, have the lifetime job of making them come true.

We don't have the option, however, of making both these ideals come true at the same time. They cancel each other out, especially in particular interpersonal moments—but on a larger social scale as well: a relational act will tend to help make manhood more true or it will tend to help make justice more true—not both. You have to decide in your life which of those two beliefs you want to make true. In a given situation, doing one particular relational act will help make manhood feel real (while making justice, in that situation, all but impossible). And doing a different relational act will help make justice more possible (and simultaneously it will make one's loyalty to manhood seem all but moot).

Actually, of course, you don't *have* to decide. "Deciding not to decide" is the default. When you opt out of consciously deciding, you default to the general tendency to favor abstract manhood and to shortchange matters of justice between human selves.

But deciding to always decide is what this book is written to recommend. Obviously that means making decisions about which *relational act* to choose. But fundamentally this book is written to recommend deciding which *belief* you'd rather make true—manhood or justice—because deciding which belief you want to make true has a surprising way of suggesting which relational act will help you do so.

THE WAY TO IMPROVE RELATIONS BETWEEN MEN AND WOMEN
IS TO EXPOSE THE CODES THAT CONTROL
RELATIONS AMONG MEN.

# 6

# WHAT MUST WE LEARN ABOUT MANHOOD FROM DAD?

A son's father can provide him with memorable lessons in loving justice and/or memorable lessons in loving manhood. Because such lessons are necessarily conflicted, the overall message may be mixed. And because the memories of these lessons are often long-buried, they are not easily dislodged and recalled. Later in his life a son may know something about how to express loving justice, and/or a son may know something about how to express manhood; yet he may not remember exactly how he learned either possibility from his father's example. Sons need to sort out both such lessons and memories—consciously and conscientiously—in order to decode their ongoing meaning in everyday life. To help prompt that process, this chapter offers a quiet evocation of the personal experience of having a father.

In your own life you may not have had a father. Or you may never have known your father. Or there may not have been an adult in your life who was like a father to you. This chapter does not assume that every reader actually *had* a father. But this chapter does assume that nearly everyone wanted *the experience* of having a father, and everyone has at times *imagined* what that experience would be like.

Some people imagine the experience of having a father even though they actually had one. There was indeed someone in their life whom they called Daddy or Dad or Father or Poppa—but he seemed somehow absent. He existed but he wasn't *there*.

To explore how we imagine the experience of really having a father, this chapter begins with a series of passages written in the form of a guided fantasy. After reading each passage, try to picture it in your mind as vividly as you can. Then pay attention to whatever emotions or memories come up for you.

You may wish to pause between each of the passages—put the book down briefly and perhaps close your eyes—to give your imagination and emotions ample time.

You may also wish to take a deep breath first. And perhaps a deep breath in between.

✧

**Imagine you had a father who liked you.** He loved you, of course, but he also *liked* you. He let you know he thought you were a very special and interesting person—someone he felt grateful to share his life with. He paid attention to the particularity of you. So when he looked into your eyes, you felt he was looking at you and you only. It was as if he completely welcomed what was unique about you—not as if he looked at you with disappointment because all he saw was someone who should be different. Imagine him looking at you now and liking you that much.

✧

**Imagine you had a father who liked your mother.** He showed her he loved her, of course, and he was unambivalently loyal to her, and he respected her, and he admired her, and he cherished their life together—but he also *liked* her. He let her know—and he let you know—that he always beheld her as a very special and interesting person—someone he felt fortunate and grateful to have known so well. He regarded her as if she was precious in her uniqueness, and he seemed to feel joy in being known by her as well—in a commitment you perhaps were too young to fully comprehend but you completely believed. Imagine him looking at her now and liking her that much.

✧

**Imagine you had a father who had work that he loved.**
He'd had the opportunity to pursue work that he cared about,
work that he was good at, work that was useful and
important—work that contributed to people's lives, not work
that hurt people—work that other people valued and recognized
him for. You were proud of him for that. And you knew he was
proud too—in a quiet, private sort of way. If someone asked
you, "What does your father do?" your answer might have been
an occupation, a job title, a craft, an art, a profession, a calling,
a service—but you knew your answer could never begin to explain *who he was.* Your father never acted as if he was identical
with his work. But you knew that part of your father's particularity was in how he did it—how he brought something special
to his work that was all his own. Imagine him at his work. Now,
imagine him coming home and turning his attention from his
work to you. Now, imagine he is full of happiness with which
to greet you.

✧

**Imagine you had a father who allowed you to find your
own pride.** He had his own hopes and dreams for your happiness, of course—how could he not? But if your path to happiness would be one you would find yourself—perhaps a path he
had not even realized was there to take—he did not hold you
back and he did not withhold his love. He did not stop wishing
you well, with his whole heart. He did not redirect you or reject
you because your path would be different from his. He did not
try to make you into someone else—someone he would like better. He did not decide on your path and push you onto it. He let
you find your own—and he let you know he was behind you all
the way. Now, imagine him standing behind you even when
you stumbled and fell. Now, imagine him helping you pick
yourself up—to find your own footing on your own path once
again—and then stepping out of your way once you are standing and striding. Imagine him supporting your *becoming.* Imagine it was because he loved your *being.*

✧

**Imagine you had a father whose emotions told the truth.**
His emotional expression did not contradict who you knew him

to be. When he smiled at you—whether spontaneously or empathetically—his eyes were full of meanings that were in sync with your experience. When he wept with you—whether in grief or unutterable joy—he did so unabashedly, his tears surfacing with ease, flowing from within as from the interior of someone who is simply honest to his soul. And when he was angry with you, you felt his hurt and pain and disappointment—not his hate. You knew that he hated, of course—he hated, for instance, the fact that some people suffer. You knew he hated injustice. You know he hated the fact that some people treat other people terribly. But you knew he did not hate you, not ever— even in times of anger. Imagine his emotions were not a mask he wore. Imagine that when he let you see his emotions it was to let you see inside.

Upon imagining the father described in these passages, you may have had thoughts about your own father or the adult who was like a father to you. You may have had memories of your real experience of him—and the similarities or differences between your memories and your imagination may have brought forth very strong emotions. If you never had or knew your father, reading the paragraphs above may have brought forth feelings that remind you of your loss. You may wish to take a moment to take note of your feelings and keep track of them. Don't let them slip away, even if they are painful.

If you are a father yourself, or if you might one day become one, you may also have had thoughts about the kind of father you would like to be. While reading the passages above, you may have reflected on how the father you imagined is like or unlike you. Keep track of the feelings you had toward this imagined father—because some of them may be feelings you hope a child will feel toward you.

Typically, when sons imagine the ideal experience of having a father, the father is portrayed as someone who passes on or bestows *manhood* in some special way. Though this ideal father may be but a fantasy figure, he evokes powerful longings; and sons often think of him as a personal initiator into the enigmas of being a real man—someone who prepares sons for the rough-and-tumble world of real other men. Sons who feel bereft of such a father may feel that their connection to manhood has been interrupted or their standing with other men has been compromised. Their image of the father they lack is very often associated with their longing for safety among other men, and surety about their gender credentials.

In the guided fantasy set forth above, however, the ideal experience of having a father was portrayed quite differently: he was pictured as an influential grownup who played a significant role in the development of a child's relation to *selfhood*. This imagined ideal father was depicted as having passed on to the child not only a core of self-esteem, but also an indelible memory of how self-esteem can be bestowed: When one is the recipient of a love that is *not* conditional upon conformity to gender expectations, one not only learns something very important about the reality of one's own selfhood; one also learns a crucial lesson in the process by which human selfhood is passed on: One human being initiates another into selfhood by beholding them, affirming them, supporting them, and not betraying them.

If we feel we lack personal certainty about our manhood, we may imagine the ideal father as someone who passes on a legacy of gender.

But if no grownup ever personally passed on to us a sense of the reality of our selfhood, we may not even be able to imagine that such a grownup could ever *be*.

Imagining the possibility of your own selfhood may mean imagining (or remembering) that someone in your life bestowed enough love on you *as you*. And their love did not depend on whether you were a real-enough man.

We all ache with the need to believe that such selfhood can be experienced, that such a love can be real. Childlike, we all wish to trust that if we can imagine such a love, it can happen.

I became convinced about the possibility of such a love in part because of two real fathers whom I know. As I began to write the guided fantasy passages above, trying myself to imagine the experience of really having a father, those two fathers inspired me. The more I wrote, the more I found myself thinking about them—how they have lived, how they seem to relate to other people, how they are with me. And the more I thought about them, the more their lives guided my writing.

Coincidentally these two fathers are about the same age, and they happened to meet each other once briefly, relatively late in life, long after their children had grown to adulthood. Their names are Vincent and Harry. I'd like to tell you more about them.

Harry, a first-generation American, graduated from college, served in World War II, and is a retired high school science teacher and guidance counselor. Vincent, a second-generation American, graduated from industrial trade school, where he trained as a tool-and-die maker, and is a retired tool engineer. Harry was married to one woman, the mother of their two children, for nearly fifty years. He is a widower. He is the father of a daughter (lesbian, divorced, now life-partnered) and a son (heterosexual, divorced, remarried, now deceased). Vincent has been married to one woman, the mother of their three children, for just over fifty years. They are the parents of a son (homosexual, divorced, now life-partnered), a first daughter (heterosexual, widowed, now remarried with one child), and a second daughter (heterosexual, married). They are both "white"— Harry's lineage is Russian Jewish; Vincent's, Norwegian Lutheran—and like other men of their generation they have lived in social worlds with women of their generation. As a result they have moved through life with commonplace but preferential entitlements of race and gender that went quite unremarked in mainstream American culture until well past their child-rearing years.

But such biographical details do not really tell their stories.

Without knowing each other for most of their lives, Harry and Vincent have several distinct and remarkable similarities. They are both deeply nonviolent, and both completely loyal to the women they married. Both have worked long, hard hours to support their families (Vincent, years of overtime; Harry, many years at two jobs at once); and they have been dedicated to providing for their children's education. Both have frequently also extended help to family members beyond their immediate household. Harry is unathletic and intellectual. Vincent is unathletic and mechanical. As it happens, neither has smoked at any time in his life, and neither has drunk alcohol except very rarely. Neither has ever bought or rented women's bodies in the form of pornography or prostitution. And neither has physically or sexually abused anyone, not once. This information is based on my personal observation confirmed with members of their families.

Still, even such biographical parallels do not tell the full story of these two fathers' atypical behavioral choices. Harry and Vincent are not perfect, and certainly neither would present himself as such; nevertheless they have been husbands and fathers of an unusual sort. And what sets them apart most profoundly—or so I now surmise—is that they have both conducted their lives and made their most important life decisions without significant reference to what any particular *other men* might think of them.

Neither Harry nor Vincent seems today to make decisions under the sway of gendered peer pressure from any particular subset of men as men. It appears they never really did. Harry's military service brought him into contact with a men-only world, but he evidences no nostalgia for that aspect of that time in his life. His passion was for his family and teaching. Vincent was exempted from military service because he had a job in a factory on the night shift making guns. And though most of his employment was in shops where only other men worked, he seems not to have emotionally idealized that aspect of it. On the contrary, Vincent's memories are clearly about the pleasure he has always taken in the work itself: operating and understanding machines, making and fixing things, inventing original mechanical solutions. This is a pleasure he has pursued outside his employment as well, volunteering his skills on countless occasions for family members, family friends, and charitable projects. If anything, Vincent seems to have taken even more pleasure in his work whenever he has found opportunities to do it outside the men-only places where he once got paid for it.

If other men's judgments had been surveyed, either when Harry and Vincent were younger or now, the consensus would doubtless be that Harry and Vincent are decent but somehow "soft"—or less kind words to that effect. In truth, whether by temperament or circumstance, Harry and Vincent have both been socially *set off* from the society of other men and also characteristically quite *different* from other men—and this has not seemed to *bother* them. Or if it has bothered them, nothing in their behavior suggests they have taken out any such feelings on the people whom they have *loved.*

For instance, Harry's daughter recalls that when she was a child, neighborhood playmates called her father names behind his back, most likely because he was mild-mannered, educated, soft-spoken, and gentle with his family. One of those names was "fairy." Vincent's son recalls summertimes as a child when their family gathered with a host of relatives who lived on farms, and all the grown-up men would disappear for hours into a room in the cellar where they would smoke heavily and play cards all through the night, and the next morning there would be a smelly barrel full of empty brown beer bottles. But Vincent chose not to join those men in the farmhouse cellar. He always found other things to do.

For another instance, after Vincent and his wife had both retired and their children had long since moved from home, he took on more and more of the homemaking: laundry, vacuuming, shopping. And when she became somewhat handicapped, he took over almost all of it (except for cooking, which became for them a collaboration). What other men would do, and what other men would think, apparently had nothing to do with Vincent's housework decisions. For yet another instance, when Harry's son died and the funeral service was to be conducted under religious customs that forbade women to sit with the men, Harry decided to sit with the women. Quite simply and unselfconsciously, he wanted to be with his daughter and daughter-in-law, and they of course wanted to be with him.

To both Harry and Vincent, social codes of manhood validation have almost always been less important criteria for their decisions than their human ties to the people they care about, and whatever is necessary to honor that connection. They did not do something because it was what other men would do or would necessarily expect them to do. Therefore—or perhaps only accidentally and coincidentally, who can really know?—every one of their children carries the memory of having experienced an exceptionally loyal, compassionate, kind, and emotionally present father.

Certainly I count it a lucky fluke that I am one of those children. And as I look back, I find myself asking many questions—

old ones and new ones. Do I ever wish my father was a man's man—someone who toughened me with his toughness, hardened me with his hardness? Maybe once I did, when I didn't know any better. Not now. Do I ever wish my father had passed on to me an impressive repertoire of manly pursuits and the social ease with which to conduct myself as a real man among men? Maybe once I did, when I was younger and confused. Not now. Do I ever wish my father had initiated me into putting down women through sexual jokes and innuendo, pornography, prostitution, ostentatious displays of heterosexual aggression, and so forth? No way. Not even when I was younger, thankfully. Do I ever wish my father had really loved me by making me a real man? Well, he really loved me. I have no doubt. Absolutely no doubt in my brain or my body—and I love him back more dearly than I can ever say. So for him to have loved me and simultaneously to have tried to turn me into a real man among men—that feels to me now like a personal contradiction. And it is . . . isn't it?

THE FATHER WHO LOVES A CHILD MORE THAN MANHOOD
LIVES A LESSON IN LOVING SELFHOOD
THAT CAN NEVER BE FORGOTTEN.

# 7

# WHAT IF MY FATHER DIDN'T LOVE ME?

An adult son who feels his father didn't love him may suppose that if only his father had really been loving, he would already "really know" his father. Such a son, feeling bereft of a father's love, may then become intent on trying to "get to know" his father, trying to understand "what made his father tick," trying to fathom what was going on inside the father during all those years the son did not get "enough" of the father's love—as if the info would make up for it.

The son may feel there was always something wrong in the relationship with his father, and the son may feel at fault—perhaps for not adequately qualifying for his father's love. So the son may long for a reunion to show the father just how well he's turned out as an adult, such that now, at last, the son will qualify for his father's long-lost love. Or the son may feel it was his father's fault that there was always something wrong in the relationship, and the son may remember having blamed and resented the father, and having felt stymied in his anger. So the son may wish to get to know his father anew in order to show he has at last set his anger aside, so as not to be stuck in it any longer.

Feeling distress about lacking his father's love, and perhaps dismay about being unable to resurrect or replace it, an adult son may spend his life trying to earn it. He may also feel a need to go into therapy, or take his feelings out on other people in his life, or take his feelings out on himself by abusing his own body, or work through his conflicted feelings toward his father in any number of other ways, unpacking hurt after hurt, betrayal after betrayal, humiliation after humiliation, loss after loss, grief after grief. Still the adult son may feel he has not yet really understood what made his father tick. And then the adult son, never "really knowing" his father, may stay bogged in the sorrow that prompted his quest for his father in the first place: perhaps never feeling that his *own* selfhood was ever recognized, perhaps never feeling that his *own* selfhood can be known.

The fact is, no son can ever "really know" his father. Even being sufficiently loved as a child by a parent does not give someone any inside scoop about what that grownup's life was like. If you feel that as a child you were not sufficiently loved—especially if you feel you lacked the love of your father—you may find this perspective very surprising, perhaps even liberatory: *no* child ever "really knows" a parent's life.

Even in the best of circumstances, "really knowing" who one's parents are—and knowing what their life was really like—is not possible. Even when there has been an abundant history of selfhood-affirming love, the circumstances of an adult's life remain an adult's, inscrutable to a child, who is simply too young to understand the most relevant biographical information.

With that perspective and proviso, this chapter introduces a series of tools for figuring out some relevant information about the effect on you of the relationship between you and your father—however fond or troubled it was. These tools are conceived to help an adult son understand what may have originally broken down inside the grown-up man he grew up with, even a supportive and warmhearted one, such that the father seemed incapable of loving the young son as a real self (rather than as, for instance, a "real-enough" *boy*). This set of tools is designed to detect what may have been going on inside your father—based on what can be observed today about the social codes of manhood verification, which your father, like you, may have been trying to live up to. The information these tools might disclose can then be available to help you better understand how your experience of your father affected your experience of yourself.


## My Father, Machines, and Me

I learned about tools from Vincent, my father. He was a machine technician and tool engineer, and tools were like a language to him. The machines he designed and built were his collected works. In our family's house, he had a basement shop with a huge wooden workbench, vises bolted onto it, a drill press standing next to it, a table saw across the room, a metalworking lathe that stretched along one whole wall, plus countless hand tools and hardware on shelves, in drawers, on pegboards, and hanging from the joists overhead—all the bric-a-brac he'd accumulated from years of working with his hands to build things and make things work and fix things.

When I was three I handed my father a flat wooden board with two curves I'd crayoned on it, two arcs that met at a point at one end. I asked Daddy if he would use his saw to cut along the lines. He did; then he handed the board back to me as the boat I'd designed, with a smooth-sanded prow.

As I grew older, Dad was to build all sorts of things for me as I explored an eclectic succession of interests: magic tricks, a toy circus, neighborhood shows, science projects. From as early as I can remember to the time I left home to go to college, I continued to come to him with a design or an idea, and he would figure out how to build it. In fifth grade a schoolmate and I wrote a puppet show that we wanted to perform for our class. I made the puppet heads myself, and I made the costumes and curtains with Mom—who was as expert at designing and sewing with fabric as my father was at designing and working with wood and metal. With Dad I made the puppet stage, in our own invented collaboration style between kid and adult with me saying something like, "It needs to be this high, and it needs to come apart and fold up so it can fit in the backseat of the car, and it needs to set up fast, and it needs to have different-colored lights on top with switches to control them and a curtain you can pull from underneath, even if you still have a puppet on

your hand." Dad figured out how to make it all work, sketching
plans as we went along. Then with the tools in his shop he built
it, and I helped.

Dad also spent a lot of time out in the garage or in the driveway working on the family car. I don't remember that he ever
took it to a professional auto-repair shop—maybe to save the
money, but also because he could usually figure out what
needed fixing, just by taking it apart and looking. Though not
trained as an auto mechanic, he could look under the hood and
take parts and pieces out and spread them on a tarp to catch the
oil and figure out what was supposed to happen between the el-
ements of this complicated machine and then figure out what
wasn't happening and then replace the worn-out part or whatever and then put everything back together again.

This aspect of Dad's mechanical genius was to remain a mystery to me. I never developed even the slightest interest in cars.
The father of one of my playmates worked at a used-car lot selling them, so this boyfriend had learned from his father how to
identify instantly the make and year of any car he spied,
whether parked or driving fast down the street. I was always
impressed with this knack of my boyfriend's, and it seemed a
very important one to have—especially if you wanted to grow
up to be a real boy. The world of cars was almost exclusively a
men-only world then. Our mothers *drove* us everywhere, chauf-
feuring us constantly to lessons, rehearsals, doctor's appoint-
ments. But the selling and fixing and tuning up of cars as
machines was a sphere women did not enter. My playmate
showed off his ability to recognize car makes every chance he
got. To this day, bombarded by automotive advertising like everyone else, I cannot tell what make a car is without getting up
close and reading the manufacturer's logo. And I am utterly
mystified when I look under the hood of a car—though if I am
discussing a problem with a professional mechanic I have
learned to appear less helpless and incompetent than I in fact
feel.

I could probably have learned how to fix cars quite adeptly,
or at least become adequate at it, if I had ever wanted to. I had
a father who was unintimidated and intuitive about auto mechanics, and I had endless opportunity to observe him and to
learn as much from him as I could. I could have learned to un-

derstand the *systems* of a car: electrical, fuel, brake, combustion. I could have learned to understand and appreciate what each part's function is, how the parts interact, what detail or interaction can go amiss, how the machine works as a whole and in all its particulars. I could have learned to take car parts apart. I could have learned to put them back together again in working order. But I never did. I simply didn't care about cars the way I cared about puppets.

One of Dad's greatest gifts to me was that he never made me feel that as a condition of his love I ought to be out with him in the driveway, under the hood or under the chassis, as a real son should, learning from his father everything he could about the nuts and bolts of auto mechanics, because it is a world steeped in masculine tradition and a world of men and men's lore that he could initiate me into step by step and safely, without any fear of failure. I just wasn't interested. He understood I wasn't interested—and I understood that was OK. He let me know I was always welcome to join him if ever I wanted, but if not, that was fine too. And when I came to him for help building a puppet stage, he was completely there, completely available to me— with all the mechanical aptitude, intuition, and dexterity he could apply under the hood of a car. And I remember having a wonderful time building that puppet stage together and making it work the way it needed to. It was a project he built expressly for me for my own special world of puppets—essentially a world of playing with dolls.

My friend Jerry and his wife have a son and a daughter in their late teens. Jerry told me he was on a business trip on an airplane recently seated beside another father, an executive who had a son about the same age as Jerry's. They began to talk about this and that and about their sons. Jerry was eating, his mouth full of airline food, when this other father asked him, "What does your son play?" Jerry needed time to chew and swallow before he could answer, and the other father didn't wait patiently or perhaps didn't notice so he pressed on, "What does he play? Does he play basketball, football, baseball? What does he play?" Jerry finally swallowed enough to reply: "He plays the piano." My friend had spoken with quiet pride, but his answer effectively ended the conversation.

A few years ago I began to wonder exactly why my father

was so accepting of my atypical interests. I've heard so many stories from so many other sons about how their fathers had forced them into having interests that they didn't really come to on their own, and they didn't especially want to pursue, but they knew they had to or else—because their father would be very angry and perhaps punitive. Some of those forced choices had become careers—successful on the outside, not so happy on the inside—and sometimes the forcefulness of the choice could still be felt as if it were a wound inflicted yesterday. So many sons have had their life choices determined by fathers such that to fail at the endeavor—or even to decline the option respectfully—is to risk losing their father's love, and perhaps to risk becoming less than nobody because he would not regard you as a real boy.

My father wasn't like that, and my life choices weren't made for me like that at all. I don't have any recollection of my father's ever telling me that I should be interested in *y* if what I was really interested in was *x*. My father's connection to me seemed to *precede* my interests—and he connected to *my* interests; he did not make me connect to his. The fact that almost all my interests were far afield of activities customarily coded "real boy's" did not seem to faze my father one whit. For instance, as an amateur photographer, he also took many prized pictures of me and my two sisters—including in costumes sewn by Mom for our dancing school recitals. I went to dancing school weekly for nine years, starting at the age of five, first ballet, later tap. Initially it was my mother's idea, she tells me. And though I was an unathletic and chunky kid—for which I was already the butt of ridicule at school—I took to dancing school like a duck to water. But I didn't dare tell anyone outside the family, because I knew for sure I'd get teased to death if anyone found out about my dancing lessons. I never told anyone—not schoolmates, not playmates, not teachers, not anyone at church. It was a secret safe only within my immediate family. Dad's many slide transparencies of me in those recital costumes help me remember that when I was the child in those photos, it never would have occurred to me that Mom and Dad would be ashamed—because they loved me and they were proud.

All of this makes my father rather an anomaly. Curious, I recently decided to ask him some questions to find out *why* he let me become myself. And I decided to start by asking him about how he himself was raised.

I learned something very interesting. I'd known young Vincent had grown up the only son of a farmer in Granite Falls, Minnesota. I'd known that Vincent's mother died when he was three, shortly after giving birth to his only sibling, a sister, and that both children were then raised by their father and an aunt. It turned out that Vincent had no interest in farming. He just didn't care for it. Instead, he liked to take things apart and tinker with them. He started with doorknobs and worked his way up to tractors. He would see what made them work and then he would try to put them back together again. Being young, he didn't always succeed.

Vincent's father paid attention, apparently, to this youthful show of interest in matters mechanical. So rather than saying, in effect, "You're my only son. I expect you to take over the family farm, and if you resist my will I'll make your life unpleasant"— and rather than saying, in effect, "What's *wrong* with you? Why can't you put things back together again when you take them apart? What *are* you?—all thumbs? Why can't you be a farmer and grow things, like me?"—instead of saying anything like that, Vincent's father arranged for him to go to Dunwoody Institute, an industrial trade school in Minneapolis. Fortunately for Vincent, he was encouraged to do what interested him and not forced to do what would have bored him. Thereupon he learned the tool-and-die–making trade and got really good at what he did best. He learned something else rather significant in that early experience, as I now surmise—a lesson about what it can mean to you if you are ever given the support and freedom to become your own best self. Very likely, that was a source for Vincent's knowledge of how he could possibly love me, when I came along.

As it turned out, I never learned from my father how to play catch, how to bat, how to shoot baskets, how to scrimmage. My father didn't do any of that stuff himself, so he didn't do it with me. But I learned much from hanging out with my dad in his basement shop and making projects together. Especially I learned from my father about tools: how to hold and swing a claw hammer to focus the effort on the swinging weight of the hammerhead, how to make a saw cut at exactly a forty-five-degree angle, how to match a drill bit to the size of the screw you intend to drive into the wood.

In my father's shop there were many tools for building things and for making things and also tools for taking things apart—often the same tools. The ratchet screwdriver, for instance, could be set for reverse and used to unscrew rather than screw. A wrench, flipped over and twisted counterclockwise, could unbolt. The claw of a hammer was a rocking lever that could remove a nail the same hammer had pounded in. Though I never became as handy as my father, I picked up a measure of his knowledge about which hand tools to use to take apart something that isn't working right—and then, from looking at the parts and insides of some mechanical device I had never inspected before, I picked up some measure of his intuition for diagnosing how something was supposed to function properly even when it was broken and not working at all. I learned that when something is broken, you use tools of disassembly, not destruction. You don't break it more. If you simply go at it with crowbar or sledgehammer, if you simply crash and bash and tear down, you won't understand how the machine was supposed to work to begin with, which part did what to which other part, which part might have got rusted or jammed. If you destroy it, you destroy all the evidence you needed to get it to work right.

Inspired by the lessons I learned in my father's shop, the rest of this chapter presents a series of questions with which to understand a father's life better, to see more clearly what was going on in him, but not to destroy him, to understand instead the workings of a father's relationship to an adult son. There's an assortment of tools here—assemblages of words that can be used like tools of disassembly—tools for unlocking and unblocking, tools for loosening up and opening, tools for untightening and uncovering. You may find some of these questions useful to see what made your own father tick—a human who was raised to be a man who then turned out to be your dad.

# A Six-pack of Tools for Deconstructing Dad

To use any of these tools properly, you also need to make use of the body of evidence of your senses, your memory of the time you spent with your father, your memory of how and who he was with others—your mother, your siblings, his friends and associates, other family members, and so on—as well as all the feelings that might come back to you about yourself when you were little. Recalling your feelings about yourself is actually indispensable to this project. You can unpack all your stuff about your father and never get behind his manhood mask unless you also use these tools to find yourself inside your own.

### Tool #1: How did you try to avoid being your father's shame?

To understand what was going on with your dad, you may have to analyze the ways he judged you as your gender, from a very early age. He may have given you to understand that you couldn't have his love unless you adopted a proper manhood mask—because otherwise he would be ashamed of you. He may have feared that if his son didn't wear a convincing manhood mask, other men might doubt the credibility of his own. He may have feared that if you wore your manhood mask (or, at the time, your boyhood mask) ineptly or meekly, other men would think your father's mask was a fake. Of course it was a fake; every man's is. But most grown-up men prefer to believe that the manhood mask is real and there's absolutely no one inside who's more real than the mask. So your father—realistically anticipating other men's condemnation—may have feared to be without a manhood mask himself. And consequently he may have dreaded or loathed the sight of you without yours.

You may or may not have been a witness to your father's intimidation by other men, how that intimidation was formed in his biography, what shape it took in his daily life. You may only have been the recipient of his gender anxiety when he let you know you were less than nobody to him unless you had your manhood mask in place.

If you can think back to particular things you did to try to get your father to love you, think back also to what happened between you and him just beforehand. Perhaps you may have felt that he would be ashamed of you otherwise, that he would not want other men to know you were his son, that he would not want other men to find out his son was such a dufus for whom manhood was so ill-fitting. If you think back, you may be able to recall some of the ways he communicated to you that you would be a humiliation to him if you were not athletic (for instance) or courageous or adventurous or excellently muscled and coordinated. And even if in your life you did in fact *become* athletic, courageous, adventurous, well muscled and coordinated, did you always know full well your father would absolutely love you, unconditionally, if you were not? Or were you always working at trying to earn his love by protecting him and you from fear and humiliation in relation to other men?

This first tool is useful because it takes you back to a time when most sons got some of their most indelible lessons in manhood from their fathers. It's a tool to help you understand his life situation in relation to other men's judgment on his manhood mask. It's a tool to help you understand how you figured into that situation when you came along.

It's a tool to help you learn whether your father ever loved you for yourself, with your mask off, you yourself. And if he did not, it's a tool you can use to help you understand *why not.*

## Tool #2: *How did your mother try to avoid being within range of your father's anger?*

To understand who your dad was in relationship to you, you also have to understand who he was in relationship to your mother. There's no other way to understand his relationship to you comprehensively, in fact. You have to use all your available empathy to try to reach inside both your mother's life and your father's life, and for the purposes of the project at hand— understanding your father's emotional effect on your life—you need to try to discern what emotional effect he had on your mother's life.

Think of this tool as triangulation: see what your father looks like from your mother's angle of vision and compare that sight-ing to the person you see when you look at him from your own angle of vision. Like a surveyor, you then establish your bearings that much more accurately.

This tool helps discover how important it was to your father that he got to wear a manhood mask and your mother didn't. This tool helps detect how important it was to his ability to wear a manhood mask convincingly that she be there for contrast—so no one would get confused as to who wore the manhood in the family. In the case of many fathers today this contrast is *very* important. Notwithstanding all the bumbling Dagwood Bumsteads in cartoons, all the television commercials showing fathers who don't know their elbow from a bottle of laundry detergent, all the helpless-househusband jokes, when the chips are down in many marriages (or, in some, when push comes to shove), husbands and fathers often have their ways of keeping the contrast uncontroverted.

Think back: Did you ever see your father let your mother know that he had sole (not shared) authority? Do you remember any times when he used that authority to get his way? Can you remember whether and how he used the authority of his mask, perhaps to clarify for all concerned (his wife, you, and/or your siblings) that he felt indomitable, that he had the right to an identity that comes with getting to wear the manhood mask and no one in the family who knows what's good for them should mess with him right now? See if by any chance anything like that comes back to you now from when you were little.

As with Dad's relation to the world of other men—which may have been relatively obscure to you—you may or may not have been a witness to the critical junctures in your father's relation with your mother when these prerogatives of his manhood mask got hammered out. You may have missed the part, for instance, when she was in tears because he raged at her for presuming to live as if she existed as a person in her own right. Or you may have missed the part when she quietly gave up some of her dreams and ambitions for the sake of domestic tranquillity. Or you may have not been around yet when, to make him feel comfortable in the driver's seat, she put much of her potential in the trunk.

You may find in attempting to use this tool that it simply doesn't work. It is of no use in your case because your father and mother each actually loved each other completely and companionably and constantly as two whole human beings—and he never used his right to wear a mask in order to threaten or frighten her into behaving as contrast to his manhood. But before you abandon your use of this second tool, recall whatever you can about the *range* of your father's anger—how scary and intense did it get? how often did it go off and over what sorts of things? Then, try to recall whether your mother ever did anything in particular to stay out of the way of it.

Let's say you are applying this tool to understand a father who, as it happened, never cursed and yelled when he was angry, never called you or other family members names, never slammed the door and stormed out of the room to end an argument, and certainly never took his anger out on anyone by physically hurting them. Let's say you are applying this tool to understand a father who let your mother know the range of his anger in more subtle and sophisticated ways. Now, assuming he was that type of father with that sort of anger range, what did your mother do—or not do—in order to keep this mild-mannered mini-volcano from blowing up in her face?

Using this tool is always a bit of a challenge for sons. It's a challenge to a son's recollection, obviously. But it's also a challenge to a son's idea of who his father was, and to his idea of who his mother was, as well.

This tool is useful because it takes you back to a time when most sons got some of their most indelible impressions from their fathers about who someone needs to be to qualify as a good woman. It's a tool to help you understand your father's life situation in relation to his manhood mask and what sort of person he needed close by, at home and in intimacy, for contrast, to keep it on—what sort of things that person was forced or forbidden to do in order to provide whatever degree of contrast his mask required.

It's a tool to help you understand how you figured into that situation when you came along. It's a tool to help you understand your own life situation today when you wear your own manhood mask—and how you may appear in that mask to the people you evaluate as women.

It's a tool to help you learn whether your father ever loved your mother for herself, with his mask off, with his anger nowhere near them, just himself and herself, gratefully together and completely loyal to each other, completely comfortable with each other, completely human to each other, completely loving justly.

And if in fact your father did not ever seem to actually love your mother for herself, this is a tool you can use to help you learn whether that might have been one of the operating reasons that he had such difficulty loving you for yourself as well.

### Tool #3: What did you have to kill off in yourself that reminded your father of your mother?

Proper use of this tool takes a bit more nerve and gumption. To wield it accurately and effectively, you really have to concentrate.

*CAUTION:* Do not use this tool before you have tried both Tool #1 and Tool #2.

In your use of Tool #1, you may have identified some things that you did—or dared not do—in order to avoid being your father's shame. Some of that stuff may have had to do with trying to earn your father's love by being as all-boy as you could.

In your use of Tool #2, you may have identified some things that your mother did—or dared not do—in order to avoid your father's anger. Some of that stuff may have had to do with trying to remind your father of his love for her as a good woman and a good wife. Some of that stuff may have had to do with trying to assure him that she was in some sense *less* than him— less authoritative, less competent in the world at large, less a person in her own right. So some of that stuff may have been about being less vocal, less large, less capable, less strong. She may have diminished her presentation of herself so that his mask would show off to best effect.

Now, the ironic thing about being stuck inside a manhood mask—especially if you're a husband and father—is that if you make your love for someone else conditional upon whether they properly diminish themselves, you inevitably end up trying to be in love with someone who keeps slipping into nonexistence, right before your eyes. If they assert their whole personhood, you find ways to make clear that you might punish them with your anger and withhold your love. Sometimes the ways you find are subtle, sometimes the ways are obvious. But in any case, the other person's only alternative, if they want your love but they don't want your anger, is to *shrink*. They must get smaller, weaker, less confident, less capable, less forthright, less intelligent, less interesting, less exuberant, less robust, less initiating—less *themself* in many ways. If you are someone who gets to wear the manhood mask, the sight of such a person shrinking will probably bring you conflicting emotions. Since you already made clear to this human being that you reserved the right to withhold your love unless she was *less,* unless she was *diminished,* you now have the problem of trying to love someone who—in your own eyes and by your own estimation—is not really worth being loved by. When conflicted emotions like that happen behind a manhood mask, you can easily end up feeling dislike—or even loathing—for the person you once loved but whose life got small for you.

*The less someone becomes for your love, the less you feel like loving them.* That's the First Law of Mechanics—if you're a husband and father who lives behind the manhood mask.

"So what does any of this have to do with *me?*" the curious son may well wonder.

If your mother's life was diminished for the sake of your father's manhood mask, your life was affected too. Here's how:

- **Your experience of your mother got short-circuited.** For significant chunks of your life with her, you only got to experience whatever was left after her diminishment. Even if she felt at liberty to be undiminished when she was with *you*—far out of the way of your father's anger, perhaps—she may not have been at liberty to be undiminished when she felt within your father's anger range. You were way too young to keep track of when she was within your father's anger range and when she was not, although like most children you probably intuited emotionally that something schizy was going on. In any case, you were probably deprived—at least episodically and maybe all the time—of an experience of your mother as a whole human being. That deprivation had to affect your perception of her, and that deprivation had to affect your feelings about her. But you were just a kid. What could you know and what could you do about it? Zippo. You were way too young to get a handle on the First Law of Mechanics in your family dynamics.

- **Your experience of your father got jammed.** How could it not? He was behind a mask so much of the time. And you weren't the only person in his life who was having a problem being loved by him. You weren't the only one who had a problem with his problem loving you. Your *mother* may have had a problem with his problem loving her. Your mother may have had a problem with his problem loving *you too. Your father* may have had a problem with his problem loving you. He was having a problem loving your mother (because he needed her to shrink for him), and he was having a problem loving you (because he needed you to be swell for him); he was having a problem loving *anyone* simply for themselves. Plus, he may not have had a clue as to exactly what problem he was having—or even that any of this was even a problem, for anyone including himself. Now, *that's* having a problem. But you were just a kid. What could you know and what could you do about it? Not much, basically, except keep trying to grow up.

- **Your experience of yourself got broken.** You were just a kid. You only needed loving. You only wanted to be loved as yourself. You only needed loving by someone who fully loved you *as yourself* and who was fully loving *as themself.* You did not *need* your father's mask. You did not *need* your mother's diminishment. You just needed their love. Under the circumstances, you probably got about as much as they could give you. It may not have been enough. It may not have been all you needed. So something of your selfhood may have broken. Something whole within you split.

Even though you were a kid when all this happened, and even though you didn't understand what was really going on, you did begin to make some important decisions to try to fix everything up. You attempted an emergency repair job, basically, but before you were old enough to handle any of the necessary tools.

One of the quick fixes you may have tried was this one: If your mother had a certain quality or a way of expressing herself, you may have tried not to exhibit anything resembling it. If your mother had a certain interest or skill or area of competence, you may have tried to make sure no one would notice its presence in you. If your mother had a certain warmth, you may have tried for emotional containment. If your mother tended to smile a lot, you may have tended toward sullen. If your mother was talkative about her impressions and feelings and experiences in life, you may have turned taciturn. If your mother expressed curiosity and concern about how other people were feeling, you may have determined that other people's feelings ought not matter to you so much. Whatever your mother was, you figured, you should perhaps *not* be. You were just a kid then. You were trying a quick fix. There may have been the explosive potential for sudden anger in the air and you may simply have been trying to keep your head down. You were especially trying to keep your father's anger from finding you the way you saw it home in on Mom. So you killed off in yourself anything that might remind your father of your mother.

In effect, you took on protective camouflage—a preliminary version of the manhood mask. You extracted parts of your potential and disposed of them outright—the parts of you that seemed too Momlike you canceled out and shucked off—in order to secure some sense of safety from the shaming anger of a grownup's manhood mask. Thus began a wrenching split in you that was to continue perhaps to today. And in spite of your concerted efforts to appear to your father to be quite *unlike* your mother—to avoid being your father's shame and to avoid your father's anger—you did something absolutely *like* your mother: *you diminished yourself in order to qualify for your father's love.* It's what she did—did it work for her? It's essentially what you did—and did it work for you?

Using Tool #3 can help you understand operationally what you did for your dad's love—and what doing that did to you.

### Tool #4: Does your father reach out to you today to try to connect with who you have become, and who you really are?

Not all fathers do. Not all fathers want to. If yours does, that's a start. That gives you something to work with.

### Tool #5: Does your father reach out to your mother today to try to connect with who she has become, and who she really is?

Not all fathers do. Not all fathers want to. If your father does, that's a start. And you could possibly be useful, like a bridge.

### Tool #6: Does your father really connect with you only when you both make a bargain that puts down your mother?

Not all fathers do this. Not all fathers want to. But it happens often enough with many fathers as to warrant regular checkups. Does your father feel at ease with you only when you are both far away from your mother? Does your father relax more around you whenever you say something that suggests you think less of her than you think of him? When your father urges you to do things with him that you both happen to share an avid interest in, does he tend to do so conspiratorially, as if "it's just between us men—and your mother is too dainty or too dim or too female to understand"? Does his enthusiasm for the shared activity *increase* in direct proportion to how much enthusiasm you exhibit about the fact that Mom is not part of it? Has he ever told you information about his betrayal of her and expected you to keep it a secret? Does he cajole you into tiny disloyalties toward her that seem so minor when looked at one by one that you feel you'd be making a mountain out of many molehills if you objected? Does he make disparaging remarks about her in front of you, then turn to you expecting a reaction of approval? Does he seem disoriented, disgruntled, or afraid of losing your affection if you show unequivocal signs of loyalty to your mother's life? Can your father believe you love him if you do not simultaneously demonstrate disloyalty to your mother? Does he frequently refer to her in diminutive terms of feigned affection—expressions that are more about trivializing her in front of you than about expressing his admiration or regard for her? Does he seem nervous or uncomfortable when you and your mother express affection for each other or a common interest? Right afterward, does he tend to do something to yank you away from your feelings for her? Do you feel this coming, when you are communicating closely with your mother? And do you then pull away from her, predicting what your father might think if you don't?

This sixth tool can be useful because it can help you understand how your father's relation to his manhood mask can be ongoing, affecting your relationship with him and with your mother throughout your life. This tool can also take you back to a time when many sons first learned the lesson that loyalty to your father's manhood mask often conflicts with loyalty to your mother. Sometimes the conflict is low-key, almost unstated. Sometimes the conflict is caustic in the extreme. But the basic outline of the lesson is the same: *to show your love to your father in terms he can accept from behind his manhood mask, you somehow have to demonstrate to him that you reject your mother.*

This is a tool to help you recognize your own role in helping your father keep his manhood mask on. If you've been using this set of tools carefully and compassionately thus far, you may have already realized that your father's lack of love for you could be a function of his love of his own manhood mask. As you grow into adulthood, you continue to try to avoid being your father's shame, of course, and you continue to try to stay out of the way of his anger. But ironically, when you join your father in a private pact between you as between men-only—a truce forged exclusively between loyalists to the manhood mask, a bargain to derogate or diminish the life of your mother—you may inadvertently aid and abet your father's blocks to loving anyone, yourself included. It is your father's love of his man-

hood mask that prevents him from showing you the love you
most need from him, the love for you as yourself, from him as
himself. And it is the same mask that prevents your father from
perceiving and receiving the whole love you might offer him—a
love that does not need to exclude your mother in order to be
your own . . . a love that simply cannot be actual without loving
justly.

IF THE LOVE OF YOUR DAD
DEPENDED ON YOUR MANHOOD MASK,
YOU CANNOT BOTH EARN IT
AND ALSO LEARN TO LOVE.

# ✦ 8 ✦

# WHAT IF I FEEL LIKE
# A FATHERLESS SON?

Sociologists, politicians, and social commentators wring their hands over the absence of fathers from children's lives. As if sounding alarums on a foundering ship of state, they cite statistics bemoaning the growing number of growing children who do not live with their "biological fathers," the rising birthrate among "unmarried mothers," the increased probability that children raised without fathers will be worse off economically, educationally, and "psychologically" (whatever *that* means) than children who grow up with their fathers around. Underlying such woeful tocsins is the presumption that a son raised by a mother necessarily *lacks* something—some ineffable, undefinable *something*—that a son can only *get passed on to him* from someone who was raised to be a man.

There are many sons who feel fatherless. Here are just a few of their stories.

## Seven Sons Who Feel Fatherless and One Who Is Too Young To

Michael and his two-years-older brother were brought up by their mother. Their father left her and abandoned the family immediately after Michael was born. Michael, now in his early thirties, has seen a photograph of his biological father, but has no recollection. The father Michael "lacks" is someone who behaved totally incomprehensibly toward Michael, his mother, and his brother—today Michael cannot even *guess* at a word that would describe his father's character or motivation. Though Michael deeply loves his mother for the sacrifices she has made and the hardships she has endured in order to raise him and his brother to turn out all right, Michael continues to feel a longing that is as much for a real father as for an answer to his bewilderment: how could someone *do* that? how could someone do that to *me*? how could someone do that to *us*? Though Michael at times wishes he'd had a father for the self-understanding he feels that would bring, Michael is quite clear that he does not wish for the presence in his life of an adult man who would behave like the father he actually had.

•

David's father and mother divorced ten years ago when he was four. David sees his father now and then. David's mother is life-partnered with Joan, and together they have raised David since he was six. David's father has a different life now with a different wife, and he hasn't called to make a date to see David for a long, long time. David doesn't really need this adult man in his life in any particular daily way; David's home life with his mother and Joan is relatively OK—just the ordinary hassles and conflicts that seem scheduled to erupt at puberty. But what David needs is for his father not to act so emotionally ambivalent, not to forget about him for such long periods, not to treat David with a distance that seems like distaste. David often seems sad, when his father's detachment makes him feel that there's something wrong with him. David can accept the changed life circumstances of his biological parents, he's doing superbly in school, he has close friends, and he can accept the love and acceptance that have come to him from the woman who has been a good friend to his mother. But David feels rejected by the adult man who fathered him, and he doesn't know how to express that feeling to anyone.

•

Billy's mother was widowed when he was five. The young family was barely making ends meet. Now Billy is ten, his mother has been working as a secretary, and lately she has been dating her boss. This man moves in a world of wealth and influence that is still unfamiliar to Billy. He and this man sometimes talk, but hardly ever about anything that really matters to Billy. He doesn't experience this man as a father so much as the man who has money and is sexually interested in his mother. Billy assumes they'll get married one of these days; he knows his mother hasn't seemed this happy in a long time. But though there is an adult man in his life who is providing him with more material comforts and opportunities than he could ever have hoped for, Billy feels more fatherless now than when his real father died. Billy feels tolerated, not known; bought, not supported. He feels like an outsider—the kid who comes along with a package deal—and he feels he has no right to his sadness because he wants his mother to be happy.

•

Stephen's mother met his father only once, the evening when Stephen was conceived. Stephen's mother is not exactly certain what Stephen's father's name was. Stephen grew up raised by his mother and grandmother along with two brothers and two sisters. The family has had a hard time financially, and soon Stephen will be old enough to look for part-time work to help out. Stephen's feelings of being fatherless are so bound up in the economic obstacles his family faces that when he thinks about having a grown-up man in the house, his first thought is that maybe then the family would not have to struggle so much for money. Already for Stephen, poverty has become a rebuke to insufficient manhood. Stephen knows generally, from hearing his mother and grandmother talk, about economic discrimination against "single" mothers. But already Stephen has begun to believe the problem at home is the absence of a male wage earner. Already Stephen has learned that in the real world, women are worth less. Already Stephen's feelings about the value of money, his mother, other women, and himself have begun to get very complicated.

•

Alex's father was killed by gunfire in their neighborhood when Alex was ten. Alex's mother is trying to figure out how to keep him and his siblings from being shot accidentally too. There is so much violence among men in the neighborhood Alex is growing up in that he stands some chance of never making it to adulthood. The additional safety and security that Alex needs cannot begin to be reckoned—his own real father was helpless to provide it; his own mother is now doing all she can on her own. Alex is old enough to intuit that there is something about adult men that tends to violent confrontations, though he doesn't grasp why. Alex is old enough to realize that the solution is not to have more and more such men drop in on "female-headed" homes. But Alex is personally confused and conflicted, because the only way out of his physical insecurity seems to be to become just like such a man.

•

George's mother got breast cancer when he was twelve. They had been very, very close and became even closer during her long illness. George would sit with her in her bedroom and nurse her and talk with her for hours. After she died when George was sixteen, he and his younger sister and brother were raised by their father, who was and is alcoholic and abusive to all the children. As soon as George could, he got away from home and made his own life. To this day, fifteen years after his mother's death, George's memory of her love sustains him. Though in reality George is motherless, George occasionally feels fatherless—his father, still living, is still abusive in their sporadic communications. But from his mother George received an original basis of self-esteem that his father has never been able to undermine.

•

Andrew's mother is twelve years older than he is. She is raising him and working part-time and going to school part-time. Andrew is still too young to think about what difference it makes whether he feels fatherless or not.

•

Rodney's father died in war when he was two. His mother went back to work full-time and has raised Rodney and his older sister ever since. Rodney would very much like to have grown up with his father, about whom his mother has told him stories with both affection and great grief. Rodney might still have the experience of a father if there were no more war. For Rodney to have the father he might have had, there would need to be predictable peace. To have predictable peace, there would need to be no more confrontations between men defending their manhood act—and there would need to be no more manhood act to defend.

•

Millions of mothers raising children today are being unjustifiably faulted if there is not a carrier of manhood in the home—someone who will dispense the essence of manhood to their sons. But nothing about a child's secure sense of selfhood—nothing about one's assurance that one is lovable, that one has been loved for one's self, that one is knowable, that one has been known for one's self—depends developmentally upon conformity to the strictures of the manhood act. Absolutely nothing.

The problem is not the lack of a bona fide carrier of manhood in the home. The problem is the societal prejudice that imputes blame and unworthiness to the millions of parents who are conscientiously striving to love and raise their children without manhood around, and without the stigma of not having been exposed to it by a real man in the house. "Single" mothers, they're often called. *Singular* is more to the point.

There are indeed certain lessons that a grown-up man may be in a better position to teach a son than is his mother. These

lessons—conveyed in the form of manhood-affirming attention—boil down to gendered survival skills. They are strategies
that prepare a boy to seek safety in the world of other men and
to avoid specific dangers that lurk there. Women by themselves
are generally fair game amid those dangers—because to the extent that there is meaningful safety for *anyone* in the zone of potential man-to-man conflict, it is available only to someone
whose *manhood act* passes muster. Therefore a father figure who
knows the ropes—a grownup well accomplished in outwitting
or vanquishing other men's aggression—may indeed induce and
induct a son into that combat zone armed with an intimidating
manhood mask, an arsenal of fighting skills, and deft maneu-
vers for guaranteeing truces (including practice in putting down
women) in order to deal safely with other men.

Whatever is special and distinct that only a grown-up man
can provide a son stems entirely from this fact about the world
we all live in: the zone of man-to-man hostility is sometimes tra-
versable by someone raised to be a man if he knows and obeys
the codes by which all manhood acts seek safety in social truces.
Therefore a father's manhood-affirming attention may indeed
occasionally pass on to a son that which no mother now on
earth can: the dream of physical safety among large numbers of
grown-up men.

But such attention is always bestowed conditionally on a
child—if and when the child measures up to the manhood
standard—and it adores that child's conformity to gender
stereotype. *Such attention is not the same thing as selfhood-affirming
love.* The love of a child's unique human self does not *come from*
a parent's manhood, and no child becomes *eligible* for such a
love by *embodying* manhood. Selfhood-affirming love is what
each child deserves, and it can be amply and variously expressed to any child by any concerned and present grownup—
someone born penised as well as the human who gave the child
birth. Selfhood-affirming love can communicate strength, honor,
courage, bodily integrity, compassion—any quality of human
character that we humans have come to value because it values
*us.* But the manhood mask *per se* is not indispensable to anyone's selfhood.

## Ten Things to Remember If You Don't Have Your Father's Love Because You Do Not Have Your Father

**1.** There is nothing you lack to be strong, honorable, and loving.

**2.** If you had a strong and honorable and loving mother; or if someone who was present like a mother to you was strong, honorable, and loving; or if someone who was present like a father to you was strong, honorable, and loving—you can be grateful for that gift. The fact that the gift did not come from your biological father is of absolutely no consequence for the loving life of your conscience.

**3.** Everyone gets two humans' genes. You needed both of their bodies to be conceived. You needed one of those human bodies to be born. After that, you don't need some magic potion that only someone specifically raised to be a man must offer you before you can be true to yourself. There is no such magic potion. There is no secret indispensable ingredient. To become your own best self, there is no mythic substance that only someone raised to be a man can provide you. There are no mysterious vibrations that you must somehow pick up only from someone in a manhood mask. You needed insemination, gestation, and parturition to get to life. How you get to love and personal identity is another story altogether.

**4.** Your mother may feel bad that there is no "male role model" in your home or in your life with her. Your mother may feel guilty. Your mother may feel that it's her fault. Your mother may be afraid for you that you somehow won't turn out OK. If that's the case, you have a special challenge and opportunity. See if you can figure out how to show your mother that she has given you all the basics you needed to begin life as a loving human being. See if you can figure out how to love her back so that she will not feel as if she did something terribly wrong to you. Because she didn't, after all. She gave you the gift of life and of her love, the best she could. That's doing something right, not something wrong—and you have a chance to prove it.

**5.** If you have memories of your father when he was in your life, and if they are the welcome memories of someone who was kind and important to you, someone who may have given you all the love he had to give you, someone you miss, perhaps someone whose absence still makes you ache with loss, you may find yourself wanting to remember his life and his loving as intensely as you can. And that's good. Feeling you want to remember him tells you something important about your own capacity to love. And when you do remember him, imagine what it would be like to see him face to face again, to really love him as himself, to look past his manhood mask as if it is not there at all, to look deep from within you to deep within him. Imagine what it would be like to *re-know* that person. Imagine what a gift that would be to you, what a gift that would be to him. Then remember that possibility. That possibility exists in you completely.

6. A human being either does or does not learn to love justly. The world is full of folks who never did, or who didn't get a chance to. Sometimes a person gets to learn the basics from a mother or from a father or from both. Sometimes a person learns the basics from someone else along life's path. Sometimes a person needs a remedial crash course and someone who decides to love you sits you down and gives it to you. Sometimes a person learns to love justly and then something terrible happens and they forget. The world being what it is, loving justice is rather flukey. The odds of learning to love justly are not great under the best of circumstances. So if you learned any of the basics from someone who raised you, you're already way ahead. See if you can find a way to show them your gratitude.

7. Learning the basics of loving justly is not the same thing as getting coached and goaded about how to wear the manhood mask convincingly. Those are two quite separate and distinct educational tracks. One learning track is about loving justice, and the other learning track is about loving manhood. If you didn't get quite as far along on the manhood track as you might have hoped, there's no reason to worry. The thing to worry about, actually, is if you get pushed *so far* along on the manhood track that you get completely *off track* with loving justice. And whether you have a father or a mother around to give you a sense of direction, it's really up to you to stay on track. You really have to want to love justice on your own.

**8.** If you did not get training into wearing the manhood mask from a grown-up man who was around when you were young, that does not necessarily mean you got no love of *you*.

**9.** If you did not get love from your father in particular, you will not find it by trying to love manhood harder.

**10.** There is nothing you lack to be strong, honorable, and loving.

THE PROBLEM IS NOT MOTHERS WITHOUT MEN;
THE PROBLEM IS FATHERS WITH MANHOOD.

# ✦ 9 ✦

## ISN'T THERE SOME WAY THAT MANHOOD CAN BE REDEEMED?

As author of a book about how men handle their problems with manhood, I feel obliged to be up-front about how I handle my own. Thus I must confess that sometimes when I contemplate the disagreeable foibles of those who uphold manhood with utmost reverence, my own mischievous irreverence becomes quite pronounced. And such is the twitting temper that I find myself in right now.

So in the legendary spirit of Deep Bob Himself, I'm going to tell another tall tale. It's a story about four men and manhood. Their names are Ron, Rick, Larry, and Joe.

The story was made up by me. The manhood was made up by them.

### Four Guys Whose Manhood Needs Help

Once upon a time, Ron, Rick, Larry, and Joe were in a men's support group together. They met every few weeks to share. They shared about this and that and then they shared about themselves. Then they shared about this and that some more.

One day they were each sharing about themselves, carefully taking turns, when *eureka!*—they realized they all seemed to be having the same problem (but until sharing one by one they had not known anyone else in the *world* was having it): They weren't feeling very good about themselves as men. They were feeling empty and worthless. They did not know how to redeem manhood—in a no-deposit, no-return world. They couldn't seem to do anything right. Other people in their lives seemed always to be complaining about them or resentful of them. Nobody who knew them seemed too happy about them. And these four men didn't feel too thrilled about themselves either. So after going around the group and sharing more about themselves, it became clear that the problem they had in common was that they couldn't seem to figure out how to feel completely OK about being a man.

Sure, some of them felt better on Fridays. And some of them felt better on Mondays. Some of them felt better about being a man in the morning. Some, at half past two.

But it was hard. They didn't know how to feel good about being a man in a predictable way.

The slightest thing could make them feel like a schmuck. Who knew? What would help? What would lock in a permanent, reliable, rock-solid, and manly self-concept? A self-esteem so metaphysical that you could look down inside your guts and honestly bellow, "I sure as hell am one hell of a man!" A self-image that could withstand all the bad press that men seemed to be getting lately, not to mention bad-mouthing from peevish women.

Maybe you know the feeling.

It comes and it goes for a lot of us.

So these guys wondered if maybe they could get themselves together in some kind of self-help group—figuring that was all the rage.

Ron suggested that they all set out to see who could feel good about himself as a man the most. A group goal, with a kind of contest built in.

Rick raised a point of order. "Isn't that being very *competitive*?" he asked. "Isn't that just typical male behavior?"

"What's *wrong* with typical male behavior?" screamed

Larry, and you could actually see veins in his forehead popping blue. "The whole trouble is, we've been so put upon by females, we don't take *pride* anymore in our biological, godgiven heritage as hunters, marauders, and *beasts!*"

Joe went *gulp*. "It's not really a competition with *each other*," he offered; "it's really with our own *pasts*. You know, like in one of those slim-support groups, where you come to the next meeting and stand on a scale and everyone applauds how much weight you lost that week? Well, we could each stand up and say how much guilt, shame, and all-around self-loathing we dropped, and everyone else can be appreciative and nurturant and *clap*."

So it was agreed. At each weekly meeting over the course of the next year, each of them would report on what they'd done—and how well they'd managed—to feel good about themselves as a man.

Each of the four men took a quite different path . . .


### Rick Gets Even

Rick went out to find other men who would validate his anger—especially his anger at the way he felt he'd been treated by the women in his life. He found an organization of men who were *very* angry—it included disgruntled ex-husbands trading bitter tales of woe with men whose girlfriends had dumped them, and divorcing fathers exchanging hot telephone numbers of sleazoid lawyers who'd fight dirty in child custody disputes. The men in this organization, it seemed to Rick, were on a righteous crusade, even though some outsiders might view it as a rampage of revenge. In fact these men were struggling amongst themselves to extract some safe and trustworthy emotional support from other men—other enraged men like themselves. Angry women were a real drag, these men agreed, because if you ever depended on a woman to stand by you, it was a setup and you would end up getting screwed. But angry *men!*—*that* could really be worth your while. Especially if they were all united in anger at someone *else*, not at you.

Rick liked hanging out with those angry fellows a lot. It gave him a feeling of security, of belonging, of fighting back, and returning to the good old days when men hung out and shot the shit, and women respected men or else.

## Larry Gets Down

Larry's path took him in search of a father. He *had* a father, of course, a biological father, but not one who really cared much for him—and all his life Larry felt deprived of some crucial connection to a beneficent and powerful male ancestor, someone benign and forgiving but manly and strong. A dad like dear Mum plus a big dose of deep dadness. Without such a father, Larry feared, he himself would never be able to feel very good about being a man. So Larry hooked up with a cult of men who celebrated their mythic communion with their wise and warriorlike father figure of choice through mystical drumming, animal-like costuming, and curious experiences in sweat-huts. Just hairy men together, sweating, grunting, reading poems, and farting, getting in touch with a good ole dad, getting in touch with Myth Man, summoning up their male ancestors' deepdown manhood (unsullied by industrialization and urbanization), not having to think about women at all.

Larry had a wonderful time. Being a man, he felt at last, was fun again.

## Ron Gets Over

Ron was an idealist. Ron had very high standards for himself. He wanted to be a *good* man. That's how he wanted to think of himself; that's how he wanted other people to think of him. But Ron was also a realist, so he didn't want to have to work too hard at this. Ron took a path toward a therapy network of "clean consciousness." Through it, Ron sought to find goodness, intrinsic goodness, in all men everywhere. It became increasingly important to Ron that he be able to find such goodness in all men everywhere; otherwise, he was afraid, he could not find any in himself—he'd be cut off from manhood if all of manhood wasn't good. Ron wanted to be *a man* and *good* at the same time. But if he looked around at *other* men, or if he looked too closely at some of his *own* behavior, he ran into mental trouble. Things got complicated. Messy. His behavior butted up against other people in ways he felt helpless to sort out. That was why he liked clean consciousness, or CC, as its adherents called it. CC means you're basically a blank slate of complete innocence, but you got scribbled on. Oh yes you got scribbled on and scribbled on; you got scribbled on so bad, you sometimes *look* bad. But *you're* not bad. You're really *good*. Deep deep down you're still a perfectly clean slate of complete goodness and innocence. If you do something bad, it only *looks* as if someone did something bad; the *thing* might have been bad (whoops), but it wasn't *you*! It was really those nasty scribbles. The *scribbles* made you do it. Once you're comfortable believing all that, all your scribbles wash clean off your slate. Then you can say, "Whew! My consciousness is clean! Your consciousness is clean! The consciousnesses of *all men everywhere* are clean." It's like no-fault gender insurance.

Ron was deeply affected by his experience in CC. Ron liked that it brought him into fellowship with other CC believers. Ron especially liked that many *women* believed in CC. They were very, very cooperative—because they were taught in CC never to express anger at men. They helped Ron off the hook. They supported him as a truly good man. And after all, Ron thought, isn't that what truly good women are *for*?

## Joe Gets Off

Joe's path led directly to sex. Joe, it turned out, needed more than anything to feel good about his sexuality. As a kid, he'd always felt embarrassed about his sexual feelings, because they weren't the ones he thought he was "supposed" to have. They made him feel odd—not, he imagined, like a real man was supposed to feel. If anyone found out the truth about his sexual feelings, Joe was certain he would be exiled from the company of really masculine men forever. So excruciating were Joe's fears that his sexuality was insufficient and substandard—and so important to Joe was acceptance of himself as a sexually manly being—that his sexuality became for him the center of who he ever wanted to be. Joe threw himself into a lifestyle that focused almost exclusively on having sex. Joe had sex as often as he could, with whomever he could, as fast as he could, as much as he could. For Joe, having sex became the sum total of his life; the only thing that mattered was whatever meant more sex. He couldn't care less about anyone else's ax to grind; the only need that counted was his own quest for validation of the masculinity of his sexual feelings, and the only validation that he could *believe* was in the hunt, the conquest, the furtive, alienated groping and pronging and then the solipsistic sexual release. *That* was when Joe felt male in his sexual organs, when his gender batteries were recharged, when he felt OK about his sexual feelings, when he felt restored to his rightful masculinity.

Joe had one hell of a time. For one brief shining moment in his meteoric sexual history, Joe got his cock and his manhood back together again.

✧

Now, the thing about these four stories is that they don't go anywhere; they go on and on and on, and they don't really have an ending. These four men could go on trying to redeem their various manhoods, and we could easily imagine more and more such men joining in the attempt. For each caricature in this lampoon, there are the cumulative stories of teeming hordes of men in real life, all of whom sense that somehow the world—and therefore their conduit to manhood—has changed dramatically because of feminism. And they don't seem to have a clue what to do about it.

They believe that manhood is a game that's still worth playing. They think their only problem is not knowing where square one is. They want to get to manhood but they don't yet *get it.*

They don't get that though they seem to be having a solitary crisis of personal and sexual identity, what they're really having is
a problem in recognizing relational selfhood.

The problem is not how to be "a real man." The problem is
how to live completely mindful of the meaning of other selves.

- *What does one ever mean when one says "I"?*
- *What does one ever mean by saying "us"?*
- *What does one ever mean when one says "you"?*
- *And what does one do to say so?*

THE QUESTION IS NOT
HOW TO HAVE A REAL SEX;
THE QUESTION IS
HOW TO HAVE A REAL SELF.

# ISN'T MANHOOD SOMETHING BASIC THAT WE REALLY NEED?

The unexamined longing for manhood leads to choices that are easily spoofed, as shown in the stories of Ron, Rick, Larry, and Joe in Chapter Nine. But simply to scoff at such behaviors—however ridiculous they may seem—yields but smug self-satisfaction for the satirist. Plus, the dissed get pissed. Worse, making a mockery of the longing for manhood offers no more practical insight into it than was evidenced by the incognizant characters themselves.

So let's have another look at what Ron, Rick, Larry, and Joe were really longing for. Each one was trying to *get* something. Each of the characters in those four stories was trying to satisfy a specific emotional need, one that goes back to very early childhood. Each was seeking a personal affirmation of some sort. This chart organizes those emotional needs so that we can take a clear-eyed look at all of them . . .

| Character | His Basic Emotional Need | His Interpersonal Objective |
|---|---|---|
| Rick | To feel safe. | To feel safe from other men's anger. |
| Larry | To feel sustained. | To feel sustained by his father's love. |
| Ron | To feel seen. | To feel seen by someone as a person worth knowing. |
| Joe | To feel sexual. | To feel sexually present with another human being. |

These four basic emotional needs—to feel safe, to feel sustained, to feel seen, to feel sexual—are fundamental to human experience, and they are felt by nearly everyone, often in combination or all at once. For the sake of our examination of the longing for manhood, however, we are going to consider these four basic needs as if they are separate, and as if they can be looked at schematically, through a scrupulous interpretation of our four virility vignettes.

In the chart, note that none of the four characters' basic emotional needs is gender-specific. That's because the need "to feel safe, to feel sustained, to feel seen, and to feel sexual" does not imply or define the gender of either the person feeling the need or the person who might possibly meet the need. But take a look at how the characters chose to achieve their emotional needs *in relation to another human being.* Right away we see that both Rick and Larry have opted for interpersonal objectives that are decidedly gender-specific:

✔ Rick's objective has to do with *other men* in general. You'll recall that Rick joined the "angry men's group" ostensibly because he was angry at women in general—and as the story reports, he was. But the *emotional satisfaction* he found among those men really had to do with feeling completely accepted within a designated group of men where he did not have to fear other men's anger—perhaps for the first time in his life. He especially did not have to fear their anger being directed *at him*. He knew he could feel safe from what he had probably learned to fear as a very young boy: angry and possibly brutal men, angry men who could hurt you real bad.

- ✔ Larry's objective has to do with *his father* in particular. You'll recall that Larry joined the "mythic father figure" movement so as to fill an emotional void in his life that may have been left when his real father abandoned or rejected or abused him. Whatever material support his father may or may not have provided (Dad's money), Larry doubtless felt deprived of the emotional sustenance he needed most (Dad's love). Now Larry spends his own money regularly and ritually to find a father's love through a secular spiritual quest for the dad he wishes he'd had. And even though Larry may never feel quite convinced that through myth-telling and drumbeats his own Loving Dad has genuinely beamed himself down into Larry's body and soul, Larry nevertheless finds enormous emotional satisfaction among fellow questers for their father's sustenance. It is the satisfaction of emotionally bonding with grown-up men who won't abandon, reject, or abuse you. They actually seem to hug you, hold you up, and let you cry when you hurt. As stand-ins for Dad, they aren't half bad.

If we next look at Ron's and Joe's chosen means to meet their emotional need, we notice that neither of their interpersonal objectives is *apparently* gender-specific:

- ✔ Ron's objective has to do with other people in general, whether raised to be a woman or a man. You'll recall Ron joined the "intrinsic goodness" therapy network because he wanted *to be seen as someone worth knowing* by people whom he could trust *to see what's really worth knowing about him*. Now, it's rare enough these days to be seen by *anybody*, much less by someone who will recognize you for who you really *are*. So on that score alone, the network introduced Ron to lots more people than he could reasonably expect to meet at random out on the street. It

was also an emotional relief to Ron when he felt he could
be seen by other people as someone worthy in his own
right, without feeling evaluated on the basis of how he
looked, how much money he made, who his parents
were, how he dressed, and so forth. Ron felt emotional
satisfaction in the freedom he found to see these self-
selected other people as themselves, to really see *them,* to
see people completely worth knowing. Emotionally, this
helped close a crucial loop for Ron: he could be seen as
someone worth knowing by people whom he himself had
come to see as worth knowing—so when he felt seen by
*other* people who were worth knowing as someone who
was *himself* worth knowing, he found intense emotional
satisfaction in this assurance that he really *was.* The circle
felt complete: he really *was* seen; he was really *worth* seeing; he really *could* see someone else; he really could see
someone else *worth* seeing. The emotions of that interpersonal event are a lot like the emotions of loving justice, as
we shall see.

✔ Joe's objective has to do with other people in general too,
although as you read his story you may have made some
assumptions as to who, exactly, he was having all that sex
with. The story never actually specified; it only disclosed
that he scored a lot. So let's take the ambiguity of Joe's
story at face value (and let's stipulate that Joe never
failed to prevent HIV transmission)—and let's look instead to the underlying and unambiguous emotional
need: Joe needed to feel sexual and not alone. Joe needed
to feel sexually *there* with someone. Joe needed to feel
sexually present *in his own body* and sexually present with
someone *else's.* Joe needed to feel sexually present *with
someone*—and *to* someone—so he could feel sexually
present *to himself.* Though it's arguably doubtful whether
Joe's ambitious lifestyle always brought him fulfillment
of those underlying emotional needs, try to use your
imagination. (Joe certainly used his.) Imagine that every
so often, Joe really met someone else who was fully human too—and they met, as chance would have it,
through an explicitly sexual encounter. Try to imagine

such a sexual experience with all the passion and compassion and emotional empathy you can muster. Try to imagine that now and then, or every so often, or *even once*, Joe experienced as close to a culmination of this human need as any human being can. Joe met someone human too. Joe's body met someone else's body meeting his. Joe and someone else touched deeply, touched each other, touched their deepest physical beings. Joe was fully there, someone else was fully there, and it was almost as if they were not having sex at all. *It was as if human sexuality was having them.* So if you can imagine such an event in Joe's life—or if you can *remember* such an event in your own—you may recognize what can only be intimated for now: the sexuality of two people being completely present sexually to each other and to themselves—human to human, self to self—is a lot like the sexuality of loving justice.

Looking yet more closely at both Ron's and Joe's stories, we notice that their interpersonal objectives are neither *apparently* gender-specific nor even *inherently* gender-specific:

✔ The need to be seen by someone as a person worth knowing is not necessarily met just because you are seen by someone raised to be a woman, and it is not necessarily met just because you are seen by someone raised to be a man. Nor can you *predict* that you will be more personally seen by one or the other (although you may, out of habit, *look to* them differently, as if you expect one to be more likely to see you and the other not to be very good at this sort of thing). Moreover, whether someone was raised a woman or a man is not what makes their *seeing* of you make you feel *seen* (although you may have slightly different emotional reactions when you feel seen by one or the other).

✔ The need to be sexually present with someone is not necessarily met just because you are sexual with someone raised to be a man, and it is not necessarily met just because you are sexual with someone raised to be a woman.

Nor can you predict that you will feel more sexually present with one or the other if you have sex. One of you may disappear to the other. One of you may imagine you're with someone else who's not there. One of you may touch the other not as another human being but as an inanimate thing. One of you may have to play dead so the other can have some semblance of sexual release. The two of you may be quite absent to each other, actually, even though you are both feeling sexual. This counts as feeling sexual, but it does not count as feeling sexually present. The point of the basic emotional need is to feel sexually *present* with someone—another human being— but that does not necessarily happen. And when you *are* sexually present with someone else, when you really are sexually *present*—completely to yourself and completely to each other—that does not necessarily happen because of how the other human being was raised based on the sexual anatomy they were born with. That does not even necessarily happen because of the sexual anatomy *you* were born with. That happens because you were both born into bodies—*human* bodies—with a *human* need to feel sexual and not alone.

None of the four characters' basic emotional needs was gender-specific. Yet two of them—Rick and Larry—*opted right off* for means to meet them that were unquestioningly gender-specific. And the other two—Ron and Joe—*decided upon* interpersonal objectives that were gender-specific as well:

✔ To be seen as a person worth knowing is not necessarily to be seen *as a man*. Ron's own moral philosophy is completely consistent with this view. He needed to be *seen by* other people *irrespective* of whether he saw them as a man or as a woman. So far, so good. But in Ron's story, he needed to be *seen as* a man—a man with intrinsic goodness. Now, what exactly does that mean? Did this mean to Ron that only *a man* is worth being seen by? No, clearly Ron did not mean that; Ron knew too many women who were clearly worth being seen by. Did Ron think he himself was not worth knowing *except* as a man?

No, clearly Ron did not think that; Ron knew too many women who were eminently worth knowing in their own right. So what exactly did Ron mean, then, when he needed to feel seen as a person worth knowing but he needed simultaneously *to feel seen as a man*?

✔ To feel sexually present with another human being is not necessarily to be *the man there*. This view not only "rings true"; it veritably resounded in Joe's own deepest longings; it reverberated throughout Joe's own sexual sensorium: he simply needed physically not to feel alone. That's basic. He needed to feel someone else was *there*. He needed to feel *there with someone else*. He needed to feel sexually *present*. So what exactly was he doing by trying to be *the man there*? Was he feeling completely present to someone who was feeling completely present to him? Or did his attempt to feel and be the man there get in the way of feeling and *being* there?

All four stories—Rick's, Larry's, Ron's, and Joe's—strike slightly different notes in a common chord:

- All four stories are about trying to meet basic emotional needs for selfhood affirmation—needs that go way back deep in childhood.
- All four stories are about a strenuous and serious attempt to meet those emotional needs by someone raised to be a man.
- All four stories are about trying to meet those emotional needs by needing manhood.

To feel like a real man is often what one longs for when what one really needs is to feel safe, to feel sustained, to feel seen, to feel sexual and not alone. When verification of manhood feels urgent, one's resulting behavior may prevent those basic emotional needs from being met. Learning to recognize one's longing for manhood as an ineffective means of meeting one's basic and human emotional needs is a crucial stage in the lifelong process of loving justice instead.

THE NEED TO VERIFY MANHOOD
STANDS IN THE WAY OF
LOVING JUSTICE THAT IS NEEDED
TO AFFIRM SELFHOOD.

# ✦ 11 ✦

## HOW CAN I BE ANYBODY
## IF I'M NOT A REAL MAN?

As we found in Chapter Ten, there are four emotional needs that are basic to every human: to feel (1) safe, (2) sustained, (3) seen, and (4) not alone. Often, however, when a human tries to meet these needs by trying to feel like a real man, the needs stay unmet in the overweening drive to validate manhood. Meanwhile manhood—the goal of a securely gendered personal identity—remains an elusive cul-de-sac.

The desire to meet basic, ungendered emotional needs is not the only motivation to verify manhood. Many humans long for manhood feeling it is somehow their "destiny." Such humans feel *born* to embody manhood in some determinative way. Therefore, such humans experience the challenge to feel like a real man not only as a social obligation but also as a physiological mission—to fulfill an innate disposition.

This feeling of gender destiny is not a "metaphorical" feeling at all; it is quite palpable; one literally feels it physically, in one's body. It is the urgent feeling expressed verbally in the sentiment "How can I be *anybody* if I'm not a man?" It is the panicky feeling of impending nonexistence when one contemplates living an instant or two without the security of verifiable manhood.

Someone else may or may not be aware when a human raised to be a man is having an episode of this hyperintensive

feeling. Someone else may only witness or experience some behavior that the feeling inspired. On the other hand, someone
raised to be a man may *also* not be consciously aware when this
feeling is getting felt. So that feeling—call it gender anxiety—is
the subject we'll look at next.

But first, a blast from the past.

In this chapter, we are going to travel backward in time, to
the origin of manhood in a human infant, in order to seek the
source of the physical feeling that longs for manhood as if for
dear life. But time travel is always an imaginative leap beyond
the known, so we must begin by getting some bearings. No
mortal has actually done it. No one knows if you get vertigo or
motion sickness and lose your lunch for eons. No one actually
knows *how* to do time travel except in word pictures. So to become accustomed to the head-spinning voyage that awaits us as
we travel back to the origin of gender panic in a penised human,
this chapter embarks first upon a practice run—a mystery joy
ride backward in time to the origin of the universe.

Our round-trip itinerary is as follows: (1) the origin of the
physical universe in space, then (2) the origin of manhood in the
physical feelings of a human. An instant cosmic epic, plus a generic, gendered biopic. The flashback of all flashbacks.

Relax, kick back, and fasten your seat belt.


## Destination: The Beginning of the Universe

### Observing the Evidence

As far as the eye can see to the outermost reaches of space, the
universe seems to be expanding. Actually, astronomers' powers
of perception left their eyeballs behind long ago; now astrophys-
icists probe space by picking up long-distance rays and waves
that human optics cannot detect. And what they have discerned
is consistent data that the universe seems to be spreading out,
speeding outward and outward, hurling beyond its own ever-
receding boundaries. The farther physicists look into the vast
reaches of the universe, the more evidence they find that the
universe *seems to have started somewhere* in time—billions of years

ago—and it appears to have been flying off in all directions ever since.


## Hypothesizing an Explanation

So the question naturally arises: At what point did all this expansion begin? When and from where and why? What *jump-started* it? Some cosmologists have proposed that the universe began with a hot big bang. It was an explosion beyond explosions. It started with a grapefruit-size ball of super-dense super-stuff, then instantaneously inflated outward into a cosmic soup of undifferentiated matter and radiation. Some three hundred thousand years later, the soup began to be the sort of broth we see as the night sky—which has been blowing hither and yon for perhaps twenty billion years. How do scientists *know* the universe began with a big bang? They don't. They hypothesize. No one was there when this big bang happened—it was obviously long before human consciousness came on the scene. But since "A.D. 1964" scientists have been aware of a mysterious faint glow of microwaves that pervades space. These emissions had been predicted by the big bang theory: they're residual radiation from the point in time when the murky cosmic soup became the see-through sky. These microwaves, scientists suppose, are to the big bang theory what fossils are to the theory of evolution: a tantalizing trail of interpretable physical evidence, a snapshot of what was going on long, long ago. Analyzing the various phenomena they can observe—the expanding universe, the background microwave radiation—scientists propose a theory that explains their observations about the universe's behavior the best they can. The theory is only a guess, but it's the most explanatory guess they can come up with that fits all the facts at hand.


## Testing the Hypothesis

There's no way to prove directly that the big bang theory is correct. Like any radically new idea that fundamentally transforms our notion of who we are and how we got here, the big bang theory is controversial (and not surprisingly, it was vigorously denounced by fundamentalist creationists). Not even all professional stargazers are certain the theory has merit. But confirming evidence has recently been rolling in, because supposing—just *supposing*—that the big bang theory may be the best bet yet, there *is* a way to figure out what evidence to look for that would be consistent with the theory. There is physical and behavioral evidence that one could look for that the theory predicts. This may be evidence no one might even think to look for unless its possibility had been suggested as a logical consequence of the radical theory. If such evidence is not found, or if contradictory evidence is found, then the theory is fatally flawed. So scientists testing the big bang theory said, in effect, "If the big bang really happened, if stars came from dispersing cosmic soup, there ought to be telltale evidence left over in the background microwave radiation. We ought to be able to detect this evidence if we can do so from a space probe far enough away from earth's interference. This trail of evidence, these ancient microwaves, will be very, very faint, but we ought to be able to perceive a pattern of unevenness in the waves. They ought to be mottled, a little warmer here, a little cooler there—fluctuating by but thirty-millionths of a kelvin. If all we find is a pattern of uniformity, there's something wrong with the big bang theory, which predicts that the original soup stock didn't fly outward in all directions evenly—instead it clumped. It organized itself gravitationally. Even as it dispersed, it gathered around itself and became galaxies. Here and there. If the big bang theory is correct, we ought to find faint traces of microwaves in a pattern of prehistoric clumping." So space scientists sent out a satellite to catch these variegated waves, and *eureka:* in "A.D. 1992" they announced that's precisely what they had found.

# Destination: The Origin of Manhood in a Human Infant

## *Observing the Evidence*

As the observed human subject approaches adulthood, the body begins to feel waves of anxiety. The body sometimes feels fear. The body sometimes feels anger. The body sometimes surges suddenly with edgy fight-or-flight reactions. Such feelings and reactions seem especially to cluster and coalesce and clump around something called manhood. The body feels especially panicked if the human perceives that this manhood is impugned or endangered. The human subject may experience these reactive sensations relative to manhood in the abstract or manhood as some personally embodiable attribute. Reaction times differ from human subject to human subject, as do intensity of reaction and violence of behavioral sequelae. But experimentally the reaction is not difficult to obtain. It's like pushing a button and *bingo:* the human defends manhood like life itself.

The observed human subject can speak rather intelligibly about the material existence of this manhood—the basis of it as *real stuff:* "Manhood is in my genes. Manhood is in my genitals. Manhood is in my gonads. Manhood is in my brain cells. Manhood is in my upper-body strength. Manhood is in my beard growth. Manhood is in my sperm—which are vigorously fertile and motile, by the way. Manhood is in my own exuberance and wild energy. Manhood is in my vibrations and wayward emanations. Manhood is in my loins. Manhood is in my very being, you know what I mean? I just can't explain it very well. Sorry."

Alas, the human subject's explanations of the material substance of manhood keep collapsing one by one. For every proposed explanation of the material basis of manhood, evidence crops up that runs completely counter to the explanation. Not a single material factor is adduced that scientifically "proves" the existence of manhood, because not a single material factor has yet been found that *ineluctably correlates with it* and that *exclusively predicts it.* And scientists have been *looking* for such a material factor *with considerable zeal.* Once they thought it was exterior genitalia. Once they thought it was a hormone. Once they thought it was a chromosome. Once they thought it was a dispositive gene. They keep not finding the sine qua non they're looking for*—and meanwhile many of these selfsame scientists' bodies are getting a bit anxious. This elusive but alleged manhood business seems to have a very unusual type of existence. It seems to have no primary cause, yet it seems to come from somewhere. Most astonishing of all: the assumed sum of the whole bears no absolute relationship to any of its catch-as-catch-can components.

Perhaps there is no there there.

Perhaps, actually, there is not necessarily a *where* at all. Perhaps manhood is simply a seemingly necessary way of being *who*.

Ah-ha.

This would mean that manhood per se does not have a metaphysical existence with any material origin at all. This would mean that the phenomenon of the so-called manhood anxiety reaction is actually the physical symptom of a biographical event. And this would mean that the physical longing for manhood has a *human history*, with a beginning in *human experience*. So the question we ought to be asking is: At what point, when and how, did this history of manhood anxiety begin?

What jump-started it?

*Something* must have *happened*—but what?

Not only does the problem now become one of hypothesizing the past conditions that prevailed when the longing for manhood began in a human biography—the problem is also how to draw a causal relation between those biographical conditions and the physical/emotional/behavioral symptoms that appear at present.

What starts human infants needing to feel like a real man? What do such children do later in life when that is what they need to feel? What's the physical link?

---

* Readers may find a fuller elaboration of this point in "How Men Have (a) Sex" in *Refusing to Be a Man.*

## *Hypothesizing an Explanation*

Someone raised to be a man once wrote a book in which he claimed to remember back to when he was a zygote, a fresh-fertilized egg in his mother's womb. I found this book rather difficult to believe. I don't have quite that much faith in human memory. So I think (I *hypothesize*) that if the history of manhood-longing begins anywhere, it has to begin sometime after birth to be within the realm of the plausible.

If whatever *happened* began sometime after birth, however, it could have been *done* very early—before the child had language, before *any* child has language. This makes data retrieval difficult. This means there may be no reliable linguistic evidence in all of recorded culture that accurately takes any of us back to what was done to that very young human. Nevertheless, our hypothetical time travel can proceed, because I brashly hypothesize the following inelaborate explanation:

1.  I hypothesize that when the human subject was born with a sufficiently visible genital tubercle (for that's the arbitrary criterion), the human infant was selected out to be taught the following two lessons:

| *Lesson A* | *Lesson B* |
|---|---|
| To be human | Not to be a man |
| is to be somebody. | is to be less than nobody. |

Each such penised human infant was taught those two lessons in a particular proportion. Some got more of Lesson A. Some got more of Lesson B.

Some got so little of Lesson A that their body has almost no recollection. Some got so much of Lesson B that their body can do little else but recall it all the time.

The proportions varied widely, but the content of the two lessons was a constant.

2.  I further hypothesize that these two lessons were learned two different ways:

Lesson A was learned pretty much the same way by all infants who ever learned it: from being kept safe and sound and sheltered, from being fed and sustained and nurtured, from being witnessed and regarded by grown-up humans as a human too, from the comforting sensual presence of other humans' breath and flesh. (These are an infant's version of the four basic emotional needs that were charted in the last chapter: to feel safe, to feel sustained, to feel seen, to feel touched and held and not alone.)

Lesson B, however, was learned quite differently; it was learned solely from rewards and punishments. For some penised human infants, the reward was a pleasant smile and a compliment and the punishment was a scowl and a stern admonition. For other penised human infants, the reward was indifference and the punishment was corporeal. At the far end of the sliding scale, the reward was episodic escape from physical trauma and the punishment was condemnatory terror, brutal abuse, humiliation, and so forth. The proportion of rewards and punishments—as well as the type of rewards and punishments—varied widely from human infant to human infant and from time to time. But if Lesson B got learned at all, it got learned in no other way: through rewards and punishments.

3.  I further hypothesize that for some human infants, the means of learning Lesson A got occasionally interpreted as the *reward* for learning Lesson B. Sometimes Lesson A was so rarely communicated in the first place—and the infant had already learned to expect so much punishment under the terms of Lesson B—that if ever simple interhuman comfort occurred, the infant assumed it as a reward under the terms of Lesson B. Sometimes Lesson B was taught with such vehemence that if you ever got any Lesson A in your life you'd hardly know it. A variety of mix-ups can occur, such that even when the infant is experiencing the means of learning Lesson A, the infant, already quite intently doing homework on Lesson B, interprets simple warmth and human kindness as a high grade in Lesson B.

4.  I further hypothesize that the learning of Lesson B would explain why most penised humans feel physically frightened that they would be worthless—less than nobody—if they are not a real man, and why they therefore evidence the observed fight-or-flight reaction (anxiety, fear, panic, anger) whenever less-than-nobodyness looms. The tremulous need to be "the man there," and to feel like "a real man," is learned to escape punishment—and the fear of that punishment is situationally recollected.

5.  Finally, I hypothesize that the words "man" and "real man" in this theory are simply placeholders, nonce words. They don't have any material meaning or substance in and of themselves. They are encrypted with no intrinsic significance. As abstractions they signify only in a particular context—in the biographical events by which these two lessons get learned, in the historical experience of the rewards and punishments needed to teach Lesson B, and in the emotional and physical sense memories of all humans whose flesh and consciousness were ever taught to memorize one or both of these two fundamental lessons to some extent.

### Testing the Hypothesis

My hypothesis is only speculation, informed by what appear to be the symptoms at hand. Perhaps it explains nothing. Perhaps it explains some symptoms but not enough. We would have to see—we would have to seek confirming evidence—by looking closely at our own lives and at the lives of other humans raised to be a man.

1.  My hypothesis predicts that if we were to look at a sampling of such human lives, we would be able to detect wide variations in the degree to which Lesson A and Lesson B have been learned. The penised humans who got a relatively high proportion of Lesson A would tend to grow up with a sense of a human identity—a selfhood—that is parallel to, or not exclusively invested in, or inde-

pendent of, their social gender identity. And the penised humans who got an overridingly high proportion of Lesson B would tend to grow up without having a cognitive clue who they are if they cannot believe themselves identical with their social gender.

2.  My hypothesis predicts that if we were to look at a sampling of such human biographies, we would be able to detect the effects of variations in the rewards and punishments meted out to teach Lesson B. We would be able to discern, for instance, that more-violent methods of punishment during childhood tended to implant Lesson B more pronouncedly. And we would expect to find that Lesson B was learned more and more intractably as childhood punishment increased, both in frequency and ferocity.

3.  My hypothesis predicts that the more indelibly Lesson B is learned, the less likely is Lesson A to be available to a penised human's sense memory.

4.  My hypothesis predicts that the more affirmingly Lesson A is learned, the less likely is Lesson B to "take." Lesson B would tend to make less and less emotional and physical sense to the human the more memorably the human learned Lesson A. And in particular, my hypothesis predicts that if we could ever discover a penised human who learned Lesson A extensively and predominantly early in life, and whose learning was subsequently reinforced rather than undermined throughout puberty and adolescence, then that so-far rare specimen would exhibit few if any fight-or-flight reflexes in defense of "manhood"—all things being equal, of course. (Regrettably, both the laboratory conditions and the subject population for such an experiment are very difficult to obtain at this time—since there's still so much that's *unequal*.)

5.  My hypothesis predicts that no matter how memorably a human learned Lesson A, and no matter how indelibly a human learned Lesson B, the net result for all is some de-

gree of lifelong gender anxiety, so long as Lesson B is taught at all.

6.  My hypothesis predicts that this gender anxiety, like residual radiation from the big bang, is detectable and perceptible—sometimes quite faintly, sometimes overwhelmingly—in a host of human events and interactions but especially in human eroticism.

7.  My hypothesis predicts that the physical sensations of this so-called manhood anxiety in human sexual expression would vary in intensity in direct proportion to the ratio of Lesson B to Lesson A. If more Lesson B was learned than A, manhood anxiety felt during sex would tend to be higher. If more Lesson A was learned than B, manhood anxiety felt during sex would tend to be lower.

*It's all just a guess*—an audacious theoretical conception—and like the theory of the big bang when first proposed, it has absolutely no "proof" yet.

But let us assume for a moment that at least some of it rings true, and let us look at some what-ifs of this theory's first premise: Lesson A ("To be human is to be somebody") and Lesson B ("Not to be a man is to be less than nobody"). What if we ask what *happens* when a human infant learns these two utterly contradictory pedagogies? What if we wonder how that *feels*? What if we were to explore how these opposite early-childhood lessons later affect one's sexual apparatus and appetite? What if we could examine how the human sexual organism—the human body electric—adapts to standing astride the chasm between the promise of selfhood (Lesson A) and the precept of manhood (Lesson B)?

HUMANS ARE NO MORE BORN WITH MANHOOD
THAN THEY ARE BORN WITH ANXIETY
ABOUT WHETHER THEY HAVE IT.

# ✧ 12 ✧

## WHAT'S SUPPOSED TO TURN A REAL MAN ON?

Human eroticism begins adapting to Lesson A and to Lesson B long before an infant ever learns language. Penised babies are dressed in blue to cue adults how to treat them: how to hold them, talk to them, touch them. The infant's nascent sexual feelings occur in a visual, aural, and tactile environment of expectations that grownups have already decided suits babies dressed in blue. Then when the child is ready to talk, the language the child gets taught is mostly loaded and coded with Lesson B.

The links between language and Lesson B get comprehended and forged ineluctably, but only baby step by baby step. Watch any child who is trying to learn the personal pronouns "he" and "she," for instance. The child is at first utterly bewildered.

A friend of mine and her husband are raising a son in a home where both grownups have made a conscientious decision not to impose social gender demands—and one of the ways they've done that is by agreeing not to bifurcate child care responsibilities. The child, just learning to talk, doesn't yet know how to use "he" and "she" but will call her "Mommy" and her husband "Daddy." Sometimes, though, when either one of these two big people suddenly walks into the room and appears to him by surprise, he will look up quickly and spontaneously say,

"Mommydaddy!" Such is that kid's simple trust in undifferentiated, unconditional love.

What happens to most children far more typically is that they learn from grownups' chiding that the categories "he" and "she" are fraught with portent. Only later—after much trial and error—does any child fathom how to use "he" and "she" with whatever meaning adults anxiously insist the concepts have. Even then, the child may be made to feel ashamed for making a mistake.*

By adolescence, induced anxiety about gender differentiation becomes especially acute among the penised. So imbedded in youthful language use is gender anxiety that certain words alone can be spoken aloud as proof of how well Lesson B has been learned. Contemptuous words like "motherfucker" and "cunt" can be handy for this purpose. Also whole hostile sentences, perhaps played back mentally from movies, such as "Shut up, bitch!" and "I'm gonna punch your fuckin' face in!"

Lesson B is in our everyday language, in the dictionary, in the verbal frame of reference for our whole culture, no matter which sexual sentences an individual may wish to speak but may not know how. Therefore, getting down to honest sexual feelings through layers of everyday language is always problematic, and honest talk about human sexuality is never easy.

---

*And gender gendarmes will doubtless have a hissy fit over this book's use of "they," "their," and "themself" in the third-person singular. But as I listen to people talking in everyday life, I hear a deep longing for a gender-free personal pronoun. Lacking authorization from English teachers or the publishing industry, the common folk have simply adopted "they" to meet a deeply felt linguistic need. Moreover, everyday speakers have discovered that the singular pronoun "they" fits easily into the same familiar rules followed by the second-person pronoun, "you" (which, happily, is already gender-free). People rarely have trouble telling from context whether "you" and "your" are singular or plural (and whenever clarification is needed, people say something like "each one of you" or "you all"). Only with "yourself" (singular) and "yourselves" (plural) does the word need to change to indicate number. In ordinary speech, many people are becoming much less adamant about gender enforcement and spontaneously subverting conventions of English grammar in order to make the language their own. Many people seem even to relish a release from gender dictates altogether, and this may be why—in so many informal human communiques—the singular "they," "their," and "themself" are fast catching on. Like children, we may simply be trying to speak of our common humanity without shame.

## What's Your Intimacy Literacy?

Our vocabulary itself sometimes creates sexual-communication problems. Most of the common words we have for sex are names of objects and things (so we keep thinking in terms of disembodied body parts) and transitive verbs (so we keep thinking only in terms of active and passive—"doer" and "done-to"). When it comes to expressing sexual feelings in a context of really deep interpersonal intimacy—where mutuality and wonder seem to overwhelm and embrace both partners at once—words often fail us. And that's because there *are* no words. The very language we speak is quite illiterate about sexual intimacy.

This language lack might be affecting your own sex and love life. To help you understand how, this chapter is written in the form of a reverse vocabulary quiz.

Most vocabulary quizzes give you a word first and then ask you to supply the definition. This one's backwards. First you'll get a definition—a short description of a sexual experience or a verbal elaboration on a sexual activity or event—and then you'll be offered some words. You'll have the option of picking which words best name for you the experience or event or activity described.

If you don't recognize the experience or event or activity, you don't have to answer. It's OK to guess. And if you don't care for the answers provided, simply make up your own.

The reason this vocabulary quiz is backwards is because translating from words to experience is always difficult when we try to talk about human sexuality. One person's nouns might not point to another person's inner feelings at all. One person's verbs might make no emotional or physical sense to someone else. And we all learned to speak words that we were *expected* to mean before any of us learned to use language to try to say what we really feel.

This backwards vocabulary quiz is designed to help remedy such practical problems of sexual communication. It begins with recollected interior experience and only *then* proceeds to nouns and verbs.

✧

**1A.** Think about your experience when you see someone and you seem to recognize them deeply and you want to take in and appreciate their being, their personality and presence, including their physicality, their particular beauty, their individuality, their quirks, their history and relationship with you, their connection with you, their commonality with you—and during the entirety of that experience you simultaneously experience a resonance of sensual or sexual presence, like a recollection from long ago brought back and intensified in the moment, a recollection that seems to have revisited you through feelings excited in your pelvis, your groin, your chest, and virtually all over.

What exactly would you call that activity and experience if you wanted to give it a name?

❑ Recognizing (literally, "re-knowing")
❑ Regarding
❑ Admiring (literally, "marveling at")
❑ Witnessing
❑ Beholding
❑ Other: _____

**1B.** Think about your experience when you look at someone's body (or when you look at a particular *part* of their body or a particular *place* on their body) and you look at that body as if it's an object or a thing—not as if it's a body someone lives in and someone is at home. Think about your experience when you look at that body as uninhabited flesh and you mentally assess its relationship to your manhood, or the manhood you are sincerely hoping to have here in this particular situation and the manhood you are sincerely hoping to feel in your own body somehow, somewhere, hopefully now. Think about your experience when you instantly do a mental calculation as to how this body ranks. Think about your experience when you look at someone's body in just that way with just that particular urgency and just that particular anxiety and with just that particularly sincere hope that you will feel yourself feeling like a real man right here and now. And think about your experience when looking at someone's body that way makes blood pump into your genitals in a particularly pleasurable way.

What exactly would you call that activity and experience if you wanted to give it a name?

❑ Cruising
❑ Scoping
❑ Just looking
❑ Eyeball target practice
❑ Sexual objectification
❑ Other: _____

**2A.**   Think about your experience when you are asleep and dreaming, or you are day dreaming, or you are in a private, personal reverie of some sort, and the memory of someone you know comes back to you and into you as if this person is there with you this very moment. It is as if they have visited you in your memory and you can almost see them and feel them and touch them. It is as if they are nearly as real to you in this memory as they are when the two of you are together. All your longing to be reunited with this person seems to have expressed itself in this near-total recall of their body and being, their presence, their presence to you, their face, their smile, their touch, their words, their breath. You *miss* this person (their absence feels like an ache), yet at the same time they seem and feel present to you, in this moment, which your memory seems to have provided you. And now think further about this event in your memory, for it brings back all the sexual and sensual feelings you recently or once felt in that person's real presence. Suddenly these feelings flood your body, and you shudder or you perspire or you feel on fire with the passion of your recollected connection with this person.

What exactly would you call that mental event and experience if you wanted to give it a name? Fill in the blank:

❑  _____

(Sorry, but the language is completely unhelpful here. Write in if you have any ideas.)

**2B.**  Think about your experience when you find a picture in your mind of someone's body, how it looks, how it moves, things it does, things it can do to you, things you can do to it. You may have this picture in your mind as if your mind's eye were a camera. Or you may have this picture in your mind because it's one you once saw that an actual camera photographed, so the picture in your mind is more like a picture of a picture. In either case, the picture in your mind is of how that person's body *looks*—moving, doing things, being done to, standing or lying still, and so forth. You may not know this person "in real life" or you may—it doesn't matter. What matters at the moment is that you have them as a picture in your mind and you have the picture in your mind as if you *took* it. Now, thinking about the experience of finding that picture in your mind, perhaps accessed from the image bank of the inner computing power that is your brain, think simultaneously about running an instant computation of that picture's relationship to your manhood, or the manhood you are sincerely hoping to have here in this particular situation and the manhood you are sincerely hoping to feel in your own body somehow, somewhere, hopefully now. Think about your experience when you picture someone's body in your mind in just that way with just that particular urgency and just that particular anxiety and with just that particularly sincere hope that you will feel yourself feeling like a real man. And think about your experience when picturing someone's body that way helps you have an erection.

What exactly would you call that mental event and experience if you wanted to give it a name?

☐ Feeling sexy
☐ Fantasizing
☐ Getting ready to masturbate
☐ Getting ready to have intercourse
☐ Other: _____

**3A.** Think about your experience when you and another person in your life are discovering and disclosing to each other the intensity of the sexual feelings you both feel in each other's presence. You both have found some words, you both have found some gestures of affection, you both have come to understand that these sexual feelings are not only especially intense, they are especially grounded in each other's individual presence: in who you see when you see that person and in who that person sees when that person sees you. Whether or not you may ever have felt this intensity of feeling before, with someone else, some other time, your body is experiencing this intensity of feeling completely in the moment with this particular person here and now. This person is as real to you as your feelings, and your feelings are as real to you as this person. Now, think further about your experience as you and this person communicate about acting on those intense feelings, as you and this other person deliberate and discuss whether, under what circumstances, with what protection, and so forth, you will likely become quite a lot more intimate physically. Try to think about your sensual and sexual feelings during these talks, as the two of you move from moment to moment, point to point, completely full of care and regard, both of you clear and direct and conscientious in responsibility-taking. And think of those feelings during this communication as a welling up with gratitude and gratification at the trust and respectful intimacy that have *already* transpired between you.

What exactly would you call that transaction and experience if you wanted to give it a name?

❏ _____

   **3B.** Think about your experience when you are with someone and you feel extremely sexually attracted to this person, and as you interpret this person's signals you think there is some chance you will have some success if you make the right moves. Think about your sexual feelings in this situation as feelings that seem to have been triggered for you by this person's body type in a particular way, as if in the image bank of your brain there is a collection of typically triggering sorts of faces and bodies and looks and appearances, and you have just found what looks like a match. This person you're now with has some or all of the physical attributes that give you the sexual feelings you always hope to have triggered whenever you review the contents of your image bank. And you can easily project in your mind some explicit sexual connecting between you, too, because this person's body looks as if it's a type that will trigger your sexual arousal in a sustained-enough way to last throughout the connection. Think about your sexual feelings in this situation as having some degree of anxiety as well. This anxiety may be anywhere on a number of various levels:

*ANXIETY LEVEL 1.* You may be anxious about whether you will be sexually rejected by this person.

- You may recall with embarrassment that you have misread other people's signals in the past.
- You may be shy.
- You may be inexperienced.
- You may not be so certain you will appear to this other person as "manly" enough.

*ANXIETY LEVEL 2.* You may be anxious about whether this person will really sexually arouse you (although this person is "just your type," or just the type you believe *ought* to turn you on).

- You may recall with embarrassment that you have become disenchanted and lost your arousal with other such types in the past.
- You may have already noted physical details, personal idiosyncrasies, or physical flaws about this person that conflict with your original, hyper-gender-specific, idealized, image-bank image—so the person could possibly become a turn-off (you never know).
- You may be high (you may have been taking something into your body to blunt your anxiety and it may also have blunted your arousal).
- Your image bank may work better for you in private, when you are masturbating, than it does when you're trying to connect to a live body.

*ANXIETY LEVEL 3.* You may be particularly anxious about your "manliness" right now.

- Something may have just happened in your life that left you feeling like shit, someone put you down bad, and you need a quick self-esteem fix through an affirmation of your manhood.
- Something may have happened in your life that left you feeling very angry and you need to deliver that anger to someone who won't physically hurt you back.
- Somebody may have recently cast aspersions on your manhood, so you need to reassert and reprove it with vigor and urgency.

Happily, the net result of any such mental anxiety—whether on level 1, 2, or 3—is to enhance your involuntary fight-or-flight reflexes, which happily include increased turgescence in your groin. Among people born with penises, anxiety is among the most effective and popular aphrodisiacs known, and handily enough you were born with a penis. Feeling your anxiety-induced arousal swell your genitals, feeling your chest pound with newfound bravado, and feeling your sexual arousal seem to vanquish your mental anxiety (the very anxiety that may have triggered it), *voilà:* you feel much better and you feel much better about yourself. So now you feel you can make your move.

What exactly would you call the subsequent transaction and experience if you wanted to give it a name?

- ❑ Seduction
- ❑ Hitting on someone
- ❑ A pickup
- ❑ Trying to score
- ❑ Other: _____

**4A.** Think about your experience in a sexual encounter with another human being when you and that person have both risen to a peak of sexual arousal and erotic energy expenditure as if in harmony or in sync, at first as if feeling one another's latent feelings stirring, then as if feeling them resound in the interstices between you, as if your sexual feelings and your partner's sexual feelings found resonance and amplification in a reverberating sound chamber that you have made between you through mutual regard. Somewhere between your bodies, you or your partner may be touching, stroking, rubbing, embracing, writhing, yet there is an undulating wave under way. Somewhere between your bodies, some part of you may be inside your partner, or some part of your partner may be inside you, yet there is a massive wave mounting. Somewhere between your bodies there may be sweat, saliva, mucus, semen, lubricant, and somewhere between your bodies there may be a latex membrane, yet augmenting all sensations and conscious awareness between you, there is a torrential tidal wave gathering velocity across a vast ocean. Someone's body becomes a near breaker beside another's, and one breaks, and then another breaks, and body to body you both are borne along by it, swollen and overflowing, as if effortlessly and mutually, drenched upon a crest.

What exactly would you call that participatory activity and experience if you wanted to give it a name?

- ❑ Ardor (literally, "great warmth of feeling . . . intense devotion . . . burning heat")
- ❑ Lovemaking
- ❑ Great sex
- ❑ Sexual intimacy
- ❑ Contact orgasm (climax by osmosis, from feeling someone beside you come—by analogy to drug-culture slang, "contact high")
- ❑ Other: _____

> **4B.** Think about your experience in a sexual encounter with a human body that you are doing things to with parts of yours, somewhat forcefully or aggressively, perhaps, but in any case unilaterally and transitively. You take it, you push it, you press it, you squeeze it, you grab it, you poke into it, you shove back and forth into it, for instance, then you clench and you spasm and you tense and you flex and you poke back and forth into it, and you poke back and forth into it, and you poke back and forth into it, and you clench and you tense, and you work at ejaculating, you work at ejaculating, you work at ejaculating, you work at ejaculating, you work and you work and you sweat and you sweat, and you push and you push, and you work at ejaculating, you work at ejaculating, until—until—you do. Think about your experience in that quasi-participatory activity as feeling that ejaculation is synonymous with orgasm. Think of fearing to feel any preorgasmic sexual feelings that do not promise oncoming ejaculation. Think of screening out all such preorgasmic feelings, canceling them, averting them, steeling your body against them, so that your body is not contaminated by them, and think, instead, of focusing sexually, strictly, on ejaculation. Think of never really experiencing your own orgasms, much less your

partner's, because to be present to another human being that completely, that vastly, that intimately, that con-
nectedly, would leave you no safe set-off space in which
to be the man there, to cum like a real man should, to
cum like only a real man must.

What exactly would you call the experience of that
quasi-participatory activity if you wanted to give it a
name?

- ❑ Fucking
- ❑ Getting laid
- ❑ Great sex
- ❑ Sexual adjacency
- ❑ Home run
- ❑ Other: _____

**Bonus question:** Compare and contrast the energy expenditure
in calories for the activity in 4A and the activity in 4B.

- ❑ 4A uses more calories.
- ❑ 4B uses more calories.
- ❑ If you're really into it, 4A and 4B come out about
  the same (in terms of caloric energy expended).
- ❑ This question doesn't belong here. It's completely
  beside the point.

✧

The point of this ostensible vocabulary exercise—trick questions
and all—is actually to depict the difference between sexual feelings in a context of intimacy (all the "A" questions) and sexual
feelings that are best felt when canceling out intimacy (all the
"B" ones). You may recognize or remember having had both
kinds of sexual feelings to some extent. When your human sexuality is experienced in a context of actual intimacy, your sexual
interaction will tend to be about being with someone else who
is just as human as you are—therefore just as real as you are (because "to be human is to be somebody"). When you try to experience your sexuality *without* such equality in intimacy—when,
for instance, you're trying to be the man there by treating someone else as *less* real than you—in effect you're getting off all by

yourself (although you're obeying your body's remembered warning that "not to be a man is to be less than nobody").

- *How did you score?*
- *How do you rate?*
- *Where do you rank?*
- Who do you *get* to be?
- Who are you *trying* to be?
- Who do you *want* to be?

SEXUAL SELFHOOD CANNOT BE EXPERIENCED
BY SOMEONE TRYING TO BE THE MAN THERE.

# ✧ 13 ✧

## WHY CAN'T I FEEL
## OK TO BE *ME*?

So-called manhood anxiety is a recurring theme of this book. Now and then, some people reading this book—depending upon their biographies—may feel the anxiety physically as well. For such readers, this poses the unfamiliar challenge of both *experiencing* the anxiety and *reading about it as a topic* at the same time.

In writing this book—for which I sought to analyze both my own experiences of gender anxiety and its presence in other men—I have become aware that some of us may need to pause now and then in order to reflect on anxious feelings that have come up not merely on the printed page.

This book is written with the conviction that if all of us penised folks stay clueless about our gender anxiety, then basically the topic remains impervious to human cognition—and the consciousness of our whole species will be perilously limited, precluding humanity's potential to evolve toward the next millennium. If, however, any of us can get a grip on it—and understand how our inculcated gender anxiety really *works*—there may perhaps yet be unrealized hope for us all.

## An Optional Feelings Check

Occasionally a reader raised to be a man will feel some nameless fear flow through, a heartbeat skip, a pulse quicken. Admittedly the very thesis of this book may prompt such periodic twinges, and an apoplectic rush of ruminations approximately like these: "What if this book really means what it says—that I can't *have* an authentic selfhood and try to be a real man at the same time? What if what this book says is true—and I might not even *be* who I *think* I am?—or I might have to be *different*?—or to be who I think I am, I am *already* different (Gosh, sure hope no one else notices!)?—or the thought of becoming who I might want to be makes me so nervous about being different that I'm not sure I want to think about *any* of this anymore?—or if I think about who I am now and who I might want to become, I just want to think about something else *(Anything* else!)."

The sudden experience of gender anxiety waves—left over from long ago—may need checking out, so that they don't unduly interfere with the experience of reading about them:

- Was the gender anxiety wave telling you to stop "for your own good"—and not go any further in your recognition of the dichotomy between manhood and selfhood?
- Or was that anxiety wave *also* telling you to go *on*? Was *your ability to observe* the feeling *as gender anxiety* actually a clue: evidence from your own senses that you may be on to some new kind of perception and a possibly new personal experience?
- Might your mental awareness of your own gender anxiety wave be evidence, perhaps, that *your own selfhood* is capable of *observing* your need for manhood?
- If you *really* know what's good for you—and if you really know what's good for everyone *else* in your life (everyone you know or ever hope to know)—might you perhaps be better off just going forward?—because might your feelings be telling you that you already have the potential to learn more about what could become a newfound sense of self?

- How do you know to trust a gender anxiety wave, any-way?

Checking out those sudden gender anxiety waves means not only keeping track of the feelings but keeping track of what sets them off. Part of practicing having a selfhood is learning how to detect those sudden gender anxiety waves and how they behave—and how those anxiety waves make *you* want to be-have.

So it makes sense to check out one's feelings every so often—one's feelings about aspirations to manhood, one's feelings about aspirations to selfhood, and one's feelings about those pesky gender anxiety waves.

It's like coming to one's senses.

It's like coming to *all* of them.

OK—now—take a deep breath. And let's go on to the real gist of this book.

## A Practical Guide to Selfhood for Men of Conscience

The following four statements sum up what you have been reading so far. Obviously you have been reading about bio-graphical experiences of other men in your life, your father, your mother, early childhood, your sexuality. Obviously you have been reading as well about emotional and physical feel-ings, perhaps comparing your own to the feelings discussed. But fundamentally, you have been reading about four main points, and here's a quick review of them:

1.  Manhood is vertical. Selfhood is horizontal.
2.  The reality of your manhood is in direct proportion to the unreality of someone else.
3.  The reality of your selfhood is in direct proportion to the reality of everyone else.

4. The reality of your selfhood is inversely related to the reality of your manhood.

A schematic diagram will help make the first point clear.

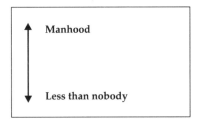

This diagram shows manhood as a vertical scale, with the abstract ideal of "manhood" at the top and "less than nobody" at
the bottom. Nearly every human who grows up to be a man
learns gender in these terms—"Not to be a man is to be less
than nobody" (Lesson B).

When manhood is viewed clearly as a vertical, it becomes
obvious at a glance why you can experience enormous discrepancy between yourself and others who were raised to be a man
but who seem to rank above you, more "manly." The top seems
to rise ever higher, always beyond reach; in daily experience,
acting like a real-enough man seems to require ever more elevation, or jacking up, in order to feel like a done deal. But the job
seems endless and the competition above is stiff. It feels like trying to rock-climb up a cliff with some churlish climbers up
above you trying to kick out your pitons. And if you dare look
down, you feel you could free-fall any instant into sexless nonexistence. Viewing manhood as a vertical clarifies why someone
raised to be a man could feel a persistent terror of being mis-
taken for someone "not a man," therefore "less than nobody," by
other men who seem to have successfully climbed higher.

Moreover, when manhood is viewed as a vertical, it becomes
clearer why someone who is never permitted elevation to manhood (a woman, for instance) would experience acutely the efforts of those being raised to be a man to attain to manhood.
Viewing manhood as a vertical clarifies why someone climbing
the ladder might be tempted to use one or more female bodies
or female life-support systems as bottom rungs. Stepping on a

female's life would niftily lift you clear of the "less than no-body" stigma: it would demonstrate there's someone below you and it's someone you're not.

The popular delusion that there is, somewhere on this planet, a path to gendered selfhood as "woman"—a path somehow independent of the ladder to manhood—has unfortunately caused much confusion, self-blame, and inchoate distress. However fleetingly one might feel one's feet upon such a phantom path, there remain daily reminders of one's standing as "woman" beneath the verticality of manhood. It is difficult if not impossible to make these reminders go away simply through earnest wishing that gender be two parallel paths. However much one might wish for gender equality by analogy (or gender parity by parroting), wishing does not make it so. Manhood's verticality has a way of crashing in upon one's most sincere yin-yang reveries. Manhood's verticality has a way of being felt and experienced bodily and emotionally in spite of one's most fervent efforts to hallucinate that gender be played in twin tag teams on a level field.

Manhood is a vertical palisades, perpendicular to a base line of female bodies.

If you were raised to be a man you will not find the path toward authentic selfhood without comprehending in personal detail exactly where you are standing on the ladder propped up to reach manhood, who is above you and why, and who is below you and why. This book so far has been designed to help you explore those questions for yourself. From here on, the book will shift emphasis somewhat to help you explore what you may tend to *do* in life to maintain your toehold on that ladder.

The ladder leads nowhere. There *is* no essential manhood. The pie in the sky is Deep Bob. But *knowing* that the ladder leads nowhere can be useful and liberating. The insight comes in especially handy when hanging on to your rung has become tiresome. Or when you have been advised that your efforts to hang on have become tiresome to someone else.

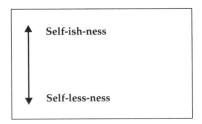

This diagram may already seem familiar to someone intrigued by the possibility of living life as a man of conscience. What you will perhaps recognize—from your own experience and observations—is that between two people, selfishness can often be interactive with selflessness. The selflessness of one person sustains what is in effect the selfishness of the other; meanwhile the selfishness of one person can be satisfied only by the selflessness of someone else. This is probably not news to you. You may have already recognized this vertical dynamic for yourself—or if not, someone may have brought it to your attention.

What you may not have realized is that this vertical dynamic, with "self-ish-ness" above and "self-less-ness" below, not only *resembles* the vertical manhood scale; it is *on* the vertical manhood scale. This diagram represents what has to happen in many people's lives for them to experience any semblance of self while remaining loyal to gender.

The words "self-ish" and "self-less" both have some shadowy sense of "self" lurking within them, and this is not a semantic fluke. The one who behaves "self-less-ly" may perhaps experience a martyrlike sense of self, and this martyrdom may secure a tether of identity attached to someone up on the cliff. Simultaneously, the one who behaves "self-ish-ly" may experience a reduction of gender anxiety in the adrenaline rush that comes from having found a handy and compliant crevice into which to drive his next piton. *Both* interacting humans obtain some sense of a gendered self in this vertical interaction. That's usually what keeps them at it, because without the manhood payoff in this dynamic, there is little to recommend it. At the end of the day, the sense of self you're left with is hardly worthy of the name.

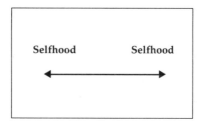

Authentic human selfhood can only be horizontal, as this diagram shows.

The diagram is a visual metaphor for this two-way truth: *Your sense of yourself as a real human self can only come from recognizing and regarding someone else as a real human self also. Your sense of yourself as a real human self can only come from being recognized and regarded by someone else as a real human self also.*

This is simply a corollary of what you may have learned as a child through selfhood-affirming love: "To be human is to be somebody" (Lesson A). If you learned that lesson to any extent, you learned it only on human-to-human terms. You learned that convincing feedback about your full humanness can be found only in relation to the full humanness of somebody else. That's why your human need *to be seen* as somebody worth knowing can only be satisfied *when you see somebody else as worth knowing.*

In principle, you can find feedback about your humanness in relation to *anyone* born human if you recognize and regard them as somebody human too. But just because *they* recognize and regard you as somebody human does not necessarily mean you have found convincing confirmation of your humanity. In your interactions with them, *you* have to recognize and regard *them* as fully human. Only in *that action of yours* does the horizontal of selfhood come into human experience.

The problem expressed in the question "How do I know I'm a human self?" is thus categorically different from the problem expressed in the question "How do I know I'm a real man?" The kinds of information that would answer these two questions are completely different. What you must do to obtain such information is completely different. And the outcome—the resulting sense of who you are—is completely different. The difference all depends upon which question you decide is more important to have answered.

When you ask "How do I know who I am? How do I *know* I'm me? How do I feel *good* about being me?" you have to decide whether you are asking a question that can only be answered horizontally or a question that can only be answered vertically.

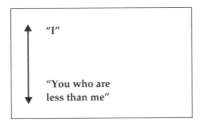

The reality of your manhood is in direct proportion to the unreality of someone else. What you must do to answer the manhood question—"How do I know I'm a real man?"—is determined by the verticality of manhood itself. Once you decide the cliff is worth being on, you have your work cut out for you: climb, keep from being kicked off into the abyss, and find secure temporary footing on your way up.

As the diagram above shows, to meaningfully call yourself "I" on the vertical dimension of manhood, you have to address your "I" to someone you select to speak to as "You who are less than me." When you say "I" on the treacherous, precipitous cliff of manhood, there's only the hollow echo of your own voice in a cavern unless you say your "I" to someone else as if they're somewhere down below. There's no other way to know with certainty that you are *anyone* once you have committed to cling to the cliffside. You can look above you for possible routes to pursue in your ascent, but you can hardly look upward for safety and security: other climbers ahead of you are already kicking down rocks. To them, you could easily become just the sort they might next select to address 'as "You who are less than me." There is no meaningful "I" for you—or for anyone, for that matter—in being named "less than" someone else so that *they* can meaningfully say "I." So you *must* look down. On the cliff, everyone must.

In the drive to scale the cliff of manhood, human beings throughout history have developed some vicious climbing techniques and have outfitted themselves with treacherous arsenals of climbing equipment, because once the cliff is deemed real, everyone needs to climb above *someone*. Otherwise you won't have a vantage point for looking *down*. Otherwise you can't say "I" with the sort of certainty that's of any significance on the bluff. Thus the verticality of manhood has profound implications for the social meaning of ethnicity and race.

Racist hatred and violence are driven by identity anxiety—a ghastly case of it. Animosities from one ethnic grouping or extended family to another are always fueled by adult men who fear that their identity will be defiled or contaminated if they do not secure their boundaries, if they do not lock up the brains and bodies of their breeders, and if they do not commit such pillage, extermination, or lynching as may be required to maintain their posture on the manhood cliff, somewhere up above the Identity Danger down below.

Once upon the vertical dimension of manhood, one *must* say "you who are less than me," or else one has no "I." Experience that confirms one's reality can be obtained in no other way.

Many of us penised folks, raised to be a man, have already looked searchingly into the training we got, the lesson we learned from rewards and punishments ("Not to be a man is to be less than nobody"), and the lifelong pressures we have experienced to conform to the manhood standard. And in that honest self-evaluation, we may have already recognized to some extent the gender anxiety waves that sometimes overwhelm us.

The panic these waves portend is always the fear of seeming to be "not a man, less than nobody": The fear of being a sissy. The fear of being or seeming a girl. The fear of contamination by anything female. The dread of being confused with anyone female.

Growing up to be a man has meant staying on guard against that hazard, learning to appear manly enough, learning ways to experience ourselves physically and emotionally as a real-enough man. Our personal embodiment of manhood may not necessarily result from the commission of a literal crime against someone's humanity, because it can be done in so many other ways so effortlessly. All it really takes is a slight negation of someone's selfhood. The real trick is managing to stay safe from the danger and rage of other men.

The Ku Klux Klan "whites" who beat and lynched African

Americans acted out of an analogous and parallel anxiety. So did the Nazi "Aryans" who exterminated Jews. They were terrified that their personal identity would be contaminated and defiled. They needed their violative rage in order to feel "white," in order to feel "Aryan," in order to still their fears that their personal identity would dissolve.

Of course it's a long, long way from one's childhood terror ("Nyah, I don' wanna be a sissy!") to an adult act of terrorization ("Take that, you bitch!"). *All* of us penised folks don't have to go the distance. We just all have to crave the *difference:* the difference between a "real man" and "less than nobody."

Dread of contamination. Differentiation through dominance. Once anyone believes in the white cliffs of manhood, the only personal identity one can obtain must come through personal disidentification. And once upon the palisades, the passion *to excise one's compassion* will self-evidently justify *whatever contempt one must exercise* in order to feel racially pure and gender cleansed.

The vertical cliff of manhood stands today as a bulwark—across most cultures, across all national borders—and an homage to that personal identity which cannot withstand equality.

The wall comes tumbling down whenever any individual born penised refuses to scale it anymore.

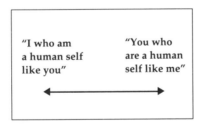

"I who am a human self like you"          "You who are a human self like me"

The reality of your selfhood, once you choose not to cleave to gender, is refreshingly found immediately in direct proportion to the reality of everyone else. As this diagram shows, your human need *to be seen* as someone worth knowing is always most effectively expressed and gratified *when you actively see someone else as worth knowing.* As humans we tend to use language, gestures, and other direct ways of actively communicating this way of seeing to someone else. Often our communication simply signals the appreciation or admiration with which we behold another person's presence. Sometimes our communication is simply a way of speaking to someone levelly as if they matter, as if they are really real to us. Sometimes our action communicates without words or language that we take their life as seriously as we take our own. The ways of saying "I who am a human self like you" to "You who are a human self like me" are so various they are almost beyond human reckoning.

Some thinkers and writers have recently put forward the view that what I have called the horizontal model of selfhood is actually a "style" of communication or a "style" of moral reasoning and that it is a "style" that "women" naturally favor and excel at. Many people like what they hear whenever any scholarly authority says that there is a primrose path to womanhood for the ladies and a parallel trek to manhood through burrs and thickets for the gents. It serves to distract people's attention from what's really going on over by the gender palisades—and that manhood cliff is a killer. Much confusion and obfuscation have been spread by authors who have suggested that although strenuous dominance is indeed required to climb to manhood, there is somehow an appropriate analog of communitarianism or connectivity for the womenfolk. Trying to hedge your selfhood bets by cleaving to gender gets people nowhere. It keeps penised people believing they must manage to stay on the cliff or else, for there's absolutely no alternative. And it keeps people raised to stay put at the bottom believing that's probably best: because climbing the cliff is crucial, and it's hard work, and *somebody's* got to do it—but however coldly anyone gets stepped on in the by-and-by, if she was raised to be a woman she has some specially feminine connectivity to keep her warm. This is an understandable and sincere attempt to locate some delusional semblance of self for those whose bodies and lives get climbed over by folks ascending to manhood. But it is otherwise unhelpful. The intrinsic verticality of manhood is the problem—and it's everyone's.

How do you balance your *selfhood* "I" and your *manhood* "I"? How does anyone?

If it's true that you can affirm and express your selfhood "I" only horizontally, and you can affirm and express your manhood "I" only vertically, what happens if you try to do both at the same time? What happens if you try to experience your human selfhood and embody manhood at the same time? What happens, for instance, if you feel a deep longing to love and be loved by someone "levelly" (human self to human self) but the only way you can think of to do that is from some higher vantage point on the vertical manhood scale? What if part of you really wants to be present with someone as your real human self (as your selfhood "I"), but what if part of you is very afraid that if you don't declare and affirm your manhood "I" you might not exist because you'll be less than nobody? So what if you try to be your "I" vertically and horizontally at once?

Well, the short answer is: you end up at cross-purposes with yourself.

Maybe if you had a clone, you could be that ambidextrous. But if not—if you are fated to be just one person in just one body in this one lifetime only—your vertical "I" and your horizontal "I" will tend to short each other out and blow a fuse.

Many people, experiencing this circuit-breaking contradiction, seek to find some compromise by which they can liberally affirm and express their selfhood "I" and their manhood "I" as well. To look at this balancing act as a diagram, picture a teeter-totter.

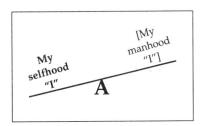

This diagram illustrates what might happen if you decided to favor, or to give more weight to, your selfhood "I." You would have decided that your selfhood "I" is very important to you, so you would tend to emphasize this sense of yourself. As you'll recall, you will tend to experience the reality of this sense of yourself in direct proportion to your recognition of someone else's reality. Therefore, when you make choices that give more weight to this sense of yourself, and when you make choices in which you can actually experience this sense of yourself, you will be giving your manhood "I" less weight. Your manhood "I" will automatically have become less important to you—at least in the particular moment when you make a choice that favors your selfhood "I."

You should keep in mind that both your selfhood "I" and your manhood "I" are relational and temporal. They are both relational because they can only happen in relation to someone else. Neither can happen in a void or in a vacuum or incommunicado in a cave. They both require some act of human relation on your part—an action that expresses your belief about who some person is to you. The selfhood "I" requires a *horizontal* act of relation to someone you recognize and regard as fully human, just like you. The manhood "I," on the other hand, requires some *vertical* act of relationship—for instance, when you find some way to address someone else as "You who are less than me."

Your selfhood "I" and your manhood "I" are both temporal because they can only happen in time, in moments of relational action, in moments of deciding which relational action you will take. You can make a choice that favors your selfhood "I" one minute and a choice that favors your manhood "I" the next. This can be somewhat confusing or disconcerting to someone who wants to see you and know you as who you are. But it is theoretically possible, because whichever sense of your self you decide to favor, you will only find it moment to moment anyway—decision to decision, choice by choice, in relational acts in time.

You may find a pattern emerging in your choices, a trend over time of seeming to favor your selfhood "I" or your manhood "I." This pattern may be either a slight or a distinct skew, and it may give both you and the people around you some provisional information as to who you really are. But the trend can be interrupted in an instant, just by making a choice that favors the other kind of "I." That's because both the selfhood "I" and the manhood "I" are always relational and always temporal.

So the teeter-totter can rock back and forth.

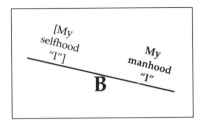

Now the diagram has changed to illustrate what might happen if you decide to favor, or give more weight to, your manhood "I." You would have decided that your manhood "I" is very important to you, so you would have chosen an act of relation that will underscore and help you experience this sense of yourself. As you'll recall, you will tend to experience the reality of this sense of yourself in direct proportion to the unreality of someone else—simply their *lesser* reality or their absolute *non*reality, as you wish. Therefore, when you make choices that give more weight to this sense of yourself, you will automatically be giving your selfhood "I" less weight. Your selfhood "I" will have become less important to you—at least in the particular moment when you choose the particular relational act that will temporarily favor your manhood "I."

Now you can understand more graphically, and experientially, what was meant by the fourth main point: the reality of your selfhood is inversely related to the reality of your manhood.

The teeter-totter rocks back and forth—and you're the one who tips the balance. You decide, moment to moment, whether to favor your selfhood or whether to favor manhood.

Now, take a moment to look back at the two teeter-totter drawings again. Take a look at the fulcrum, the point upon which the teeter-totter tips.

You'll notice that when you decide to give your selfhood "I" more weight, the decision turns on Lesson A ("To be human is to be somebody"). You have allowed this lesson of personal equality to live through your relational action. Through your act of witnessing or recognizing or beholding the humanity of someone else, you have given expression to your own human needs to be safe, to be sustained, to be seen, and to be with. You have found and identified your reality in finding and identifying with the reality of someone else. This someone else could be any number of human individuals in your life, because the reality of your selfhood "I" is in direct proportion to the reality of all other humans.

You'll notice that when you decide to give your manhood "I" more weight, the decision turns on Lesson B ("Not to be a man is to be less than nobody"). You have allowed this lesson of personal identity anxiety to live through your relational action. Through your decision to be the man there—for fear of seeming less than nobody—you have found and identified your reality in an action that disidentifies with someone else whom you thus designate as unreal to you, or less real than you. The designated nobody could be anyone, though you would be unwise to try this on climbers above you on the cliff. Much of your upbringing has been to prepare you to tell the difference between people you can safely try this relational act on and people who, if you foolishly thought to try it on them, would doubtless do much worse to you. You are always safer and more secure when you perform a relational act that reifies your manhood "I" on someone who already seems closer to nobody than you.

You'll notice that when you decide to tip the balance toward your selfhood "I," your choice of relational acts will seem to have a "right" and a "wrong," or perhaps a "more appropriate" and "less appropriate." Some relational acts will seem more like "the right thing to do" than will others. Some relational acts will seem more right under some circumstances than others. Since your objective in favoring your selfhood "I" is to act relationally toward someone else as if they are as real as you are, your own sense of what's right and wrong will tend to emerge from how *you* would prefer to be regarded by someone choosing to favor *their* selfhood "I" as well. As a corollary to that, your sense of "right" and "wrong" on the horizontal plane of selfhood will necessarily emerge from as much knowledge as you can muster about other people's feelings, life situations, recent experiences, and so forth.

You will also notice that when you decide to tip the balance toward your manhood "I," your choice of relational acts will seem to have a "right" and a "wrong" as well—or perhaps a "more effective" and "less effective." Some relational acts will seem more like "the right thing to do" than will others. Some relational acts will seem more right under some circumstances than others. Since your objective in favoring your manhood "I" is to act relationally toward someone else as if they are not as real as you are, your own sense of what's right and wrong will tend to emerge from how *you* would not expect to be treated by someone who valued and regarded your reality. Perhaps it will emerge from how you yourself were once treated by someone who was intent on experiencing their own manhood "I." As a corollary to that, your sense of what's "right" and "wrong" relational behavior on the vertical scale of manhood will necessarily emerge from paying as little attention as you can to certain other people's feelings, life situations, recent experiences, and so forth. The "certain other people" are of course the ones it will be quite safe for you to discount and knock down, insofar as you can reasonably predict. This explains why for some people who are *very* dedicated to the manhood "I," rape is safe sex. If you follow the manhood "I" all the way in the direction it logically leads, there is nothing wrong with rape.* This can seem troubling or confusing for anyone who is sincerely trying to find and identify a real manhood "I" but who would not dream of raping anyone. Not every "effective" or "right" thing to do looks right or effective to everyone who is trying to find and identify their manhood "I." There is a broad range of ways that different people *experience* the manhood "I" subjectively, a few of which were touched on in Chapter One: Believing in a god who *deifies* manhood. Raping someone. Lynching or exterminating someone. Forcing someone to give birth. Masturbating to a picture of someone being harmed. Masturbating inside someone you're hurting. Hitting or having sex with a child. Leaving a mess for someone else to clean up. Laughing at or telling a joke that only another manhood "I" could possibly find funny. In every case it means feeling like an "I" who is higher up the vertical manhood scale than someone lower down. Since "doing the right thing" for a manhood "I" means, basically, doing whatever gives you the subjective experience that you're not lower down—you're not like someone who's less than nobody—there is quite a wide range of possible actions that will momentarily achieve this fleeting subjective experience for you in just the way you like it.

Can a single interpersonal decision, a single relational action,

*See also "Rapist Ethics" in *Refusing to Be a Man.*

be both "right" in terms that will help you realize your selfhood "I" and "right" in terms that will help you realize your manhood "I"? That question may arise in specific situations.

The logical answer would seem to be "It's very doubtful," because the horizontal structure of selfhood is at cross-purposes with the vertical structure of manhood. Nevertheless, human life isn't always logical, so you may feel a strong tug to have these two "rights" coexist now and then. And wouldn't it be nice if you could pull them together in a single relational act that you have conscientiously chosen to unify your selfhood "I" and your manhood "I" once and for all?

Here's the problem with that:

Your selfhood "I" and your manhood "I" are not merely different from each other. Night is different from day, but there is dawn and there is dusk. A head full of hair is different from a bald one, but there are thousands of hair strands in between, and no single strand converts a coiffure to a scalp. Your selfhood "I" and your manhood "I" are not merely different; they are opposite and contradictory. They cannot both be true for you at the same time, in the same decision, in the same relational act, in the same momentary experience. Sequentially, of course, you can experience now one, now the other—however much vertigo that may give you, however much distress it may give someone who'd like to know you. But physically, emotionally, and interactionally, you can't experience your selfhood "I" and your manhood "I" simultaneously.

At best, you can but rock the teeter-totter back and forth. There's no midpoint of equipoise where you can give both equal weight.

When you know who you are in terms of Lesson A ("... human ... somebody"), the things you must do for the sake of Lesson B tend over time to simply stop making much emotional sense, as you discover more and more self-confidence in being a real self to other real selves. When you know who you are in terms of Lesson B ("... a man ..."), the things you might do for the sake of Lesson A lose more and more emotional resonance as you carve out, self-consciously, more and more certitude for yourself in your niche on the cliff.

✧

## Another Optional Feelings Check

For some readers raised to be a man, it may be time to ac-knowledge those waves of gender anxiety again. Those flustery, sometimes blustery feelings of nervousness or discomfort or an-ticipation of punishment. Those feelings that seem to *physically* revisit your body whenever certain questions come up about your manhood "I." Questions about whether you are who you would like to be on the vertical scale of manhood. Questions about whether the vertical scale of manhood is real and whether you're really on it. Those waves of personal identity anxiety.

There's no magic wand* to make those waves go away. And even if you think you've cleverly managed to keep your gender anxiety feelings at bay ... *they'll be back.* You can count on it. You've got Lesson B in you, right there in your flesh-and-blood feeling body. And if you were lucky, you've got some Lesson A too. One human body, two contradictory lessons. Now and then you're going to *re-feel* them. And the waves of anxiety from Les-son B can really *get* to you sometimes.

Though you can't make those waves go away, you can be-come more alert to what you're feeling when they come for a visit. You can remember to run a self-check routine whenever they show up. You can ask yourself, for instance,

- *"Who* am I deciding to be—right here and now?"
- *"To whom* am I being myself—right here and now?"
- *"How* am I being myself—right here and now?"

Getting a handle on such moment-to-moment relational deci-sions can be a way of getting a handle on the waves. It's a way of reminding yourself that *you exist in your relational acts*—and you *are* who you really are—*at least as much as you exist in your physical body.* Maybe even more so, from the point of view of other people who have come to care about you.

---

*No pun intended. Sometimes a magic wand is just a magic wand.

IF YOU NEED INEQUALITY
TO FEEL OK ABOUT YOURSELF,
THERE IS NO WAY
THAT YOU WILL EVER FEEL OK.

# ✧ 14 ✧

## HOW CAN I GET ALONG BETTER WITH MY MEN FRIENDS?

When someone decides to practice living as a man of conscience, personal friendships may take on an intense new emotional relevance, as if to the core of one's being. This vibrancy between friends may require some getting used to. As one slowly but surely cedes the gender-centered personal identity that finds its only replenishment in relational acts of disidentification, even the most casual acquaintanceships may suddenly seem momentous. And significant *romantic* attachments may seem so full of portent that one's brain goes into turbodrive trying to track all the critical interactional action in conscientious detail.

Life as a man of conscience can get a bit overwhelming at times.

Assuming for the moment that you want to have loving and trusting friendships both with humans raised to be a man and with humans raised to be a woman, the practical prospect of actually doing so as one's selfhood "I"—face to face in everyday life—may seem nearly as daunting as it seems indispensable to one's selfhood. The decision always to act relationally "selfhood to selfhood" with one's friends is indeed a monumental challenge: how does one pay complete attention in this profound new way to the people in one's life whom one cares about the *most* (not to mention all the people whom one encounters incidentally)?

This chapter and the next discuss some of the practical issues involved in close personal relationships with other humans raised to be a man. The chapter after that focuses on practical issues involved in close personal relationships with humans raised to be a woman. These seemingly separable practical issues are significantly linked, as we shall see.

But first, a closer look at relationships with other men who are not necessarily one's friends . . .

## The Question of How Not to Be a Coward in Relation to Other Men

The fear of other men's judgment on one's manhood act—the fear of other men in general—takes quite a toll. Not only does this fear prompt a constant defense of one's manhood "I"; it also gets in the way of close friendships with any particular other men. To see how this double dynamic works, let's take a quick, candid inventory of how, exactly, someone raised to be a man might tend to get along with all those other masked men out there. Here's an assortment of common ways . . .

1. With trepidation
2. With bravado
3. With suspicion
4. With *je ne sais quoi*
5. With extreme caution
6. With piss and vinegar
7. With knots in stomach
8. With enough wealth and violence so no one will mess with you
9. Without very much conventional power, relatively speaking
10. With as much actual power and protection as wealth and capacity for violence can implement

For many would-be men of conscience, their typical ways of relating to other men as a bunch may feel at times very odd.* Meanwhile angrier, perhaps more vengeful sorts of men always seem able to get even with ease.** Little wonder, then, that the would-be man of conscience may deliberately avoid the company of threatening other men altogether. Especially mindful of the Three (and Only Three) Things That Can Happen When Two Men Face Off in Defense of Their Manhood Act, the would-be man of conscience might wisely stay the heck away from volatile situations in which one of the Three Things must occur . . .

- **You lose.** A masked man manages to address you as "You who are less than me," so you are humiliated or put down and he comes off the man there.

- **He loses.** You manage to address *him* as "You who are less than me" in such a way that he will learn not to challenge your manhood further if he knows what's good for him, the twerp.

- **You both agree to pick on someone else.** With (and only with) some third party you both agree to address as "You who are less than *us*," you and another man both come to feel at ease in each other's company (i.e., safe enough from each other's manhood act to entertain the notion of not doing each other harm).

No wonder men of conscience feel odd man out when it comes to loving friendships with other men. Given the alternatives one has for dealing with all other men out there in general—lose, lose, pick on some other loser—how can one reasonably expect to find loving friendship with even a handful of men in particular? How can one be certain that an other man will not suddenly slip into Defending His Manhood Act? How can you know that you won't be trounced?—or that you won't feel you have to trounce him?—or that you won't end up colluding with him to trounce someone else?

Once you detect that someone is an *other* man—a masked

*See nos. 1, 3, 5, 7, and 9.
**See nos. 2, 4, 6, 8, and 10.

man who *gets off* on treating human beings as *other*—you already have all the information you need to know that this guy could be a danger to someone's selfhood, including yours.

No wonder men of conscience approach relations with other men feeling trepidation, suspicion, extreme caution, knots in stomach, and relative powerlessness. The odds do not appear to be too terrific for the odd.

So how does a would-be man of conscience ever get out of this no-win trap? Here's an important clue: Most humans raised to be a man are not only combatants in the manhood drama; *they are the picked on and put down as well.* Most humans raised to be a man tend to be combatants now and then and the patsies now and then—sequentially and simultaneously.

So to understand what stands between you and loving friendships with other humans raised to be a man, one of the things you need to figure out is what's really going on when you're being made a foil for some other men's truce. To live in selfhood mode takes practical courage not only in order *not to put someone else down* but also in order *not to be put down.* Just as one needs to waive one's manhood act so as not to diminish, pick on, or trounce someone else, one needs to know how to act in selfhood mode when one is being diminished, picked on, or about to be trounced by someone else. We're talking now about serious *selfhood defense:* how do you act relationally in selfhood mode when all of your impulses are screaming flee or fight back (but if you flee your name is mud)?

Somewhere above you on the vertical scale of manhood, you'll find more-powerful men who are combatants in their own manhood drama. You'll find some other more-powerful men who have agreed to pick on *you* so that they can make believe they're best of chums. And if you take a clear-eyed, clearheaded look upward at the Manhood Gladiators ranged above you, you can find amazingly useful clues that will help you not only survive but love justly.

The first thing we need, though, is some inspiration. We need some models of real-life practical courage. We need to find examples of humans in history who (a) were raised to be a man, (b) were seriously persecuted by other, more powerful men, (c) exhibited practical courage such that they didn't roll over like wimps and say "Pick on me some more," and (d) exhibited practical courage such that *they disarmed the very manhood act* that was knocking them upside their heads.

## The Question of Practical Courage in Relation to Other Men Who Could Hurt You

History gives us the stories of many exceptional humans who were raised to be a man and who exhibited exemplary practical courage. We need not look to myths or fairy tales or make anything up. You may already personally know some historical or contemporary models of such practical courage. You may, in your lifetime, personally become one as well.

I've selected three (you will surely think of more): Socrates, Jesus of Nazareth, and Dr. Martin Luther King, Jr. In their various dealings with other men who could hurt them, these particular humans exemplify just the kind of courage in relation to other, more-powerful men that would-be men of conscience can usefully apply in their everyday lives.

Let's take a brief look at these three sample profiles in practical courage. And let's take a look at how they kept their teeter-totters tipped in their dealings with other men.

**Socrates (ca. 470–399 B.C.).** Greek philosopher and gadfly. Went around asking nettlesome questions, like "What's truly a good life? What's truly justice? What's truly courage?" Liked to lead young people in mega-mental rap sessions. Dubbed "wisest man alive" by Delphic Oracle, but bothered all believers of conventional wisdom. Bothered civic authorities especially. Was charged with corrupting youth, for teaching them to question authority and to think for themselves. Was put on trial and sentenced to death. Drank hemlock, rather than escape or opt for exile.

*Teeter-totter position at time of trial,* when confronted by authorities coming down on him on charges of trumped-up crimes: Offering his own lucid oral defense, stood fast and firm with teeter-totter in position weighted toward "My Selfhood I"; presented simply and unsentimentally the facts about how he viewed his mission: "to persuade every man ... to seek virtue and wisdom before he looks to his private interests." For that, *hasta la vista.*

**Jesus of Nazareth (ca. 6 B.C.–ca. A.D. 30).** Jewish carpenter by trade, switched careers to enter prophecy field. Went around telling cryptic parables and asking nettlesome questions. Bothered all believers of conventional wisdom. Bothered religious and civic authorities both. Charged by secular authorities with fomenting civil disobedience and resented by religious authorities as yet another messianic wannabe with dubious credentials. Put on trial by Roman state for insurrection and sentenced to death. Execution involved carpentry, with iron spikes driven in on orders from Rome.

*Teeter-totter position during three-year period of itinerant preaching,* when faced with mounting threats and pressure from powerful sacral and secular authorities to cease and desist: Apparently tilted toward "My Selfhood I" with unusual constancy and in ways that were extremely atypical for their time. Communicated with a woman as another human self, for instance; did not consort with her as a prostitute. Genially washed feet of colleagues—even though that's what only a servant would do for a master. Enjoyed company of kids. Did not blame loving mother for Dad's aloofness. Kind to many strangers. Quoted by several fans as having coined pithy pro-selfhood one-liner: "Love your neighbor as yourself." Nonplussed that few fans ever got it.

**Dr. Martin Luther King, Jr. (1929–1968).** American cleric, orator, and interpreter of dreams. Went around advocating nonviolent resistance to discriminatory separate-and-unequal policies in public places. Preached equality of opportunity and human harmony—and conscientious civil disobedience to bring it about. Bothered fundamentalist believers in First Amendment, which legally protected segregationists' right of free association. Bothered believers in "racial purity." Bothered believers in skin-pigment superiority. Bothered some descendants of slaves, too, by not minding his station in life. "Colored" by birth, but became Negro, then black during lifetime. Posthumously recognized as African American. Assassinated by a rifle fired in hate by a "white" man.

*Teeter-totter position on freedom marches, when jailed,* and at sundry other times when faced with imminent threat of bodily injury from race-hate groups, other defenders of conventional wisdom: Tilted toward "My Selfhood I" position almost always. If threatened by physical attack or put-down, stood firm in own selfhood, did not attack back or put down in reply. Inspired by Moses, Jesus, and Mahatma Gandhi. Influential in creating new term of art in U.S. law: "civil rights," which at last legally recognized the principle of selfhood as human equality—not a notion pale male slaveowners had in mind when authoring their Constitution.

✧

The teeter-totter positions noted above pertain only to relations with other people raised to be a man. For supplementary information about how those teeter-totters wobbled with respect to women, here are some important historical facts:

Two of these men were married but were not especially honorable or exemplary in their personal affairs with women. Socrates' wife, Xanthippe, was regarded by him as but shrewish breeding property; he much preferred fraternizing in the homosocial world of philosophers. Dr. King was privately cautioned by co-workers that his sexual conduct with women other than his wife, Coretta Scott King, was at odds with his public image; also, once a woman in prostitution informed police that Dr. King had been violent with her, and once an associate saw him angrily assault the woman with whom he'd had an intimate friendship for several years. The third, Jesus of Nazareth, was unmarried and, according to followers' reports, appears to have acted in selfhood mode with women and men alike. However, at a professionally preoccupied moment Jesus snubbed his loyal, loving mother, Mary; and no women were allowed into the inner circle of disciples whose feet he so gladly bathed.

Practical courage in relation to other men does not predict practical courage in relation to women, and that is a challenge for modern men of conscience that is explored in subsequent chapters. Meanwhile what about this business of trying to relate to other men in selfhood mode and with practical courage—isn't it sort of . . . well . . . *dumb?*

Two of these three historical humans were executed, Socrates in his seventies and Jesus in his thirties, and one, Dr. King, was assassinated at age thirty-nine. Indeed, extrapolating from these three deaths would seem to produce a rather grim actuarial table—titled, perhaps, "Practical Courage as High-Risk Behavior." But before you dismiss keeping your teeter-totter in "selfhood" position as a quite rash way to handle your fears of other men's power to *crush* you, consider this: If you are confronted by the anger of an other man who has more conventional power than you do, and if he is seriously threatening to injure you (for the sake of his alliance with some other man's manhood act, some other man you may not even know), and if you try to confront *this man* with your teeter-totter in the "manhood" position, what can you realistically expect to happen? Your chances of not getting crushed are *not any better.* The odds might actually be dead set against you. A lot depends, of course, on whether he needs to pick on you just a little bit, or whether he needs to wipe you off the face of the earth. (That's another sliding scale. Another slippery slope.) But whether he's bullying you small-time or big-time, you can pretty much bet that as soon as your teeter-totter tilts to manhood mode, you're done for.

If you set out to trounce more-powerful men in manhood mode, you are more likely to *get* trounced. History has been much influenced by Peremptory Trouncers in Manhood Mode, of course: the Goths, the Nazis, European homesteaders in what became the United States of America, etc. But Socrates, Jesus, and Dr. King do not seem to have been the trouncing sort. Trouncing other men was not what they were into. Perhaps they were aware of the extremely long odds on trouncing. We can't actually be certain. So we just have to guess—from what we ourselves can glean about how touchy and nasty men tend to get when they're coming at you in manhood mode. And most likely, what these three exemplars of practical courage discovered is that they had a choice in their lives between doing nothing (and being picked on some more)—or acting self-confidently in selfhood mode.

So we have quite another irony on our hands:

On the one hand we can observe all the humans in history

who were raised to be a man and who became lifelong combatants defending their manhood act. And they defended their
manhood as if it was their life. And they could conceive of no
other existence for themselves except on the vertical scale of
manhood: manhood "I" versus manhood "I."

On the other hand we can witness a few courageous humans
in history who were raised to be a man but who became lifelong
nonviolent resisters to the manhood act. They defended *selfhood*
with their lives—in selfhood mode—and in so doing they disarmed the manhood act; they disconcerted and discombobu-
lated other, more-powerful men by not playing according to
Men's Rules of Combat on the Cliff. Subversively, they helped a
good many other humans conceive of an existence for *themselves* too. And they help us even today to conceive of an existence for ourselves that is *not* on the vertical scale of
manhood—it is on the horizontal scales of justice: Level. Equal
in humanity. Selfhood to selfhood. Real human self to real human self.

If one is living in selfhood mode, one is more likely to find
loving and trusting friendships with other humans who were
also raised to be a man. Living in selfhood mode, one is more
likely to find one's own sense of personal power, one's own human worth, one's own sense of efficacy and competence, one's
own sense of having contributed to human existence. Living in
selfhood mode—loving justice—one is more likely to have a self
worth having.

Many humans raised to be a man assume that they lack such
selfhood courage—the practical courage to stand up to those
who abuse you through their power over you, just because they
*get* to, because they're higher up the vertical scale of manhood.
Many humans raised to be a man assume they lack the courage
to face down their own fear of what an other man would do if
he really got it in mind to blow you away.

As a result, many humans raised to be a man look for everyday ways to keep their head down. They look for ways to
stay out of the line of fire, out of the danger range of other
men's anger. They may seek career paths that bring them less

into conflict with other men's manhood act. They may attempt to find institutional supports for their own manhood act such that they reduce their risk of losing at it—they accumulate wealth, for instance, or they amass their own power to do harm. They may simply, through dress and deportment, send signals that announce, "You'd better not mess with me." But they know, bottom line, that when an other, more-powerful man is picking on you and the difference between his power and your power is great enough, you could get yourself killed if you confront him in manhood mode. As a result, many humans raised to be a man sometimes feel they have no choice but to put up with being picked on. And this makes them feel really lousy about themselves. They know in their guts that they've been craven cowards. They feel they've caved in to someone else's manhood. To save their own life, they feel they've all but given it up.

When you examine your own experiences and choices in this regard, when you check yourself out, when you study how *you're* living your life, you can often employ some useful analytical tools. They're good for selfhood defense. I call them . . .

## Six Tools for Deconstructing an Other Man Who Has Gone Into Manhood Mode

1.  **Who else besides you does he bully?** Likely as not, you're not alone within his anger range. The manhood act can't be carried off very convincingly with only one patsy. The manhood act generally requires quite a number of humans to be "less than" it. That's because there are so many other potential combatants out there, so many other Gladiators With the Manhood Mask On—so many truces to forge, so little time. So, who else does he put down? Who are all the people who are third parties to his manhood-versus-manhood truces? This information is useful. It helps you recognize other humans who are similarly situated, and perhaps your logical allies.

2. **Who doesn't he dare to bully?** Obviously, there are specific other men in his life who are even more powerful and more dangerous and from whom he will put up with shit if he has to. He probably has to. There are a few men in the world who don't have to take shit from nobody nohow—a few have buttons nearby for nuclear warheads, but such men are probably rather far away from you on the fool chain. So if you watch any particular lower-ranking man in manhood mode closely enough, you'll probably have no trouble sussing out who he takes shit from. This information is useful. It helps you diagnose why he's scared shitless.

3. **What's behind his seeming confidence?** Is it really your misreading of an arrogant belief in his own insular reality, a belief that develops over a lifetime from disregarding the reality of others?

4. **What's behind his seeming strength?** Is it really your misreading of a trigger-happy aggressiveness that will lash out in rage and threaten harm if its will to domination is at all challenged?

5. **What's behind his seeming courage?** Is it really your misreading of the way he backs up his dominating anger with whatever injury to other people's self-esteem is necessary to ensure their subordination and awe?

6. **What's behind your fear of him?** C'mon, what're you afraid of? Are you chicken? Are you a scaredy-cat? Sissy? Momma's boy? Girlie? Or is it really your own long-ago fear of ever letting go of your *own* manhood mode?

## Another Checkup on Those Feelings That Are Not Entirely Optional

Those anxiety waves keep coming back, unbidden, unannounced. Panic waves. Low–self-esteem waves. Seethingresentment waves. Crawl-up-your-asshole waves. Scared-shitless waves. Please-god-make-me-not-be-less-than-nobody waves. And *nothing* brings them back to your body and your brain like an other man in full-blown manhood mode who's fixing to define his manhood over and against *you*.

Absolutely nothing.

Those waves were not wired to your autonomic fight-or-flight reflexes by coincidence.

Those waves were taught to you to keep you stationed on the cliff—and to keep your ass in line.

TO CREATE THE POSSIBILITY FOR LOVING FRIENDSHIPS
WITH OTHER HUMANS RAISED TO BE A MAN,
DISARM THE MANHOOD ACT
WITH YOUR SELFHOOD.

# ✦ 15 ✦

## HOW CAN I GET WOMEN TO TRUST ME?

The previous chapter stopped rather abruptly, I'm afraid, with some loose ends left over. It had started out promisingly enough, with the heartwarming question about how to have loving and trusting friendships, but somehow we got bollixed up on different questions entirely: How do you save your ass? How do you survive on the vertical scale of manhood? How high is your "station"? How do you not get trounced out of it? How do you muster the practical courage not to trounce some-one else? How do you disengage your brain from the dynamics that are keeping you stuck on the manhood cliff long enough to imagine what a trusting and loving friendship even *is*?

It appears that we are still a ways off from the subject of forming loving or trusting friendships with anyone. It appears that in order to consider the practical question of such friend-ships, we must analyze in yet more detail what's really happen-ing among the folks out there on the cliffside of manhood.

## Who Can You *Trust* in Relation to Other Men?

Whenever you're in manhood mode, you really have to know who to trust—or else you're sunk. When you're hanging out there on the manhood cliff, when you've rocked your "I" toward manhood, you need reliable cues about who's *for* you and who's *against* you. Much of your upbringing has been to download those cues to you. You now carry those cues in a data base in your brain, sorted by body type, age, temper, and so forth—so you can tell the difference between who might try a manhood act on you and who might not. Whenever you meet anyone new, you run a search to see where they stack up. In nanoseconds, you assess their trustworthiness—the relative likelihood they could do you harm.

To climb the vertical cliff of manhood, you not only need agile climbing techniques and effective equipment (like more money, preferred pigmentation, calluses), and you not only need to learn to keep your head down, to duck the rocks kicked down from up above. You also need superkeen peripheral vision. You need to be able to check out climbers alongside you, and even climbers somewhat down below. You need to be able to tell *with exactitude* which nearby climbers could suddenly sabotage your climb, which climbers will give you a leg up if you need it, and which climbers somewhat down below will let you stand on them or step on them when that's the boost you must have.

Exactly who might help you climb toward manhood and exactly who might make you plummet? Viewing the much-touted Upward Bound Experience in this harsh light of sheer survival, you find yourself scrutinizing fellow climbers as if your life depends on it. And indeed, if your entire sentient life depends upon your quest for manhood, your manhood "I" cannot survive without knowing how to tell your fellow climbers apart: which are the safe ones and which are the lethal ones?

## Checklist for Safe Friendship With a Fellow Man

❑  1. Will this man not put me down because he thinks I'm lower down the manhood scale than he is?

❏  2. Will this man not need to form a climbing alliance with *another* man such that *they both* need to pick on me?
❏  3. Will this man's ranking on the manhood scale give me a leg up?
❏  4. Better yet, will hanging out with this manly man give me a "lift pass" upward?
❏  5. Will I feel better about myself—more securely gendered—when I'm with him and when I'm seen with him?
❏  6. Will he not hurt me to prove his manhood?

These six criteria for assessing the safety or lethality of someone raised to be a man will be applicable mainly with people nearby or only slightly overhead. You would probably be taking your gendered life in your hands if—to seek companionable company—you lobbed a grappling hook too high above you on the cliff. Minding your station on the manhood cliff means not expecting safe friendships with anyone who, to get so high up, has a track record of trouncing types like you.

Your manhood "I" does not depend on recognizing *anyone* as a real human self. Once you have decided that your station in life is somewhere on the manhood cliff, you have decided that the dopey fact of someone else's fundamental humanness doesn't matter diddly—and your humanness doesn't matter diddly either. It's your decision, and once you make it, you live or die in terms of it. So you will tend to be friendly to fellow climbers whom you can trust with your life—the life of your manhood "I."

Meanwhile, scanning your options for safe friendships with women, your criteria for assessing safety or lethality will tend to be applied to people who are slightly below you. Or perhaps way below, depending on your taste . . .

## Checklist for Safe Friendship with a Woman

❏  1. Will being seen with this woman not make my manhood ranking drop?
❏  2. Will I be able to prevent this woman from forming a

climbing alliance with some other man who is higher up the cliff?

- ❏ 3. Will this woman's body rating on a scale of 1 to 10 give me a leg up? (... or something else up?)
- ❏ 4. Better yet, will having this comely woman around give me a real "lift"—a subjective sense of elevation toward ever-greater manhood?
- ❏ 5. Will I feel better about myself—more securely gendered—when other men know I have tied a knot with her?
- ❏ 6. Will she not hurt me, ever, in a way that gets in the way of my need to climb toward manhood?

Interestingly, all six of these criteria have the same point of reference as the six before: When you're scoping out your options for friendship in manhood mode, your point of reference is never an actual human raised to be a woman; your point of reference is always the judgment of other men—what they will think of you, what they will think of her. You never befriend *her*, because your attention stays stuck on your status in relation to other *hims*.

No wonder we never got to loving and trusting friendships. That crazy-making cliff kept looming up and getting in the way. Once you're committed to the manhood cliff, there's *no way* to loving and trusting friendship.

In perilous service to the vertical scale of manhood, most humans growing up to be a man learn to be terrified of other men's judgment on them—on their sexuality, on their sexual identity, on their very validity as "men." With other men's explicit encouragement, you will take that fear into your most intimate relations with a woman—a situation that can be very hurtful and damaging to her while closing you off from everyone. The imprint of your lifelong fear of other men's judgment, plus the potential for violence between men that backs up that judgment, overrides your selfhood "I" in ways that women are rarely aware of.

Imagine for a moment that you have a woman friend who trusts you. Perhaps she loves you as well. She thinks of you as her partner, an ally of her life. And you and she are very, very close. One evening you happen to be apart; you're out for a night with the guys, let's say. Good friends, good buddies. And you all laugh a lot, you tell a lot of jokes, and, let's say, some of the jokes are put-downs of women. Not specific put-downs of the woman who trusts you, exactly, but general put-downs that clearly include her too. And you feel torn between your loyalty to the woman who trusts you and the men you're laughing with. And rather than seem odd man out, rather than not laugh at the guys' jokes, you laugh along, you don't know quite why. The thought may not cross your mind that you are laughing out of loyalty to your men friends' manhood. The thought may not cross your mind that you are laughing out of fear that if you don't, they will cast aspersions on your masculinity. Then again, such thoughts may be somewhere on your mind. In any event, imagine that later that night you and your woman friend rendezvous. But she senses that something about you is not the same. She senses you seem to have disappeared to her somewhat. She does not know what happened, but she senses that things are not quite the same between you as they were before your evening apart. She does not know, nor can she, what you did that sold her out, and she does not know, nor can she, that you sold out your loyalty to her for the sake of your loyalty to your men friends. She stays in the dark, because you do not dare tell her. And if she asks you if something is wrong, you say no. You deny—both to her and to yourself—that what you did earlier that evening was in order to defend your manhood "I" to other men. And now you feel stuck, because your teeter-totter got stuck, and your woman friend misses your selfhood "I"—and so do you, come to think of it.

Only through decoding and deconstructing how men act with other men (most of which behaviors are forms of loyalty to the manhood "I") can a man of conscience ever hope to recover the possibility of a selfhood that can relate intimately and responsibly with anyone.

## Who Can Trust *You* in Relation to Other Men?

I began this book with several provisional assumptions about who a man of conscience might be. Now is a good time to assess whether any of my provisional assumptions apply to you . . .

- **There's a discrepancy between a man of conscience and the manhood standard.** (You often feel there's a discrepancy between yourself and masculinity, or between "who you really are" and manhood.)

- **A man of conscience has firsthand knowledge of specific other men who have done things for the sake of their manhood that the man of conscience does not think are right.** (You know of men who *for the sake of their feeling really masculine* have done things to other people that hurt them in some way. You may or may not have said something to them about it; you may not even know any of these men well enough to talk to them. But you are fairly certain that they did wrong things—hurtful, unfair, unjust— because doing so made them feel more like real men.)

- **A man of conscience has clear recall of specific things *he* has done for the sake of manhood—things that he does not think are quite right.** (You have done some things for the sake of your manhood too. Maybe not the same things as other men exactly. Maybe things that were not *as* hurtful, not *as* unfair, not *as* unjust. But you have some idea that just because other things might be *worse* doesn't make the things *you* did A-OK. You're not keen about admitting any of this, perhaps. But if and when you're really truthful with yourself, you're aware that there sometimes seems to be a you inside you that knows the difference between hurting someone—being unfair or unjust to them—and being good to someone. You care about that difference, and you care about your capacity to perceive that difference.)

- **A man of conscience wants loving and trusting friendships.** (But even though you long for loving and trusting friendships—and even though you seem to have some internal gyroscope that cues you to what's harmful, what's unfair, what's unjust—sometimes something comes over you and throws the gyroscope for a loop. And it's like a wave of anxiety, like a force field of dread. And your teeter-totter goes tilt. And you do something for no other reason than that it will shield you from some other man's judgment on your manhood. And some of those things you have done when that happens have hurt people you love. Have hurt them really bad.)

To restore balance to your inner gyroscope, to tilt your teeter-totter back to selfhood mode, you will need to reexamine what sorts of things make you suppose you can trust another man at all. The following checklist recaps the six Criteria for Safe Friendship in Manhood Mode, but each one is recast in terms that might now seem more emotionally familiar.

## Checklist for Men Friends (Would-be Man of Conscience Version)

☐ 1. You may have been checking out other men to make sure they will not trounce you. To make sure they are not the trouncing sort. To make sure they will not pick on you or put you down. To make sure you will be safe with them because they will not endanger you by trying to affirm their manhood.

☐ 2. You may have been checking out other men to make sure they will not hobnob with other men who would pick on you or put you down in a minute. To make sure they are not the betraying sort. To make sure they are not the bonding-against-you type. To make sure you can feel safe with them because they will not affirm their manhood with someone else, in a pact against you.

☐ 3. You may have been checking out other men to make sure they will not embarrass you by appearing to be too low down the scale of manhood. To make sure that no-body's less-than-nobodyness rubs off on you. To make sure all your men friends have a level of manhood that is a credit to you, not a debit.

❑ 4. You may have been checking out other men because of a slight sense of . . . because of a tiny twinge of . . . be-cause of a now-and-then-fleeting-feeling-which-shall-remain-nameless of . . . Oh, you know. You just like being near the guy 'cause he exudes confident physicality and . . . well . . . his body is . . . you know . . . strong . . . mus-cled . . . straight-acting. And . . . well . . . being around him is like . . . getting your batteries recharged. So that gives you . . . er . . . that makes you feel . . . uh-h-h . . . it gives you a kind of . . . tingly feeling. But only every so often, not all the time, you know?

❑ 5. You may have been checking out other men, other men you might select to consider your friends, simply out of a shared sense between you that you are men, not women—therefore safely far more than nobody.

❑ 6. You may have been checking out an other man to size up his disposition to violence. Does he do it? Does he get off on it? Will he do it to you? Might you have to do it to him back? Or can you count on a détente?

These six criteria can be used to check out fellow men as po-tential friends just fine. Lots of men would be grateful to find just one such climbing buddy in a lifetime—one real man who really fits all those criteria. Quite a sweep, actually. There's only one slight problem: Each of these criteria keeps your teeter-totter stuck in manhood mode. Applying any or all of them, you stay emotionally at the mercy of other men's judgment on your manhood—not to mention those insistent anxiety waves. And you have not yet made a conscientious move *to free yourself*—to live *in and through your selfhood.*

The chances for loving and trusting friendships on the man-hood cliff are zero to none. Someone stuck in manhood mode can but dangle precariously somewhere in that fictive hierarchy, with or without safety ropes affixed to other men. At the end of such tenuous tethers will be but men whose love of manhood you trust not to kick your ass off the cliff. And that's *not exactly* loving, trusting friendship. Whenever you assess reliability and dependability in gung-ho climbers on the cliff, you grant the hierarchy of manhood the power to *define* you and *control* you. As a result, you cannot observe what keeps men's teeter-totters tilting—as if in tandem—into manhood mode. And you cannot discern the shared delusion that keeps you clambering up the butte.

One's commitment to the cliff also precludes loving and trusting friendship with any human raised to be a woman. Applying any or all criteria for Safe Friendships in Manhood Mode to any particular woman in your life, you effectively make a decision to maintain allegiance to other men's judgment on your manhood—and you leave yourself wide open to the virtual inevitability that at some point you will act untrustworthily or unlovingly to her to appease the judgment of other men.

Whenever you're being "the man there" with *anyone* you think you love—whenever you are privately defending your manhood somehow—you've got the hierarchy of other men on your mind, and you are being haunted or shamed by that hierarchy.

Living in manhood mode, defending your manhood "I," you cannot possibly act as a trusted friend to any woman. To remain loyal to your own manhood means you will inevitably remain loyal to the manhood of *some* other men—perhaps the ones you think you trust the most—and your loyalty to that truce will put any woman friend at risk of betrayal.

So when you truly decide to tilt your teeter-totter toward your selfhood "I," you will necessarily reexamine some of the forces that keep tripping you up, some of the forces that keep putting a temporary lock on your conscience, some of the forces that keep tipping your behavior toward injustice. And some of those forces might be some of your best friends.

You may find yourself in need of more than practical courage to face the climbers stacked above you. You may find yourself needing some truly dependable allies. To find them, you will need to be truly trustworthy yourself.

You may have to consider a brand-new criterion for all your

friendships with humans raised to be a man. You may have to check out potential men friends on a completely different basis. You may have to ask yourself:

❑  *Will he put someone down to be someone to me?*

and you may have to ask yourself *about* yourself:

❑  *Will I put someone down to be someone to him?*

Until, as a man of conscience, you have decoded the truce in your friendships with men, you remain without practical courage in *all* your friendships—and your observable behavioral character gives no woman you know any grounds to believe you are a trustworthy ally. She has no reason to assume you will not eventually put her down to seem "someone" to a man.

THERE CAN BE NO TRUST
IN A TRUCE WITH MANHOOD.

# ✧ 16 ✧

## WHY DO COMMUNICATIONS IN MY LOVE LIFE BREAK DOWN?

The dichotomy between manhood and selfhood results in many seemingly incomprehensible crises in interpersonal relationships. What seems most incomprehensible about these crises often manifests itself first in the form of a "communications problem." Both people in the relationship will experience—though likely for quite different reasons—a rather mysterious breakdown in communications. Where before the two people talked back and forth quite genially in a common language, suddenly each seems to be speaking in a tongue the other finds unintelligible. And once communications have been thus rent, there appears little hope of finding out what went wrong—so things get worse.

For the person in the relationship who was raised to be a man, it is particularly useful to analyze such "communications breakdowns" to check out how the dichotomy between manhood and selfhood has been a factor in the rift.

Let's take a look, for example, at a typical everyday crisis in a real-life interpersonal relationship where two humans happen to have come together to be trustworthy allies to each other. Let's say that each of these humans checked out the other and on the basis of their observations they decided to get to know each other better, perhaps quite well, perhaps quite intimately, obviously with much trust. Let's say they are lovers, or best friends, or married to each other, or dating. Let's say one of those humans is you. And let's say your mate has just brought up a serious point with you and she is confronting you on it and it has something to do with something that you either did or failed to do.

If that sounds only dimly familiar, or if you can't completely imagine yourself in this situation yet, here are some phrases to help jog your mind:

> "You hurt me ... you put me down ... you made me
> feel completely unimportant to you ... you dismissed
> or trivialized what I said and made me feel invisible
> to you ... you didn't keep your promise to me and
> made me feel like I'm nobody to you ... you forgot what
> you promised to remember and you made me feel like
> you don't hear me when I talk ... you made fun of
> me in front of other people as if they are more real
> to you than I am ... you told me one thing and then
> turned around and did just the opposite ... you told me
> something that wasn't true—you lied—as if you think
> I'm not worthy of your honesty ... you betrayed me
> to your friends as if I'm always in the background—or
> as if I don't figure in your landscape of human beings
> at all ... you pay attention to me only when you want
> sex ..."

If you've filled in your own personal mental blank with one or more familiar particulars, you may have noted a familiar feeling rising up in you, the premonition that you are being critiqued *by a woman* because you happen to be *a man*. You may recall previously experiencing such a critique as a reprimand of your manhood. Or you may literally hear the bombshell generality that occasionally accompanies such appraisals:

> "And ... and ... *you acted just like a man.*"

Whether or not you hear those exact words, you hear their explosive meaning in her report. *Ka-boom.* Attempting to act decisively in selfhood mode—with practical courage, the best she knows how, the best she can manage under the circumstances—she confronts you about something you did or failed to do, not comprehending how you in particular could ever act that way toward someone you love. Lacking any other rational explanation, she attributes your behavior to your conformity to your social gender. But the words do not applaud you; they do not cheer your derring-do on the cliff. Quite the contrary. The words cut to the quick as a rebuke—and you cannot *stand* to hear her say them.

To figure out why that may be so, let's go back to that incendiary incident, that flash point, that moment when she says to you, "You acted just like a man"—or words to that effect. At this point in the dramatic action, you might feel a need to hit the PAUSE button and monitor the presence of anxiety waves—or perhaps hit FAST FORWARD and skip past the hard part. But here in this chapter we can slow emotional events down—or even rewind—and replay the scene frame by frame.

*What she says*—the literal sentence she speaks—goes up into the air between you, like in a cartoon character's balloon . . .

*What she probably means*—the true subtext of what she is saying—can be read only if you pay close attention. It's like when you're watching a foreign film and you need a translation of unfamiliar idiom into vernacular you can understand . . .

*What she's probably thinking*—what's really going on in the back of her mind—may be difficult for you to discern, because it appears to go up into the air between you like a cartoon character's thought cloud . . .

Actually, however, if you could get an instant readout of what she might really be thinking, it might look more like this . . .

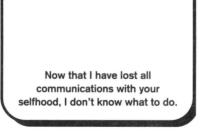

So there may be a moment here when she reviews her options. Some of her options may look better to her than others. She may or may not indicate to you which options she is considering or why. But if she could call up in her mind a computer screen—and on it find a menu of all the options she has right now—it might look something like this (we'll zoom in now for an enlarged view) . . .

---

## MENU OF AVAILABLE OPTIONS

**Make do.** Accept that it's his nature as a man to behave this way. It's his "style of communication." It's his "style of moral reasoning." So if you want to have anything more to do with this human being, you're simply going to have to accept that it's your nature as a woman to put up with being put down now and again.

**Make up.** Take the blame. Act like whatever happened was all really your fault. Forgive. Pretend it was nothing.

**Make out.** Try to reach him through sex. ("Hello? Hello in there? Is anybody home?")

**Make over.** Change your life so he will find you more interesting or less repellent. Change your appearance. Change your attitude.

**Make room.** Make yourself smaller so he can be big, diminished so he can be expansive. Give him more of your space.

**Make believe.** Put on a happy face. Show the world that everything in this relationship is hunky-dory.

**Make a wish.** And/or pray to a higher power who will listen.

**Make scenes.** Rant and rail. Exhibit extremity of emotional distress through extremity of emotional expression. Try to reach him by disclosing a depth of pained anger that, presumably, someone else human might recognize as pained anger. ("Hello? Hello in there? Is anybody home?")

**Make it without him.** Leave him and make a life for yourself that no longer needs, or wants, to have anything more to do with his.

---

That's about it. That's about all the options she has available. There is also, of course, "Make mincemeat of him." And perhaps we should consider that option for a moment, since it may spring to your mind more readily than it may occur to hers, on her mental Menu of Available Options. In point of fact, since her

objective is to reestablish communications with your selfhood
"I"—with practical courage, acting decisively in selfhood
mode—making mincemeat of you is nowhere near what she is
trying to do. You may *feel* it's what she's fixing to do—it may be
*your first thought,* actually, just as soon as she brings up any critical point about your behavior—but it's probably *not* what she
has in mind. The basic problem with it is, she would have to say
good-bye to her *own* personal moral identity in order to blow
you away that definitively. So realistically speaking, since we're
presuming she is still within the realm of trying to *reestablish*
communications selfhood-to-selfhood ("Hello? Hello in there? Is
anybody home?"), the option "Make mincemeat of him" is not
likely to show up on her mental menu until she has consistently
tried several others without success.

Now we come to a point where there are two interior mono-
logues going on: yours and hers.

Her interior monologue, freely translated, is basically as follows:

"How can I get you to recognize me as a
human being? How can I again feel *safe* with
you, *sustained* by you, *seen* by you, *not*
*alone* with you? How can I get you to feel
safe with me, sustained by me, seen by me,
and *with* me again? How can I get your
*selfhood* back?"

Your interior monologue will tend to go on simultaneously.
Freely translated, it basically goes like this:

"You're attacking me. You're attacking my
*manhood.* You're attacking everything I stand
for, everything I strive for. You're
attacking everything about me that made
me fall for you in the first place. How can
you double-cross me like this? I feel
completely blindsided and endangered.
I feel like you're yanking out every piton
that's holding me up 'cause you want to

make mincemeat of me. You want to make
me go splat."

What we have here, of course—somewhere in a thought
cloud, somewhere up there in a haze in your brain—is the mak-
ings of a familiar diagram. Perhaps you can already picture it . . .

Perhaps you can guess which way it seems to want to tilt. Perhaps you can feel it flutter in the prevailing winds of those
waves from way back. Perhaps you can feel it crash with a thud
when it tips to default position.

At this point in our frame-by-frame analysis, we hit PAUSE
and stop playback for a moment, because there are two surprising observations to be made:

1.  None of her options will return you to selfhood
mode. Absolutely none. There is nothing she can do to "get"
you to be yourself to her in selfhood mode. Absolutely nothing. You have to tilt your own teeter-totter. You have to decide to be your self yourself.

She may succeed temporarily in "getting" you to change
some of your behavior, perhaps—in particular the behavior that
prompted her to appeal for the return of your selfhood. She may
"get" you to stop picking on her for a time; she may "get" you
to stop putting her down for a while, for instance. She may not,
of course, but let's say she does. *Even if she does temporarily succeed in effecting some alteration in your egregious behavior*, she will

not get you back in selfhood mode. You do not get back into selfhood mode unless you decide for yourself to get back into it.

You decide *when* your teeter-totter tips and you decide *which way it tilts.* Day by day. Decision by decision. Moment to moment. Frame of mind by frame of mind. Relational act by relational act.

Nobody else decides but you.

Ever.

We discover another surprise at this point in playback:

**2.** You felt attacked as if by someone else in manhood mode. You were reminded of how it feels out there on the cliff, rocks raining down on you, sure footing crumbling to dust, sussing out your surroundings for safe and lethal fellow climbers. Instantly you re-felt all the emotions that flood your body and your brain when you espy another climber in full-blown manhood mode who's fixing to define his manhood over and against you.

It was not your fault you felt those feelings. Those waves of anxiety were burned into your brain and perhaps bruised into your body a long, long time ago, and *they will be back;* you will re-feel them situationally—perhaps as long as your body and brain go on living. You can't stop the waves completely. But you can stop them from telling you how to live. You can stop them from telling you who to be.

No one is perfect. Everyone is human.

- Living as a man of conscience does not mean that you never—or you never will—cause anyone pain.
- Living as a man of conscience means there's something different about how you deal with your knowledge of the pain you may have caused.

All your communications with someone you love are relational acts, and you always select whether you will be communicating with this person in manhood mode or in selfhood mode *before you ever decide what you'll say.* When you decide to tilt your teeter-totter back to selfhood mode, you decide to reestablish communications with another human being whom you love *as* another human being. When you decide to tilt your own teeter-totter back to selfhood mode, you decide to recognize another human being's pain as if it is completely real, because that other human being is completely real to you—because only when you regard someone else's full human reality are you completely real to yourself. And only then are you fully human to that other person.

We will be moving onward to explore exactly how this interpersonal process feels, exactly what selfhood mode feels like for someone who would live life as a man of conscience. But we pause again just briefly to examine in sharper focus the choice that is taken when your wobbling on your teeter-totter results in a crisis in your interpersonal relationship. According to conventional wisdom, you have the opportunity to blame the crisis on "a communications problem" (instead of, for instance, taking responsibility for your wobbling). If you opt for the euphemism of "communications problem," there are many people who will buy it. Scads of magazine articles and self-help books will talk you and a gullible loved one through your ostensible "communications problem." It's probably the most popular all-purpose equivocation for what just went wrong between you and the person you love. Even you can buy it—but only if you love manhood most of all.

When you choose to sell out your selfhood this way—when you thus evade the opportunity to be somebody to somebody, in love, with another human self, justly—you may feel guilty. You may feel as if the *person you love* has made you feel guilty. You may react with anger or counteraccusation, feeling that you should *not* feel guilty and you should not be *made* to feel guilty and anyone who keeps *trying* to make you feel guilty is just trying to make mincemeat of you. Only in manhood mode do such dodgy and disingenuous stratagems make sense, for it appears that manhood mode speaks a syntax all its own: manhood maintenance through selfhood deception.

Deciding to love manhood more than selfhood, manhood more than anyone, manhood more than love, manhood more than justice, would *of course* make one feel guilty. When one has cast off precious human selfhood—all potential for safety and sustenance, all possibility to be seen and not alone—for the sake of survival on a mythical cliff, one would *of course* be racked with pain so excruciating as to be beyond ordinary words. The name of this pain may never be fully known to the man who feels it, but experientially, emotionally, physically—perhaps even spiritually—his decision to stand fast in manhood mode feels as close to perdition as one can probably know on earth.

THE END OF "COMMUNICATIONS PROBLEMS"
IN MANHOOD MODE
IS THE BEGINNING OF TAKING RESPONSIBILITY IN SELFHOOD MODE.

# ✧ 17 ✧

## WHY CAN I FEEL NOTHING WHEN SOMEONE I LOVE FEELS PAIN?

The choice to live as a man of conscience may bring with it many perplexing recognitions. Every would-be man of conscience will stumble upon his own puzzlements in the process. This chapter is about one such personal matter that still stumps me: why can I sometimes feel nothing when someone I love feels pain? If I've decided to live as a man of conscience (and I have), then that should not ever happen (right?). Yet it does. Much more often than I care to admit.

Indifferently, I'll feel myself stand gawking at another human being's expression, realizing intellectually that their affect clearly indicates that they are in some pain, but feeling all the more remote from that person. It's almost as if the other person's pain must not trespass within an emotional boundary that at this particular moment I feel preoccupied with defending. Or it's almost as if not feeling the other person's pain prevents my borders from blurring. With my intelligence I can even observe—when the extremity of my emotional distance also becomes evident to the person in pain—that the other person's pain increases, evidently because they feel additionally isolated in their anguish, now out of touch with the one who ostensibly loved them, now outside of a comforting and healing companionship altogether. And then, bizarrely, I who stand there gawking drift further and further into a private reverie, trying only to feel more distinct in my bearing—not feeling my loved one's pain.

I almost never understand this phenomenon when it happens. If I realize what's going on with me at all, it's only some time after, which is usually too late. The person in pain already witnessed my emotional departure and saw me off.

I know of no other way to explore this peculiar behavior than with evidence from my own life.

## The True Story of a Young Boy's Search for Manhood (*continued*)

Remember little Johnny? We first met him in Chapter Four tormenting his sister who was younger by two years. This was a habit Johnny developed when he was around the age of five, and he continued at it till he was ten or eleven. The more his teasing got a rise out of his younger sister, the more he did it. The more he "got her goat," the more satisfaction he found. For all he knows, looking back today, he may actually have learned to calculate whatever parental reprimand he might receive for hurting her, and weigh that reprimand against the satisfaction he could receive by hurting her, and then hurt her just enough to get the satisfaction while avoiding scolding too harsh to make such satisfaction worth the trouble. He's an interesting case. Especially on the subject of how a kid makes decisions in relation to other people's pain. Plus, obviously, how a kid's relation to other people's pain flows into that kid's emerging personal identity.

Johnny became who he became in part through what he did to his sister when they were both little. Johnny's sister became who she became in part through the same sequence of events.

"Sequence of events" is a euphemism. It means the decisions that little Johnny made to deliberately hurt her.

During this period of Johnny's youth, which included more such "events" than Johnny can now recall, a related incident occurred. It happened like this, when Johnny was about six:

One evening Johnny and his sister were both playing quietly with their various toys in a room in their family's house—playing quite amicably, as was often the case in between episodes of Johnny's tormenting her. For some reason Johnny had some thumbtacks—perhaps to make puppets out of wooden clothespins. On this particular evening, Johnny knew that their father would soon be coming into the room where he and his sister were playing—it would soon be bedtime, time to say good-night. Johnny remembers knowing that Daddy was already in his pajamas and bare feet. And Johnny remembers doing something with a thumbtack on that particular evening. Completely deliberately, Johnny set a thumbtack on the floor in the doorway to the room where he and his sister were playing. He set down a thumbtack with the business end pointing up. He set it there intentionally in case Daddy might happen to step there. And Daddy did. When Daddy came into the room, the thumbtack went all the way into his bare heel and it bled. Daddy thought the thumbtack had fallen on the floor there by accident. Johnny never told anyone that he had put the thumbtack there on purpose. Daddy was in pain. And Johnny watched. And Johnny never told another living soul what really happened. (Johnny's father will find out this information here for the first time.) And Johnny loved his daddy. And Johnny's daddy loved Johnny. And although later in life, Johnny tried to tell himself that what happened that night to Daddy actually had a great deal to do with random chance—Daddy could have stepped anywhere, and there was just one tack, one single tiny tack—Johnny came to understand from that event how remarkably easy it is to coolly decide to cause someone pain when you think you can get away with it—even when you love them and they love you.

## The True Story of a Young Boy's Search for Manhood (continued some more)

Several years later, we find John playing with his toys again. He was twelve. He was playing with some toys on the concrete floor of a screened-in porch that was connected to the kitchen by two poured-concrete steps. It was a hot summer's day. Dad was at work. Mom was doing laundry in the basement. John's sisters were both away—one was at camp and the four-year-old was playing elsewhere in the neighborhood. There was an electric washing machine in the basement, but Mom had to carry basketfuls of wet clothes up the basement steps, out through the kitchen, and through the porch, to hang them out to dry from clotheslines in the backyard. This was how Mom always did the laundry, several times a week.

On this particular summer afternoon, while John was playing on the porch, Mom stepped down from the kitchen carrying a heavy laundry basket of wet clothes in front of her, and she stepped wrong, and she fell down on the concrete in a heap of wet laundry, and her leg turned under her somehow, and John looked at her in fright, and he saw that her leg had a broken bone sticking out the shin, cracked and sticking through the skin bone white and bleeding, and John screamed out to his mother, and she stayed calm and brave and told him what to do, and John screamed and cried, and John could not bear to see his mother in such dreadful pain, and John felt the pain of his mother's broken leg almost as if it had happened to him, and he cried out in great sobs, and his mother tried to figure out what to do next, and she consoled him, and she tried to assure him she would be OK, and she probably didn't feel all the pain yet herself, and she told him how to go to the telephone and dial emergency for an ambulance, and John did so, choking back sobs, and then he called Dad at work, trying to be brave, trying to be strong so he could get help for his mom, terrified, then waiting with his mother for the ambulance to arrive, holding her, being held, her trying to comfort him, him trying to be brave and strong for her, him feeling so bad for her, him feeling so scared for her.

John knew his mother was in great pain. Even though she was being brave and strong, even though she was not crying, even though she was talking to him like he was still John and she was still Mom, John knew his mother was in more violent physical agony than John had ever witnessed up till then

in his life. Almost in shock himself, John felt a kind of emotional and physical connection to the pain that must have
been seizing her body from her broken, bleeding leg. Helpless to make her pain go away, John felt completely confused
and incompetent in that connection—feeling pain that was
happening to someone he loved, feeling pain that was happening to someone who loved him. Not knowing how to
stop the pain. Not knowing if it would ever stop. Not knowing if his mother would ever be OK again.

## The True Story of My Search for Manhood
### (beginning to be discontinued)

As I look back, I am startled to discover, tucked away long ago
in my memory, the story of a thumbtack in my father's foot and
the story of my mother's broken leg. No sooner had I given this
chapter its title (for I had planned to expound on the topic of
empathy) than these two stories flashed back to me and seemed
to write themselves.

How did my body and brain ever learn so completely to disconnect from the pain that someone I loved was feeling—pain I
knew that I had *caused,* pain I had to disconnect from *in order* to
cause? And yet, how did my body and brain still remember,
years later, a connection to someone I loved that was so deep, so
profound, that when that human being was in pain *I seemed to
feel it too,* almost as if the pain was my own, such that even at
the time I searched my memory to see if somehow I might have
been responsible for this terrible injury? (If only I hadn't been
playing on the porch, I remember thinking, she would not have
looked up to see me and missed the step!)

As I look back, I am startled to discover how various is my
range of possible relationships to other people's pain. Observing
very young children, I can see a similar gradation—from emotional aloofness to emotional identification, from childish cruelty
to a child's version of compassion—sometimes apparently already gender-coded and sorted boy or girl, but often clearly not.

The puzzlement of recognizing the full range in my own biography is not resolved. Each child's capacity both to feel and to

not feel someone else's feelings seems variable and malleable—it may be shaped and shunted one way or the other during early training into social gender. But did we all come with the whole gamut? Perhaps. Perhaps it may be impossible ever to know.

And so I wonder, today: Do I still carry in my body and brain the potential to disconnect—and to hurt someone I love? (Yes, apparently yes. I'm afraid so. Obviously yes.) But do I still also carry in my body and brain the potential to connect—to emotionally register fully the knowledge that someone I love feels pain? (I very much hope so. I very much hope the answer is yes.)

How does anyone's body and brain decide *whether* to disconnect or connect? How is anyone ever able to run a check on not only their *own* feelings but also the feelings of someone *else*? Is there such a thing in us as "conscience"? That is the question we turn to next.

WHEN SOMEONE YOU LOVE FEELS PAIN,
MANHOOD'S FIRST NEED IS TO HAVE AN IDENTITY;
SELFHOOD'S FIRST NEED IS TO IDENTIFY *WITH*.

# ✧ 18 ✧

## HOW CAN I TELL THE DIFFERENCE BETWEEN WHAT'S RIGHT AND WHAT'S WRONG IN MY MOST INTIMATE RELATIONSHIPS?

"Conscience" is a word with many meanings I don't like. "Conscience" is often thought of as a spectral axiom, an angelic good-conduct guard, a sanctimonious superciliousness—an abstraction with no guts to it. As used in this book, however, the word "conscience" denotes a physical and emotional way of knowing—a specific sensorial capacity. This chapter looks at what conscience means concretely in real-life human feelings—and what conscience may mean in a real body and brain such as your own.

Justice and manhood *are* both abstractions. Through our moment-to-moment relational acts we decide—by loving one more than the other—whether we wish to make justice or manhood real in everyday life. So if someone has decided to create justice by trying to live as a man of conscience, the question might naturally arise: how do I ever *know* which acts to choose?

The answer is not in any instruction manual or rulebook. The answer is in our own biographies. If we have some memory of the guiding principle of selfhood—loving justice—then we can learn through our acts how that memory feels to other folks as well.

**As human infants born penised, some of us started out prepared to love both justice and manhood to some extent.**

We learned the very basis of human selfhood—"To be human is to be somebody"—through human touch, through our developing experience of other humans' bodies and voices, through being recognized and communicated with, through being sustained and safely held, through being supported and nurtured.

If we were lucky, our basic human needs to feel safe, to feel sustained, to feel seen, and to feel not alone were sufficiently met such that as we grew up, we could meet those lifelong needs in other human beings as well. If we were lucky, we got a start in life that helped us tap *our capacity to reciprocate*—a human trait that foreshadows loving justice. The capacity to reciprocate sometimes seems so flukey you might imagine it's a miracle, except it's no mystery at all if ever you got the lesson of selfhood along the way. If selfhood was ever passed on to you, you can pass it on.

If you were unlucky, no one passed that lesson on to you personally very well at all—or something else may have gone quite wrong—and as a result you have no memory of it.

But let's assume that you are someone who was at least somewhat lucky, and let's assume you are someone whose body and brain remember that "to be human is to be somebody"—at least now and then if not all the time. Let's assume your body and brain still remember what it was like to feel safe, sustained, seen, and not alone—for no other reason than that you came into this world a baby human. And lucky you, there were one or more grownups around who were delighted to give you a head start in figuring out what this human-self-to-human-self stuff is all about.

We all learned the contradiction to selfhood, too—we learned that "not to be a man is to be less than nobody." We learned that stern lesson as the very fundament of social gender, and we each learned it through rewards and punishments—for some of us, rewards quite lavish; for some of us, punishments severe. It got you started out intent on climbing the vertical scale of manhood as nimbly as you could—with foreknowledge of the peril that will befall you if you fall, the shame that awaits if you don't climb as high as you should, and the pain you will feel if someone uses your body to climb above you. This lesson of manhood prepares you for "the real world"—the social world of men. Not incidentally, it also teaches you to regard the social world of men as "real"—vastly more real and relevant than any personal experience inconsistent with it (such as any experience you may recall or long for of human self to human self).

To whatever extent you learned the lesson of manhood from rewards and punishments, you were left with a recurrent experience of gender anxiety waves, in your own individual pattern: a tension in your chest or throat perhaps, a palpitation in your heart, a spring tension in your musculature, some episodic heebie-jeebies. Anatomically, these hot buttons are remnants of your autonomic reflex system, with the social gender schema branded onto them. For you to "get" the meaning of manhood so you would never forget it, the lesson had to boot to your body and brain in a physical, palpable way. That's what those weird waves do now and then—make you feel like fighting back or ducking for cover when your abstract manhood seems in danger.

This explains why you might feel someone is trying to kill you when all they're doing is trying to have a personal chat about—let's say—your having treated them as if they were nobody. You probably *did* treat this person as *less* than you—since only through such relational acts do you ever get to feel the subjective sensation of your manhood "I." Once you do such an act, it pitches you into manhood mode, and immediately you get a reinvigorating rush—so *of course* you felt as if the person having this chat with you was trying to "unman" you. The logic is silly and circular, but the physical feelings are real. This other person, though acting with practical courage (perhaps to head off being put down by you further), was challenging the very foundation of your chosen identity mode: to be the man there, in that moment, through that particular relational act. Your life was not literally in danger—this was a conversation, after all, with words. But it sure fooled your body and brain, which had been hot-wired during your upbringing to react offensively and/or defensively against just such challenges to the transactional foundation of your social existence as a man. Those fight-or-flight reflexes keep kicking in to keep you ever vigilant, ever on the alert for Gender Danger.

One of the reasons so many humans feel manhood like a fire in the belly is that when waves of gender anxiety strike, they seem emotionally and physically overwhelming—because when triggered they play out involuntarily through your blood circulating, your breath inhaling, your nerve signaling, your muscle contracting. Just because manhood is make-believe—it has no material basis whatsoever—that does not mean your body and brain cannot be tricked into responding as if manhood is as vital to your survival as is keeping your body out of the way of speeding trucks. So powerfully is the lesson of manhood imprinted onto your autonomic nervous system that you can sometimes feel as if you would be utterly numb, plowed down, limp, or dead without your manhood (1) to keep you fortified, (2) to keep you from free-fall, (3) to keep you recognizable, and (4) to keep you sexed. Such are manhood's corrupted versions of the four basic human emotional needs.

**Just as there is a physically resonating reminder in us of the lesson of manhood—those persistent anxiety waves—there is also a physically resonating reminder in us of the lesson of selfhood.**

The body's memory of human selfhood is not always as easy to detect, and it does not announce its presence with all the bamboozling and hullabaloo of gender anxiety waves. The lesson of selfhood is nevertheless resident in us—both physically and emotionally. However slightly or intensely, it's in us and it's between us. But so far as I am aware, it has no adequate name yet.

*What shall we call it when . . .*

> we feel someone else's feeling?
> we feel someone else's sadness?
> we feel someone else's happiness?
> we feel someone else's pain?
> we feel someone else's pleasure?
> we feel someone else's calm and contentment?
> we feel someone else's excitement and energy?

*What shall we call those feelings* that seem like emotional mirroring, emotional mimesis—except that they are not imitation; they are as real as your own?

*What shall we call those feelings* that seem as though a viaduct has opened between you and another, a flooding passageway for fluent emotional exchange, or as though you and another have suddenly grown a common skin, a membrane for emotional osmosis—except that the feelings seem not so much to be *transferred* as to well up from within you, *in yourself, with* another self, *in joined witness* to your joint selfhood?

*What shall we call those feelings* that seem so consoling, so reconnecting, so comforting, so reuniting—and yet vaguely discomfiting, awkward to inhabit for too long a time—because they resonate so profoundly of human life, of life with life, of human through human, of one's self in thrall to another?

*What shall we call those feelings* that do not compute as feelings on the terrain of social gender—and so they sometimes frighten us; they were not the feelings we were expecting; they were not the feelings we had been expected to have; they were not the feelings we needed in order to feel certain our manhood was real?

*What shall we call those feelings* that so transparently tell us we are in the presence of another living human being, and we are the very being to whom that very life is present?

*What shall we call those feelings* that so rock us and astonish us with our common humanity that we are speechless, agog?

So dumbfounded are we as species that we have not yet devised a way to *tell* one another of this experience. We have not yet found precisely the word or the name that would mean exactly everything that some of us already seem fortunate to know. Fortunate to remember. Fortunate to have learned. Fortunate to have not forgot for fear.

These feelings simply do not have an adequate name in the English language. Some of us feel these unnamed feelings more deeply than others do. Some of us feel them more or less often. Some of us feel them in some situations but never in others. There's an enormous range of people's experience of these feelings, just as there's an enormous range of people's experiential learning of selfhood. Some of us never got much. Some of us got just barely enough. Some of us got selfhood nearly squished out of us because the trauma that taught us manhood blew all our loving-justice circuits.

But just as gender anxiety waves arise as a physical reminder of the lesson of manhood (because our autonomic reflex system was variously terrorized into reverence for the hierarchy that sustains the social fiction), these unnamed feelings arise in us as a lucky physical and emotional reminder that, in simple point of fact, "to be human is to be somebody."

Groping for a name, I found in my Random House Webster's College Dictionary four words in the general neighborhood of such "feel-with" feelings—four words that all "denote the tendency or capacity to share the feelings of others": SYMPATHY, COMPASSION, PITY, and EMPATHY. None quite says what needs saying.

My dictionary says that SYMPATHY "signifies a general kinship with another's feelings, no matter of what kind." But "no matter of what kind" seems totally wrong for the purpose. "What kind" of feelings these are really does matter to you; you can tell that they are the exact kind of feelings another human would have *as a human*, because they are exactly the kind of feelings *you* would have as a human. Obviously, you would not be feeling these "feel-with" feelings in "sympathy" with someone's *anti*human feelings—murderous rage, for example, or the impulse to sexually violate someone else's body. That would be completely impossible, completely outside your experience of those unnamed feelings—because the lesson of selfhood never taught you any feelings but human-to-human ones, somebody-to-somebody ones.

My dictionary says that COMPASSION "implies a deep sympathy for the sorrows or troubles of another, and a powerful urge to alleviate distress." So far, so good, as "feeling-with" goes. But "compassion" may mislead by suggesting that our "feel-with" feelings only respond when someone human is in sorrow or in trouble, or when a "distress" needs "alleviating." Our "feel-with" feelings do that, of course, and human selfhood lives on in and through you when they do. But our "feel-with" feelings also resonate when someone is exhilarated, playful, ardent, or affectionate, when someone is uncomfortable, timid, or alarmed—whenever someone human is feeling some human emotion in some human dilemma or delight. Not all human emotions need to be "alleviated." Some do. Some don't. Some we can just let be—and feel them in ourselves through our beholding.

My dictionary says that PITY "suggests a kindly, but sometimes condescending, sorrow caused by the suffering or misfortune of others." And the condescension edge of "pity" is what makes it the wrong name for our "feel-with" feelings, all of which are horizontal, human to human, not from some imagined top down. The power we feel when we feel our "feel-with" feelings is the power of our fundamentally level connection to another human life, a connection that empowers us to experience more fully our own life as human. Whereas in pity one might feel the power of one's privilege or prerogative (one's power *over*, perhaps), in "feeling-with" you feel the power of your humanity *with*. Selfhood does not say, "There goes a human being, poor thing." Selfhood says, "There in that human being goes my human-beingness too."

My dictionary says that EMPATHY "refers to a vicarious participation in the emotions of another, or to the ability to imagine oneself in someone else's predicament." Alas, this word will not suffice either. When we are "feeling-with," we are not voyeurs, we are not spectators to some different being's emotional state, we are not "imagining" what it would be like to be them. When we are "feeling-with," we are recognizing, we are registering, we are resonating, we are actively engaged in receiving certain signals from a real human life—certain signs, perhaps, certain evidence of experienced feelings—and *we are reminded of the lesson of selfhood.* We do not need to have the exact same feeling as that other human being to be reminded of our common humanity. We do not have to wait until we have had exactly the same feeling we perceive in another before such time as we are willing to concede that their selfhood has some merit that may be applicable to our interaction. Just because we may never have had precisely such a feeling as we perceive and behold in the human being we're with, that does not mean we leap to the conclusion that loving justice cannot occur between us. "Feeling-with" does not hold out for simultaneity, synchronicity, or perfectly calibrated synonymity between your feelings and someone else's. "Feeling with" is simply a physical reminder of selfhood. Once upon a time, you learned it: "To be human is to be somebody." And now and again, these "feel-with" feelings help you to remember.

So, lacking a usable label from my dictionary, and bearing in mind the full range of situational meanings and emotions described above, I propose a new term: MORAL SONORITY.

**mor·al so·nor·i·ty** (*moh*-rull suh-*nohr*-i-tee) *n.*
**1.** Feelings that are resonant with interhuman af-
filiation. **2.** Feelings that are therefore communi-
cable from one human being to another. See
*loving justice.* [From MORAL, implying "conscience," or a sense of right and wrong in selfhood mode; and SONORITY, meaning sound
vibration and resonance.] *We sometimes feel our
moral sonority alongside our waves of gender anxiety. Even though selfhood mode and manhood mode
are contradictory, moral sonority and gender anxiety
can be experienced simultaneously.*

When you give more weight to your selfhood "I," you will
necessarily choose relational acts that clarify a human identity
for yourself on the horizontal plane of selfhood, in horizontal
relation to someone else who is also human, whom you see as
a real self. When you choose such relational acts, your choice
turns on your knowledge that "to be human is to be
somebody"—and your teeter-totter tilts to selfhood mode. On
the contrary, when you give more weight to your manhood
"I," you will necessarily choose relational acts that will establish an identity for yourself such that you can feel higher up
on the vertical scale of manhood than someone else, someone
whom you will necessarily elect to see as having less of that
identity, and therefore someone whom you elect to treat as less
real than you (less real by whatever margin you like, since
you're calling the shots). When you choose such relational
acts, your choice turns on your knowledge that "not to be a
man is to be less than nobody"—and your teeter-totter tilts to
manhood mode.

You can seesaw between selfhood mode and manhood mode
however much you like, but you cannot logically be in both
modes at the same instant, in the same relational act, in the same
decision. A single relational act will pitch you into one or the
other mode (depending entirely upon whether it expresses
equality or inequality). There is no such thing as a relational act
that will stabilize your seesaw in both selfhood mode and manhood mode simultaneously.

Interestingly, however, although the teeter-totter of your relational acts is either in selfhood mode or manhood mode, your perception of both moral sonority and gender anxiety waves—physical signals reminding you of selfhood and manhood—may be in your body and brain at the same time and in all sorts of proportions. This emotional and physical phenomenon is sometimes surprising, sometimes confusing. To picture it for yourself, imagine two oscilloscopes, side by side ...

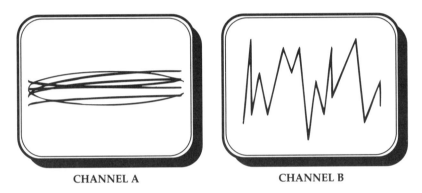

CHANNEL A                    CHANNEL B

An oscilloscope is like a TV screen that displays patterns of variation in whatever you tune it to receive. If you tune an oscilloscope to moral sonority on Channel A, for instance, you might picture your reception of these "feel-with" feelings as if they were emotions in motion between you, ebbing and flowing, rising and falling, just like the variable waters in between bobbing or tempest-tossed boats. On your Channel A, you would stay tuned to emotional news from other human selves—buoyancy, distress signals, smooth sailing, small-craft warnings, lost anchors, and such. Channel A is where you would stay tuned for physical reminders of Lesson A: "To be human is to be somebody," which under duress sometimes translates as "I feel adrift and out to sea" or "Mayday! Mayday!" The apparent motion of emotions between you—your perception of your "feel-with" feelings, your reception of moral sonority—is how you know whatever you can possibly know, human self to human self, emotionally and physically.

If you tune another oscilloscope to gender anxiety waves on Channel B, you might picture your reception of these feelings as if they were spiking, peaking and plummeting episodically, rising with Gender Danger, then subsiding through some resolution, some tension release, then rising again in panic or anger if the foregoing resolution was ineffective. On your Channel B, you would stay alert to emotional news from your fight-or-flight reflex system, so that your niche on the cliff feels as snug and secure as possible. Channel B is where you would stay tuned for physical reminders of Lesson B: "Not to be a man is to be less than nobody." Emotionally and physically, the apparent resolution of your spiking gender anxiety waves—and whatever means you need to use to keep them from spiking anymore—is how you know whatever you can possibly know about how it feels to be the man there.

The informational readout from Channel A feels completely emotionally real. The informational readout from Channel B feels completely emotionally real. Physically, emotionally, experientially, you can *feel* moral sonority and you can *feel* gender anxiety waves. Lesson A is in you and you can feel its physical reminder. Lesson B is in you and you can feel its physical reminder. Theoretically, you can stay tuned to both channels at the same time. And since each channel has a volume control, you can decide which one you prefer to amplify, which one to give more of your attention to. This is a handy feature. It's especially handy when you are deciding between different—and contradictory—relational acts.

**Selfhood mode and manhood mode each have a distinct and different "right" and "wrong."**

When you're in selfhood mode, your choice of relational acts will seem to be on one dimension of "right" and "wrong." When you're in manhood mode, your choice of relational acts will seem to be on an entirely different dimension of "right" and "wrong." One of the reasons these contradictory dimensions of right and wrong make sense to you is that you quite literally *sense* them—you experience them emotionally and physically, in your body and in your brain. When you've decided to act in selfhood mode, and you've turned up the volume on Channel A as high as you're able, and you've turned down the volume on Channel B as much as you can for the time being, your feelings—your reception of moral sonority from in between you and another human self—will provide you with emotional guidance as you deliberate upon which relational act will probably be more appropriate and which relational act will probably be inappropriate. It's only emotional guidance, of course; it's not a set of rules. And your monitors must be rather carefully calibrated, for the validity of this emotional guidance system depends greatly upon increasing the acuity of your reception on Channel A as well as upon reducing interference from Channel B. Then, with your feelings tuned to Channel A—either predominantly or exclusively for the time being—you will *sense* the seeming rightness or wrongness of a relational act you may be considering. Then, when you decide upon an appropriate relational act and your Channel A screen picks up signals that it was indeed appropriate (for instance because another human self subsequently did indeed experience more safety, more sustenance, more recognition, less aloneness), you would yourself feel moved emotionally, because in that very interaction—when you become the very human who acts humanly to another human self—you become your most real self. If, however, your Channel A monitor picks up signals that your relational act has turned out to be inappropriate (for instance because it is being experienced by someone else as contributing to less safety, less sustenance, less visibility, isolation) you would immediately act on that feedback from another human's feelings—for the sake of their feelings and for the sake of your own. Their feelings and your feelings are connected in a common fate once you're in selfhood mode. If the other human feels bad, you cannot feel good. If the other human feels pain, you cannot feel pleasure. Given the way Channel A monitors the apparent motion of emotions between you and other human lives, such a vast emotional disparity could not possibly happen. To feel pleasure in another human's pain, you would have to tune out Channel A completely, and decide to forget Lesson A by whatever means necessary.

Conveniently, there is a way to do that, if and when you choose. Just as you can decide to tilt your teeter-totter from selfhood mode to manhood mode, you can decide to turn up the volume on Channel B. The volume on your Channel B monitor can go quite high, so you really don't have to turn down Channel A to get the effect of no interference from it. But if you *can* turn down your Channel A as well, it will help, because then you will feel that much less conflicted about the emotional guidance coming in on Channel B.

Once you've decided to act in manhood mode, you will make your choice of relational acts on the basis of whether your action will achieve that objective either more effectively or less effectively. "More effective" translates into "right," and "less effective" translates into "wrong," because in manhood mode, the problem is how to be the man there, how not to be less than nobody; and the solution is whatever relational acts will establish your identity at the expense of someone else who is closer to nobody than you. Your emotional guidance system on this mission is the spiking pattern of gender anxiety waves coming in on Channel B. When you begin to detect signals of an uncomfortable elevation in those anxiety waves—for instance because someone has impugned or threatened your manhood, from above or beside or below you on the cliff—you will immediately begin your search for the relational act or acts that will effectively recertify your manhood "I." You will feel you *have* to. You will feel you have no choice. You will feel these gender anxiety waves like a death knell. You will feel your very life hangs in the balance. You will feel you must find an effective relational act or you will surely perish as an independent, sentient creature. When those gender anxiety waves spike, they can be quite frisky. Every so often, they spike so high they go off the screen, and you can't even monitor them again until you take someone down all the way.

When you are deliberating upon your choice of effective and ineffective relational acts, the emotional feedback coming in on Channel B is highly informative as to what's "right" and what's "wrong." Usually, you can feel immediate feedback as to whether a particular relational act has reduced your gender anxiety level. And if you feel that it hasn't—if your gender anxiety waves are still spiking—all you have to do is try another. And then another. Sooner or later, if you apply yourself to the problem of recertifying your manhood "I" in manhood mode, you will—if only through trial and error—discover some especially effective relational acts that will bring someone down and bring down your gender anxiety level as well.

As you probably know from tuning in Channel B now and then, those gender anxiety waves rarely fall below your at-ease threshold for very long at a time. Rarely do they languish in the safety zone for so long that you can relax your attention to the Channel B monitor altogether. You never know what someone will do or say next that will send your gender anxiety waves spiking again. And you never know what you will feel compelled to do or say next in order to bring your gender anxiety level back down. That's what makes life in manhood mode, and life on the cliffside of gender, such a thrill.

You will recall that gender anxiety waves come in on your autonomic fight-or-flight reflex system, the same one that evolved in the human species for keeping you alive. In its unenhanced, flesh-and-blood state, this reflex system keeps human critters from inviting a saber-toothed tiger to dinner, and it keeps warm-blooded humans from jumping into bubbly volcanoes for a swim. It's built in, sticker-price standard equipment, to keep us out of harm's way. And so you will naturally feel your fight-or-flight reflex kick in now and then when gender is the furthest thing from your mind. This happens a lot in life—on battlefields (even though a duel between manhood acts may have got you there), when you are knifed and bleeding to death (even though a turf war between masked men may have prompted the dispute), when you are being beat up with a baseball bat because of the color of your skin (even though the demands of the white cliffs of manhood simply had to put you down somewhere below). When your precious human life itself is actually in peril, actually in pain, actually in extremis, your fight-or-flight reflex will try to be there for you, as long as it can be, as long as you have not been pummeled to numbness, past feeling alive at all.

Far afield of Gender Danger, your fight-or-flight reflex will respond to other sorts of risks and hazards having nothing whatever to do with saving your ass on the vertical scale of manhood. When you're a child, for instance, your fight-or-flight reflex can kick in when you are riding fast on a toboggan or a dirt bike, when you are watching a horror movie, when you are being chased by the neighborhood bully, when you are being called on to recite in class, when you are a witness to some violence in your home, when you are being spanked, when you are on a roller coaster, when you are driving dangerously fast in a car, when you are watching a slasher film, when you are catching a ride between subway cars, when you are wrestling, when you are being tickled hard, when you are in a fistfight, when you are blocking a tackle. Many varied childhood experiences commonly set off your built-in fight-or-flight reflexes. And then, once your body and brain figure out that your *gender* depends on the same emotional-and-physical reflexes, something remarkable happens: you find yourself *repeating* whatever risk or hazard made your fight-or-flight reflex go off, and you find yourself *repeating* whatever resolution you found in order to *reiterate* the control it seemed to give you over your gender anxiety waves.

When you were a kid, one of the things that happened in your body was that when your autonomic reflex system went off, nerves all over your body went on tingly alert, your lungs seemed to gasp till they'd explode, and blood pumped torrents throughout all your plumbing (presumably to speed emergency reserves of oxygen and blood sugar to your musculature). And since you are a human who happened to have been born with elongated tissue around your urethra, that part of your body went on tingly alert and got pumped too. Human infants born with that particular tissue formation start having erections soon after birth. And those same humans grow up having erections in all sorts of situations that apparently have no connection with Gender Danger.

What happens, though—if the rewards and punishments meted out to you teach Lesson B correctly—is that from various childhood risks, perils, and hazards you learn what makes your tiny penis throb up and what makes it stay up. Later on, when you fear the punishment that awaits you for acting not enough like a man and too much like a nobody, you know which situations you can count on to make your penis throb reliably. You learn which sorts of situations you can revisit to avoid the punishment that awaits you for not being adequately gendered. In a pinch, you can even count on your fear of the hazard or punishment—your reflex reaction when you're in harm's way—to make your penis hard.

A lot of the sports and adventures enjoyed by men have this private payoff: Such activities make you feel your fight-or-flight reflex kicking in. Such activities then help you feel a pleasant relief when the reflex subsides. Such activities seem to keep your genitourinary system fit—they give your autonomic reflexes a workout and so seem to give you control over your gender anxiety waves. Most of these sports and adventures are intriguing and exciting and rewarding in their own right, of course. And because nobody does any of these activities "with" their penis (the way you might throw or catch "with" your arm, or run "with" your legs), whether you get a kick out of them has nothing whatever to do with any given genitourinary system. But for many humans who were raised to be a man and who got a heavy dose of Lesson B along the way, certain sports and adventures have an added appeal. They seem to prompt emotional feedback on Channel B. They seem to make you feel more real as a manhood "I."

The subjective experience is fleeting, of course, and not a terribly convincing one at that. The only way those spiking gender anxiety waves will truly decrescendo is when you select an effective relational act and you select the person or people you're going to do it to and then you just go ahead and do it—so they absolutely get the message that you just regarded them as closer to nobody than you. The subjective sense that your manhood "I" exists—and that you exist as your manhood "I"—can only occur emotionally and physically when you are acting in manhood mode and when you are tuned in to Channel B and when you have effectively executed the relational act that will effectively reduce your level of gender anxiety waves temporarily. No touchdown will do that. Only a put-down.

This can be frustrating, especially if you expected the sport or the adventure to tone down those gender anxiety waves once and for all. This can be especially aggravating as well to the athlete's date, or the conquering hero's spouse, when the game is over, when the match has been won, when the derring-do has been done—yet the good sport's emotional and physical sense of his manhood "I" continues to elude him. If he is watching Channel B—"just to see what's on"—and if he feels those gender anxiety waves still spiking, he may not rest content until he has acted like the man there. Decisively. Definitively.

He may have neglected to turn down the volume on Channel A. He may be getting interference. His reception of the status of his gender anxiety waves on Channel B may occasionally feel out of sync with his perception of his human-beingness via Channel A. The discombobulation he experiences is why he feels he can't seem to do anything "right." Whenever he does something "right" in manhood mode, for the sake of his manhood "I," he feels his gender anxiety waves diminuendo but he gets conflicting interference from Channel A: he feels the pain of another human being. Drat! He can't seem to do *anything* right within manhood mode, on the dimension of effective and ineffective. He keeps sensing a contradictory emotional guidance system. He keeps sensing moral sonority. He doesn't like what's coming in on Channel A because it always conflicts with his manhood acting, but he can't figure out how to turn the damn thing off.

Each monitor has only one channel: moral sonority or gender anxiety waves. Both monitors are difficult to turn off, though the volume on each can be turned way up and the volume on each can be turned way down. It all depends which one you want to pay more attention to. It all depends who you want to be.

No one is perfect. Everyone is human.

- Living as a man of conscience does not mean that you never—or you never will—cause anyone pain.
- Living as a man of conscience means there's something different about how you deal with your knowledge of the pain you may have caused.

How you deal with your knowledge of the pain you may have caused is largely how someone close to you can surmise who you really are. In your most intimate relationships—with someone who wants to know you, someone who wants to be with you, someone who would like to love you—how you act *after* you've hurt them is the only clue they have as to whether you're likely to hurt them again. No one else can predict *any* of your behavior with any certainty, of course. *You* call the shots. *You* tip your teeter-totter. *You* decide whether to act relationally in selfhood mode or manhood mode. No one decides but you, so no one else can know for certain which *way* you will decide, which relational acts will seem "right" or "wrong" to you, which relational act you will choose next. So from the point of view of someone else in your life, it's a complete crapshoot. But how you deal with your knowledge of the pain you may have caused suggests whether the odds are in favor of justice or manhood.

How you deal with your knowledge of the pain you may have caused is largely a matter of whether you decide to stay tuned to Channel A, the moral sensorium that is your "conscience," as a constant in your life. To do this, you may have to turn down the volume on Channel B—and this may seem tough to do, especially in the company of other men who have their B channels blaring. But in your most intimate relationships especially, staying attuned to your sensorial conscience is not only the only way to tell what's "right" and "wrong"; it is also your only lifeline to selfhood. Because to whatever extent you try to turn that conscience down or shut it off and say, "I refuse to feel *with* this person; I refuse to identify with such feelings. It is more important to me to feel I am identified as a real man"—to that extent you have cut yourself off, emotionally and physically, from your human capacity to know another's selfhood and your human capacity to know your own.

HOW CAN ANYONE IN CONSCIENCE NOT LOVE JUSTICE?
HOW CAN ANYONE IN CONSCIENCE STAND
TO LOVE MANHOOD MORE?

# ✧ 19 ✧

# HOW CAN I HAVE BETTER SEX?

In many people's experience, sex and selfhood are separate, never together. Many people have given up hope that sex and selfhood might ever be experienced between two human beings in the same place at the same time and in the same way. Many people believe it is not even possible to feel our full humanness, including our sexual humanness, in a relationship with another human being where there is complete, reciprocal fairness: where each sovereign self feels safe, sustained, seen, not alone—and where no one would even dream of getting his rocks off somewhere up on a cliff.

What would it mean to reconnect sex and selfhood—in our bodies, in our relationships, in our world, in our lifetime?

What would the eroticism of loving justice be like?

Who would we be to one another when we behold and are beheld as fully human, fully somebody?

How does our sexual selfhood *feel*? And how can we possibly find out?

These are a few of the questions this chapter seeks answers to.

This is not a chapter about how to have better sex in manhood mode. There are plenty of books for that. Instead this chapter is about how to recognize the difference between sexual feelings in selfhood mode and sexual feelings in manhood mode.

To live as a man of conscience means understanding in yourself and for yourself what that difference is, and how that difference affects your relationships.

The difference between sexual feelings in selfhood mode and sexual feelings in manhood mode may at first seem very nuanced, very subtle, not easily apparent, not easy to detect—until suddenly it becomes obvious. Like, *click*. And then one's newfound capacity to recognize the difference will tend to stay in one's mind, as if on file, available to be consulted for all the moment-to-moment choices one might ever make thereafter in one's sexual relationships.

The discussion here is not intended as a how-to sex manual—although some passages will be sexually explicit. The point is not to answer questions like "What are the best sexual positions?" The point is to help you answer, for yourself, questions like these: "What's my position sexually in relation to selfhood or manhood? When I'm having sex with someone, am I feeling emotionally and physically that I belong to an affinity group of human selves? Or am I having sex as if I'm a contestant or combatant—as if sex is a qualifying round for membership in a climbing team on the vertical scale of manhood?"

No one is perfect. Everyone is human. But the decision to act relationally in selfhood mode or in manhood mode always has consequences in one's interpersonal intimacy. I know of no sex manual that helps anyone locate their position sexually in terms of that decision. Therefore this chapter also offers some practical guidelines for recognizing *which* position you are in sexually— whether, at a given moment in a relationship, you are acting as your selfhood "I" or as your manhood "I"—so that you can *change* your position, if and when you choose.

Everything this book has said so far about manhood mode applies to sexual relationships as well. Basically, for anyone to be the man there, for someone to feel closer to manhood than to nobody, someone else (someone *human*) has to be treated, at least momentarily, like an underling (not like *somebody*).

And everything this book has said so far about selfhood mode applies to sexual relationships as well. Basically, for anyone to feel human there—to feel sexually present *as* oneself in one's own body and *to* another self who also feels present in *their* own body—there has to be a relational context of justice created through acts of reciprocal regard for one another's selfhood. That context does not change, nor would anyone *require* that context to change, as sexual arousal and expression intensify.

Understandably, some humans raised to be a man would prefer to know in advance what it would be like to have sex in selfhood mode, to see first if it's what they might enjoy. Understandably, too, some humans raised to be a man, having read thus far, may have surmised some implications for their own sex life already, but they could use more clarity about how to reconcile sexual sensations with the full range of other feelings we have been discussing—basic emotional needs to feel safe, sustained, seen, not alone; inculcated gender anxiety; and the emotions in motion between us that are the way we know our moral link to other human selves.

Before obliging such readers' concerns, let's recap what has been said so far about the decision to act relationally in manhood mode and observe in more detail how it applies to sexual relations.

## A Personal Checklist of Some Reasons You May Feel That You Ought to Stay in Manhood Mode During Sex

- ❏ Many other humans raised to be a man intimidate or scare me.
- ❏ I must always act like a man or else they will judge me and humiliate me.
- ❏ My manhood act during the rest of my life is shaky enough as it is. I need to succeed in it during sex at least.
- ❏ I must not be my father's shame. I must kill off in myself whatever resembles my mother.
- ❏ I believe that there is such a thing as real and deep manhood. There *has* to be. I can't exist otherwise.
- ❏ Those damned gender anxiety waves—I don't know how else to quell them except by getting off in manhood mode.

❑  I have no idea what sexuality in selfhood mode is or what it might be like—but it scares the shit out of me. How can you be that open with someone, that intimate with someone, that erotically communing with someone, that orgasmically transported with someone, that *human* with someone—and not feel as if you will fall off the edge of the knowable universe?!

❑  I think my partner expects me to act like the man there— and I would feel funny if I refused.

Each human growing up to be a man probably has additional reasons that were not reflected in that list. If such a personal reason occurs to you, feel free to fill in the blank.

❑  _____

Mentally keeping track of the social pressures that keep you acting in manhood mode is a good idea at all times, not just when you're having sex. Your own personal checklist of such pressures can help you recognize more clearly whatever might be hanging you up. That doesn't get you off the hook, but the more you've stayed alert to those social pressures while you're *not* having sex, the less likely it is that they'll hang you up when you *are*.

Like almost everyone raised to be a man, you may feel some pressures to stay in manhood mode during sex and not be consciously aware of them. That's partly because there are some heavy-duty pressures that we haven't even gotten to yet.

## Seven Mysteries of "Male" Sexual Anatomy (Or, Why Humans Don't Come the Way We Sometimes Think We Do)

One of the most viscerally significant pressures to stay in manhood mode during sex may be your belief that there is such a thing as a "male" sexuality. The social notion of "male" sexual feelings—a corollary of reverence for Deep Bob—seems to receive widespread confirmation during the selection made at birth when humans who shall be raised to be a man are sorted out from humans who shall not. Upon visual inspection, these latter humans are simply deemed not penised (though later in life they are reckoned to be clitorised, vulvaed, breasted, uterused, etc.). The only sorting factor that pertains at birth is an exterior genital tubercle that can be judged by the attending physician "long enough." That bit of flesh then bears an awesome burden as the human to whom it's attached begins believing that with this anatomic organ comes a separable sphere of sexual sensation that is, unambiguously and unquestionably, "male."

Nothing in an overview of human anatomy supports this social notion—only belief in Deep Bob does, plus all the relational acts in manhood mode that make the notion feel real. Nothing observable about "male" sexual anatomy leads logically to the conclusion that there is a discrete set of sexual feelings that are "the male ones," which when felt can always be clearly delineated from "the female ones." The following seven points show how improbable any such category is. A human raised to be a man might try very hard, acting relationally in manhood mode, to make certain (or make believe) that the sexual feelings he is having are only "the male ones." But he will be up against intransigent facts about his sexual anatomy that will make this effort extremely frustrating.

1. **Penises are transformers and transducers—just like clitorises are.** Nobody knows why, but the nerve hookup inside both penises and clitorises has a similar capacity to receive and retransmit sensation from one place in your body to another and then to another—and to amplify all that sensory information simultaneously. The feelings are experienced subjectively as intensifying whole-body or full-pelvic arousal, whether with or without direct stimulation. The transformer and transducer capacity of the penis has been observed clinically (by William H. Masters and Virginia E. Johnson) and described anecdotally in erotic literature as well as life. But it may go relatively unfelt by an individual human raised to be a man to the extent that he chooses to concentrate more on the mechanistic or operational capacities of the penis.

2. **Nipple eroticism is experienceable by a high proportion of penised humans.** Nobody knows quite why, but a penised human's nipples and pectoral area occasionally become extremely sensitive to touch; such touch is experienced subjectively as contributing to an overall feeling of sexual arousal, during which the nipples themselves become tumescent. Again, this sensitivity has been widely reported in sexual literature, but it may go unfelt, especially as other anatomical operations are being judged the main event.

3. **In people born penised, the accompanying prostate gland is located much more conveniently for pleasurable stimulation via the rectum than the clitoris is located for pleasurable stimulation via the vaginal canal in people born vulvaed.** Nobody knows why. And many penised humans do not even suspect that this is so. Or if they do, they don't give it a lot of thought. But anatomically there is no unequivocal foundation for fundamentalists' belief that society must be organized the way it is because of some heterosexual manifest destiny. It just ain't so. As most penised adults are well aware, a proctologist can quickly obtain a sample of seminal fluid simply by donning a rubber glove, inserting a finger or two into the rectum, and gently palpating the prostate. Presto. The prostate is just about the first thing you come to. You can hardly miss it. If you're in a sexual mood, if your sphincter is relaxed, and if your rectum is lubricated, even the gentlest probing of the prostate can push your buttons in an instant.*

4. **During human orgasm, contractions may occur in the outer vaginal canal of humans with "female" sexual anatomy and in the sphincter muscles of humans with "female" or "male" sexual anatomy alike, and when these contractions occur, they come at exactly the same interval: every eight-tenths of a second.** Nobody has a

---

*For anyone who cares to believe in a creator deity, this experience may cause one to appreciate divinity all the more.

clue why this is. Perhaps it's some sort of biological clock that goes off when we all get off.

5. **Researchers use arbitrary criteria and fudge human experience in order to make "scientific" distinctions between "female and male categories" of human sexuality.** For instance, a couple of renowned clinical researchers who studied "female" sexuality (Masters and Johnson again) first eliminated from their subject population all humans with a clitoris that was too long. Those same redoubtable researchers decided they would study only episodes of "male" sexual arousal wherein ejaculation and orgasm were experienced simultaneously (see point 6, below). The subject population was thus skewed even before they screwed.

6. **Ejaculation and orgasm are not the same phenomena.** They can be experienced independently of each other. Their neurological hookups are separate and enter the spinal cord in different places. **Penile erection runs on yet another neurological and vascular system.** Erections come and go. They don't always come, and they don't always have to. So if you're keeping count, that's three independent bipolar variables; and that makes at least ten possible combinations of experiential events in a human with "male" sexual anatomy:

   ✔ There can be penile erection without ejaculation and orgasm.
   ✔ There can be penile erection and ejaculation without orgasm.
   ✔ There can be penile erection and orgasm without ejaculation.
   ✔ There can be orgasm without penile erection and ejaculation.
   ✔ There can be orgasm and ejaculation without penile erection.
   ✔ There can be orgasm and penile erection without ejaculation.

✔ There can be ejaculation without penile erection and orgasm.

✔ There can be ejaculation and penile erection without orgasm.

✔ There can be ejaculation and orgasm without penile erection.

✔ There can be penile erection and ejaculation and orgasm pretty much all at the same time. (This last experience is the only one that most penised humans—including most sex researchers—ever pay conscious attention to.)

7. **Nonejaculatory orgasms in penised humans are not only possible, they are frequently multiple.** Nonejaculatory orgasms have doubtless been widely experienced but without a name to call them, so they have not often been noticed as such. They have been reported anecdotally and in sexological literature; a few therapists and workshop leaders teach sensate-focus techniques to have them, and they have been advocated in the teachings of certain Eastern traditions and some Western sects. But because there is no commonly understood name for them—and because they seem so far off the map of what "male" sexuality is alleged to be—they don't get mentioned much in everyday communication about sex. I came upon them myself rather by happy accident and wrote about my experience in an essay first published in 1974*—but I had no idea then what to call them, I'd never heard or read anything about them, so I just described the feelings. Subsequently some who read my essay told me they'd experienced similar feelings. Subsequently I came to know intimately a few other penised humans who were also experiencing them—and I realized this because when my body was naked next to theirs, I felt them—though as I recall we had better things to do at the time than to think up words for what

---

*The essay, titled "Refusing to Be a Man," was later anthologized in *For Men Against Sexism: A Book of Readings,* edited by Jon Snodgrass (Albion, California: Times Change Press, 1977).

was happening. Subjectively the experience feels somewhat like a full-body pulsing, an intense wavelike feeling
of orgasm but without release of ejaculate; hence there's
no refractory period. Continued stimulation can result in
recurring orgasmic waves. Occasionally ejaculation may
be retrograde, which means the seminal fluid doesn't
squirt out, it stays in. The extent of one's penile tumes-
cence is variable, and not especially central to the experience. Rather more relevant seems to be the intensity of
one's subjective receptivity to the transformer and transducer capacity of one's genitals as expressed and experienced far beyond one's groin. Researchers seem to have
settled on the term "nonejaculatory orgasm," an awfully
academic-sounding mouthful. Slang, to my knowledge,
has not yet offered an expression that is any more com-
municative or truthful. Alas, once again, life eludes the
common tongue with which we might hear tell of it.

Each of these seven "mysteries" is in fact an exception that
*dis*proves the rule: taken together, this list refutes the social notion that there is a boundary where so-called male sexual feelings absolutely end and so-called female sexual feelings
absolutely begin. Most penised folks share a passionate inner
conviction that you can go looking for that boundary in your
body when you have sex. You can't. There is no such boundary
to be found. A penis marks a human body as "male" (by social
convention); therefore the adjective "male" can meaningfully be
applied to a human body that is penised (a tautology, nonethe-
less true). There are physical and emotional feelings that help
you socially to feel more "a real man" and not "less than nobody." But logically and physiologically, there is no circum-
scribed set of sexual feelings that are definitionally "male." The
presence of a penis does not correlate with the definitional presumption in any meaningful way.

Believing that you dare not feel other than a decidedly
"male" sexual feeling will surely make you decide to have sex in
manhood mode, however—and perhaps go into overdrive to do
so.

In order to learn whether you might prefer sex in selfhood
mode instead, you would first need to reexamine your convic-

tion that coming with a penis automatically makes one feel sexually "like a real man." You would need to re-observe all your
own sexual feelings, alert to the possibility that none may be
distinguishably "male" even though all are distinctly human
and sexual. Even if you believe yourself "a real man"—an avid
devotee of Deep Bob, rock-solid in your resolve to be the man
there—your sexual feelings might not be containable in a canis-
ter marked MEN'S. All your sexual sensations may in fact be relative and relational. And realizing that fact might allow you to
try feeling sexual in selfhood mode for a change. But before you
do that, there's more to consider . . .

## Yet Another Reason You May Feel That You Have to Stay in Manhood Mode During Sex (Or, The Erotics of Economics)

In Chapter Thirteen we found a diagram useful to show that
manhood is vertical and manhood is the constant content of Lesson B—"Not to be a man is to be less than nobody."

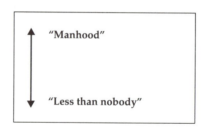

Nearly all humans raised to be a man learn gender in those
terms, through rewards and punishments, through trial and error. Only upon that vertical scale does manhood have any recognizable social meaning—and more important, only upon that
vertical scale does manhood make any *sense*: it's the only way
social gender can have emotional and physical meaning to individual bodies and brains. Of course there is a wide *range* of
emotional and physical experiences of manhood that individual
bodies and brains may have, but everyone penised is having
their sensory experience of manhood somewhere on the same

vertical scale—depending upon whether they are feeling closer to "manhood" or closer to "less than nobody" at the moment.

At the top of that vertical scale is the abstraction "manhood," perhaps the most widespread delusion in human history. Deep Bob is aloft and in charge up there, setting the manhood standard, setting the pace for everyone who has been duped to live in manhood mode. The fact that "manhood" is a fiction does not seem to deter many people from assiduously trying to approximate it—to feel closer to it emotionally and physically, however they can. If anything, the fact that "manhood" is a sham seems so buffaloing to so many that all they want to do is stampede all the harder.

Indigenous North American Plains peoples, in order to obtain necessary food and fur, would round up buffalo and drive them toward a cliff—with the wind blowing from behind so the animals could not smell the carnage up ahead. The alarmed herd would be steered toward a land formation where the grassy plains became a sudden ledge, and there at the brink the stampeding buffalo had but to plummet to death upon the boulders down below. Curiously, tourists today are told that such sites are called "buffalo jumps"—as if the dumb animals were not routed there to *drop*. Perhaps, too, a tourist observing teeming life on a much more metaphorical cliff might surmise that when someone ascending to manhood takes a nasty tumble, he had free will and it was all his own fault—whereas in fact the fellow fell victim to his own inculcated compulsivity, plus that of all climbers ranged above.

There are many personal reasons you might feel compelled to bring along manhood into the bedroom—to prop it up like a totem in the shadows, perhaps: There's the judgment of other men to consider, and what *they* might think about, or say about, your sexual identity. There's whatever humiliation you may have recently experienced in the rest of your life, and your perhaps urgent need to compensate as soon as possible. There's your own history with your father, and whatever ways *he* acted out his personal identity problem in relation to you, and in relation to your mother as well. There's your own emotional and physical memory bank of gender anxiety waves, left over from long ago, sometimes spiking unpredictably, giving you the fright of your life. There's also fear of the unfamiliar: What would

your sexuality feel like if you weren't using sex in order to experience your ranking on the vertical scale of manhood? What if
you stopped *caring* about the vertical scale of manhood—and
what if you and your partner simply cared about *each other* instead? What would human sexuality feel like if we were
experiencing—physically and emotionally—one another's complete human-beingness, our completely common humanity?
There's also, perhaps, your partner's expectation and anticipa-
tion that you will act like the man there—and your desire not to
disappoint someone you love.

For the social fiction of manhood to feel real and make sense,
it has had to resonate in your brain and body for most of your
life in at least some of the ways we have discussed. You've experienced your own personal assortment of ways, and you've
experienced each element in your customized assortment with
its own intensity. But there's yet another way the social fiction of
manhood resonates, and for once language helps us name it.

- Have you ever had the sexual feeling that you needed to
  *have* someone? Or have you ever had the sexual feeling
  that there was someone you wanted to *have* you?

- Have you ever had the sexual feeling that you wanted to
  *take* someone? Or have you ever had the sexual feeling
  that there was someone you wanted to *take* you?

- Have you ever had the sexual feeling that you wanted to
  *possess* someone? Or have you ever had the sexual feeling
  that there was someone you wanted to *possess* you?

Recall for a moment the specific sexual feelings that seem to
be nameable in any or all of those ways. Recall some emotional
and physical experiences you may have had that might be triggered by those phrases. Recall as much of what was going on in
your brain and your body as you possibly can. And don't be
shy—nearly everyone has had such feelings to some extent;
that's one of the reasons the language happens to be so helpful.
Don't assume that your sexual anatomy has "made" you have
the set of sexual feelings of wanting *to possess* or the set of sexual
feelings of wanting *to be possessed*. Don't assume that one set of

sexual feelings can be experienced only with one set of sexual anatomy or another. And don't be surprised if you—like many other penised humans throughout history—may have had some of these emotional and physical associations about or during the act of intercourse. In English—as in other languages—the verb "to possess" literally means both "to fuck" and "to own." That semantic coincidence is not an accident. This next diagram will help us understand why.

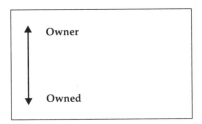

   Not only must the social fiction of manhood resonate within our human bodies and brains *emotionally and physically*; it must also resonate in between human bodies *economically*. The economic relation of owner and owned is on the vertical scale of manhood, just as "self-ish-ness" and "self-less-ness" are. And when the objective economic relation of "owner" and "owned" is viewed on the vertical scale of manhood, one can see exactly why they take on subjectivity as well. On the vertical scale of manhood, "owner" and "owned" begin to make emotional and physical sense in human bodies and brains. They begin to be felt with the same urgency as social gender itself. For one human being to "own" another is otherwise an utterly meaningless and incomprehensible proposition. Owning a live human being makes no *sense*, it doesn't have any emotional or physical resonance, unless economics has erotics—unless "owning" becomes the same sexual turn-on as "being the man there."
   Now, to "be the man there" is of course meaningless as well, unless one is acting in manhood mode, attuned to one's gender anxiety waves, and choosing an effective relational act that will establish one's manhood "I" on the vertical scale of manhood above someone designated closer to nobody. Conveniently, the economic relation of owner to owned helps one avoid having to

make so many such nuisance decisions. The economic relation of sexual "owner" to someone else's sexually "owned" body is a great expedient. You don't have to decide every little detail of every relational act. With your proprietary ownership of another human being's body established in how you have sex, you can devote more of your attention elsewhere—to competition and combat with other cliffhangers, for example.

But owning has to make you feel closer to manhood; owning has to make you feel you're a man, not less than nobody; owning has to convince you erotically—emotionally and physically—that you have an authentic manhood "I." Otherwise owning isn't erotic. Otherwise economics aren't sexy.

The erotics of economics have emerged in human history on the vertical scale of manhood—in the private-property sense of the verb "to own." And they arise there in the biography of nearly every penised human—in one's personal erotic adaptation to the shaming lesson of manhood. In no other way could the economic relation between owner and owned come to feel so sexy to so many human beings. In no other way could some few human beings find their way upward on the cliffside with such apparent passion, flushed with such a prideful sense of power.

This explains yet another reason you may feel pressured to stay in manhood mode during sex: To personally perpetuate the erotics of economics, to do your part, you may feel you *have* to have someone. You may feel you *have* to take someone. You may feel you *have* to possess someone. You may have to go so far as to feel that the other person's body is really *yours*—to do with what you want. Like an ownable object. Like an ownable thing. Like your private personal property. You may feel that if you *want* to have it, then obviously you should just be able to *take* it. You may feel packed solid with the emotional and physical feelings of *owning*. You may feel utterly terrified to experience any other kinds of emotional and physical sensations, for fear that if you do, you will feel *owned*. You may also feel that if you don't *want* to have or take or possess someone, then there might be something wrong with you, or your partner will think there is something wrong with you, or your partner will feel inadequate.

For countless humans raised to be a man, that's what *having* sex means: *Having* it. *Having* someone. Having someone—

owning someone—as an *it*. Having *more* of it—having more *its*—to feel more real, to feel more real a man. Having sex to have a gender.

## The True Story of My Own Search for Manhood *(resumed)*

My own sexual history encompasses both the feeling of wanting to possess and the feeling of wanting to be possessed. I can re-call both sets of feelings vividly. This may come as no surprise to many readers, though there were times in my life when it came as quite a surprise to me.

I mention this fact of my personal sexual feelings in order to make clear a point of view: I do not assume that *any* given con-figuration of sexual anatomy determines or predicts how one can or will negotiate one's way through life erotically when one is intent on feeling as close to manhood as one possibly can.

I can observe anomalies all around me. I have known some. And for that matter, I am one.

The only thing that can be predicted with certainty is that if you're trying to feel close to manhood, then your emotions and physical feelings (including your personal eroticism) must adapt somehow on the vertical dimension between owner and owned, between one who wants to possess and one who wants to be possessed. If you don't, you don't stand a chance of feeling manhood the way anyone might reasonably want to.

You can, of course, find yourself feeling close to manhood in a way you absolutely *don't* want to. Those who have been raped or sexually abused or incested, for instance, know this for a fact. You know the manhood so close to you was *not* what you wanted. For a while, or for some time afterward, that particular relational act may have made you feel utterly like a nobody. Un-fortunately, that is how you can be certain it helped someone else feel closer to manhood. And *nothing* in you needed to be so useful to *anyone's* climb up the cliff.

Notwithstanding all such completely nonconsensual rela-tional acts in manhood mode, many penised humans attempt sexual relations in manhood mode as if meaningful consent can occur. By definition the transaction must include *someone's* being treated as closer to nobody, otherwise *no one* gets closer to manhood—a real bummer if anyone had their heart set on it. So such transactions really do strain the concept of knowledgeable and informed "consent." Yet the only way one can feel sexually close to manhood is either as *owner* or as *ownable,* so this means *someone* must do the sexual owning and *someone* must be sexually owned. The deal doesn't come off otherwise. But surprise, surprise, an ownable's eager participation in this climbing formation can feel extremely sexual.

Human sexuality is malleable. All our built-in sexual-response reflexes can be taught to trigger in all sorts of ways, and it would be hard to chart all the possible stimuli that human anatomy can respond to. So just as one can learn to feel quite sexual in the act of owning another human's body, one can learn to feel quite sexual when another human's body is owning yours. You may feel "sexy." You may feel "desired." You may feel "wanted." You may feel "good-looking." You may feel closer to manhood than to nobody because someone higher up the cliff likes how you "look," likes "looking" at you, wants you to "belong" to them. Someone wants to "have" you (yes you, just you!). Someone wants to "take" you (yes take you, overwhelm you!). Someone wants to "possess" you (yes possess, yes possess, yes please yes possess!). Someone wants to *own* you, if only momentarily—own your body, use it, do things *to* it, act *upon* it, perform sexual acts *to* it, as if it were theirs, not yours, as if it were an actual *ownable,* even as if it were an object. The entire experience (however long it lasts) can be quite a turn-on, as many humans—including myself—well know. There's so much erotic buy-off in it that many humans spend much of their lifetime trying to perfect their sexual ownability. Concurrently, many humans spend much of their lifetime trying to increase their market share as sexual owners.

But the experience necessarily occurs somewhere on the vertical scale of manhood, not on the horizontal dimension of selfhood. The experience necessarily occurs, if it is to occur at all, through feeling in one's body and brain the erotics of economics. *Feeling* sexual ownership. *Feeling* sexually ownable. *Feeling* sexually owned. Because not to feel close to manhood is not to *feel* social gender. Without sexual ownership, there can be no sexual experience of manhood. Not to feel like an owner or an ownable is not to feel anywhere *near* manhood. And the more you can feel sexual possession, the more you can feel social gender, the more you can feel close to manhood, the less like a nobody you'll feel.

It's a sliding scale. A slippery, precipitous slope. But it holds out the promise that you too can approach Deep Bob. Or at least you can come close.

## Sex and Selfhood (Or, The Revolution from Between)

Because you can switch back and forth between selfhood mode and manhood mode in an instant, from decision to decision, from relational act to relational act, even from moment to moment in the same sexual encounter, you might not always recognize which mode you are in. Sometimes you may feel sexual vis-à-vis another self-possessed whole human being—and sometimes you may feel sexual as possessor or possessee. Sometimes you may feel sexually like somebody human. And sometimes you may feel sexually like "the man there"—or like "there's a man there" just above you—and you're in flight from nobodyness.

The human capacity to feel sexual is neither intrinsically horizontal nor vertical. Sexual feelings in and of themselves don't express either equality or inequality, and sexual feelings are not intrinsically in either selfhood mode or manhood mode. But because so many of us grow up believing that sexual feelings equal an experience of "real manhood," we don't pay as much attention as we could to the practical possibilities of sexual feelings as an experience of selfhood. Unfortunately, people sometimes deliberately turn off or turn down such possibilities, thinking that sexual feelings belong with gender anxiety waves. Sexual feelings don't "belong" to either moral sonority or gender anxiety necessarily. Sexual feelings don't have a one-track will of their own. *People* do sometimes, but not sexual feelings. From tender to ardent, the full range of human sexual feelings can accompany a relational act that affirms human selfhood—justly, lovingly, mutually, reciprocally.

Sexual feelings can also accompany a relational act that affirms the possession of one human's body by another. But with the sexuality of possession there is a critical, practical limit as to when such relational acts *stop* feeling sexual for the owned one, becoming pure pain, pure dread, pure nobodyness. From the point of view of the sexually owned one, negotiation of that limit is a very high priority—and very tricky, since your limit can be crossed in an instant and all you have to go on is your trust in the one whom you might want to be sexually owned by. If your trust was misplaced, or if negotiations break off, you may be badly hurt. You may also feel real dumb, unlucky in love, and responsible—at least until you realize what a game of chance you were playing with the eroticism of possession and how slim the odds were. Some people find that sex in manhood mode is way too risky for their taste. It's a gamble by definition, and not a win-win situation by any stretch. From the point of view of the sexually owning one, however, negotiation of the ownable's limit is not the same priority. For the owner, the only incentive to negotiate an ownable's limit is to maintain sexual access. If negotiations break off, you can always decide to sexually own someone else—and, with any luck, begin a new round of negotiations.

Feeling sexual in manhood mode can sometimes feel like a vanishing act. Especially during the act of intercourse, sexual feelings in manhood mode sometimes cannot be aroused or cannot climax unless you have mentally gone away someplace else, even though your body is physically existent beside another human being's body. Feeling sexual in manhood mode sometimes feels as if your actual partner has had to disappear from you, or you have had to disappear from your partner, in order to experience your sexual sensations as distinguishably "male." It feels as if you're not so much intimate as adjacent.

The experience of feeling sexual as an owner in manhood mode is an acquired taste, and not everyone who tries it has mastered the knack. To do it right, you really *have* to be elsewhere in your brain, since emotional and physical receptivity and responsiveness to another human's experience are contraindicated. Feeling *with* someone—moral sonority—is a no-no in manhood mode. Those meddling feelings on Channel A mitigate aphrodisiac reception of gender anxiety on Channel B. And it's necessary to tune out moral sonority now and then, so you don't get mixed messages about "right and wrong," especially during intercourse, and frequently in order to come. Afterward this erotic disappearing act can leave you feeling somewhat estranged from your partner as well as from yourself—but that's the breaks in manhood mode.

As a practical matter, you may feel that the coordination and physiological functioning of your sexual anatomy requires so much concentration that you have little left over for your partner's feelings. This may indeed be the case, since to feel sexual in manhood mode at all, your physiological functioning must hit all three bases at once (erection, orgasm, ejaculation), and you will feel obliged to give your complete concentration to the challenge.

Occasionally, however, your concentration may become so intensely focused on the operational or mechanistic potential of the penis that—simply as a matter of practical expediency—you will close down your receptivity to the transformer and transducer potential of the penis. To put this phenomenon more bluntly: in order to keep your sexual motor driving, you will focus feeling on the penis as a single-chamber piston, to the exclusion of feeling the penis as a distributor issuing energizing and tantalizing signals to various points in the engine block.

Physiologically the penis has but one built-in either/or: the urethra can be available for the passage of urine or else it can be available for the passage of seminal fluid—not both at the same time. There's a reliable valve for that purpose, and you don't have to think about it (except when you wake up "piss proud" due to bladder pressure on the prostate and you can't pee until you detumesce). But apart from urination, the erectile and sensate potential of the penis is quite various and variable. Physiologically, nothing *prevents* you from experiencing the transformer and transducer potential of the penis during engulfment in intercourse, or during any other sexual activity for that matter. Physiologically, nothing *requires* you to shut off or edit your sensual experience in that way. It is a choice that *you* make; your body does not make it for you. It is a choice that you make even though you may not even be aware it's a choice you *can* make. You make the choice in what feelings from your body you wish to give more attention to, or which feelings you wish to give no attention to at all. You make the choice in how much attention you give to feeling *with* someone. The transformer and transducer potential of the penis—while by no means the only way to experience the tactile presence of another whole human being—happens to be extremely sensitive to the motion of emotions between two partners. The transducer and transformer potential of human genitals sometimes feels like circuitry central meets circuitry central, like all systems are in touch and aglow, like all systems are pulsating, and all sensory systems are amplifying and reverberating back and forth. Physiologically, then, that's a major reason you will need to tune out moral sonority in order to have sex in manhood mode, especially if you have elected to perform the act of intercourse.

If all you decide to feel, basically, is whether you are erect and ejaculating, and if you decide not to feel *with,* or not to feel what your partner may be feeling, or not to feel what you and your partner may be feeling together, you may now and then experience difficulty getting to what you might call first base, erection, or even to second, ejaculation. You may require some other sorts of masturbatory aids, some of which, conveniently, you may have on file in your memory. This may account for why you sometimes have to disappear during a sex act with someone—why you sometimes seem to go away somewhere else in order to get off on your own. Perhaps you may simply have to consult your private image bank to see what could help you get up or stay hard or come. Having chosen to eliminate an enormous and significant range of sensory information both from your own body and from your partner's—but not having turned down your gender anxiety waves—you may feel you have no choice. And your partner, perhaps not aware of all the complicated computations and amputations going on inside you, may have no choice but to await your return (Hello? Hello in there? Is anybody home?).

Not surprisingly, some people find it difficult to own their own sexuality if they are *being owned* by someone else. And some people find it difficult to own their own sexuality if they are *trying to own* someone else. Deciding to commit one's body and brain to *possession* as an erotic transaction is to decide to stay stuck in manhood mode, by definition, and not everyone feels entirely comfortable there; not everyone sincerely desires to stay there.

Throughout human history, there have been individuals who

have recoiled from sexual possession—whether as possessor or possessed. This decision—a kind of "conscientious objector" stance—may be experienceable or interpretable as a preference for the sexuality of selfhood.

Over the past dozen years I have been told by quite a number of humans born with "male" sexual anatomy that they have opted, for the time being or over the long term, not to attempt to perform the act of intercourse. By way of explanation, they have sometimes confided in me that in order to complete the act of intercourse they have felt they had to regard or treat their partner's body in ways that they no longer felt comfortable doing. I infer that because they conscientiously reject the economic relationship of possession between the two of them, the erotics of that economics have also had to be put on hold. I doubt that I would have heard from any such individuals had I myself not spoken out publicly and recommended "choosing . . . not to fixate on fucking."* Originally I imagined I'd meet outrage for expressing such heresy. Instead, as it turned out, I heard from penised people who hadn't had the nerve before to talk about such personal feelings.

Some humans born with "male" sexual anatomy have realized that their preferred experience of coitus is as an embrace, not a stab. For them, the subjective feeling that one is violating another person's body is simply emotionally impossible. These are humans who, when the act becomes one of penetration-past-resistance (rather than explicitly invited entry and engulfment) simply cannot feel emotionally and sensually present in the physical act. So unless they feel a full participant in the sexuality of selfhood, they demur or abstain from any relational act that they sense is being driven by desire for sexual possession.

When such humans make such choices as relational acts of conscience, they may not have a language with which to communicate to their partner what is going on inside them. Some such episodes have resulted in hurt feelings, especially if the partner is inexperienced or confused about the difference between the sexuality of possession and the sexuality of selfhood. Communications can become quite botched, actually, and what was intended as a

*In a speech I gave on dozens of campuses called "How Men Have (a) Sex," published in *Refusing to Be a Man.*

relational act to acknowledge the partner's selfhood becomes interpretable, inadvertently, as sexual rejection.

As I've listened to such stories, I cannot help recalling the range of my own experiences in the act of intercourse, in particular the pleasure I have experienced when my erotic desire to feel ownable has been met by a partner's considerate and consensual and not-too-clumsy desire to own somebody. Having been in the so-called driver's seat myself, I was perhaps more able to interpret some of the mysteries one frequently comes upon on the passenger's side: when, for instance, the driver might resent directions, or when, for instance, the driver seems so preoccupied with testing the speed limit that communications with the passenger are all but out of the question. I understand intimately, in other words, something of the solipsism and self-absorption that are emotionally and physically necessary, simply as a practical and physiological matter, in order to drive the point of one's manhood home. And as much as I have enjoyed being taken for such rides, I have begun to reflect uncertainly about my own responsibility for, in effect, expecting someone else to do driving under conditions of detachment and self-involvement that in conscience *I'd* find hard to do. I *know* I found such driving hard to do emotionally and physically, which was why I got off the road.

But I digress. I had meant to talk about sexuality in *selfhood* mode.

Feeling sexual in selfhood mode is not at all the same as feeling sexually "possessed" or "owned." Sometimes people feel afraid that it will be, and so they avoid even the premonition of such feelings. The misconception is easily explained: If all you are familiar with is sexual feelings as "owner" in manhood mode, you might assume that the only alternative is to feel sexual feelings being "owned"—and this may feel emotionally and physically impossible for you. And if all you are familiar with is as "ownable" in manhood mode, you might assume that the only alternative is to feel sexual feelings as "owner"—and this may feel emotionally and physically impossible for you.

Often a sexual embrace will begin in selfhood mode, but then one or the other partner panics, because suddenly it feels as if you stepped away from the cliffside of manhood and so you are nowhere, even though you are both exactly there, human to

human—loving each other more than manhood. As if in an an-
imated cartoon when characters step off a cliff into midair and
it takes them a while to discover there's no familiar footing underneath, you have time for a momentary experience together,
the two of you, your sexual selfhoods meeting, perhaps ardently,
ecstatically, human to human, somebody to somebody. Then one
or both of you get flustered at the unfamiliarity, so you reach
back to the cliffside and try to hold on for dear life. You may not
have known you would not have fallen into any abyss. You may
not have known you would have both been fine: safe, sustained,
witnessed, sexually intimate, somebody to somebody. Sexuality
in selfhood mode isn't about climbing or falling or owning or
being owned or putting down or being put down. But if all
you've ever experienced is sexuality via possession on the cliff,
how would either of you know what to expect when—perhaps
intentionally or perhaps by happy accident—you discovered another way to be altogether?

Sometimes people will come together as if sexually attracted to
each other in manhood mode, as if one will probably be owner
and the other will probably be owned, because they might have
liked each other anyway but that was the only way they knew to
express their liking sexually. Then, as they get to know each other
more personally, more deeply, it becomes quite impossible, emotionally and physically, to continue seeking sexual feelings together as possessor and possessed—and so they evolve or invent
for themselves a sexual expression that is premised on mutual
self-possession, they discover or reclaim for themselves a sexually
intimate self-revelation, until it suits them, until it becomes them,
and they feel whole unto themselves and even more whole together. And so begins another Revolution from Between.

Just by looking at people, you cannot tell who has begun
such a powerful revolution. You cannot tell from any of your assumptions about their sexual anatomy, their pigmentation, their
money, their clothes, their age, their anything, that they may
have discovered or invented the sexuality of selfhood for their
very own selves. Just by looking, you cannot necessarily tell
who really prefers the power *between* us and who still really prefers power *from the top down*. The Revolution from Between is
not yet that far advanced. But soon. Very soon, I believe. And
you may find yourself amazed to be in it.

## A Personal Checklist of Some Ways to Tell Whether Your Sexual Feelings Are Occurring in Selfhood Mode or in Manhood Mode

As you look over the following clues, reading one from Column A, then one from Column B, you may find yourself experiencing a click of recognition at how clear-cut the difference can be. In your own life, the difference between feeling sexual in selfhood mode and feeling sexual in manhood mode might not always seem so clear-cut. But if you can spot the contrast when you read this "I" chart, you'll know you've got the acuity to detect the difference in your life.

You may also find yourself filling in some autobiographical details. For instance, you may recognize some relationship clues from Column A that at first frightened you when you experienced them—because they did not compute on terms that would make you feel like a real-enough man—and so they scared you to cross over into the sexuality of possession. Scared you into turning down your moral sonority. Scared you back to competition for your manhood. Scared you into splitting sex apart from selfhood.

Just because you're feeling sexually aroused does not necessarily tell you which mode you're in. That's why these clues are not about your body's sexual feelings as such—they are about the relational context in which you feel sexual.

Feeling sexual in manhood mode is driven by a real desire, of course. The desire is to experience social gender sexually, emotionally and physically, so that it will seem to feel real, so that *you* will seem to feel real. Feeling sexual in manhood mode is driven by the need to experience social gender on the vertical scale of "manhood" versus "nobody." The desire to believe and actualize this social fiction is called *loving manhood.*

Feeling sexual in selfhood mode is also driven by desire. It is as powerful and as passionate a human longing as our human bodies were born capable of feeling. Feeling sexual in selfhood mode is driven by the need to experience our humanity emotionally and physically on the horizontal dimension of selfhood—to feel safe, to feel sustained, to feel seen and not alone, and to bestow the same human entitlement upon each one we love. The desire to honor this human reality is called *loving justice.*

When you detect yourself feeling sexual in manhood mode, you may remember—*click*—that you have another option: You can tune in your moral sonority. You can tone down your gender anxiety. You can tilt your teeter-totter. You can reclaim your sexual selfhood.

The core of your being can love justice more than manhood.

| RELATIONSHIP CLUES FROM COLUMN A (You may be feeling sexual as your selfhood "I") | RELATIONSHIP CLUES FROM COLUMN B (You may be feeling sexual as your manhood "I") |
|---|---|
| There has been honesty. You have told your partner the complete and significant truth. | There has been deceit. You have kept a significant secret or told a significant lie. (When you think you can get away with lying, you tend to think of your partner as someone who isn't worth as much as you. If you have not come clean with that person, having sex with them tends to be a continuation of your false pretense.) |
| There has been beholding between you. You have been a witness to each other's subjectivity. You have recognized yourselves as two subjects, two whole human beings. | There has been objectification. Although one of you may have seemed to regard yourself as a subject, one of you was definitely regarded as an object. (Whenever someone in a sexual relationship is regarded as an object, whether willingly or not, they tend to become situated as ownable. This can present a problem if they later presume to assert themself equally as a full human subject. For the sexual owner, such assertion presents relational difficulties—it turns him off. Sexual objectification only works so long as it turns on the owner, which may be contingent on various market factors—youth, beauty, etc.—but it becomes inoperative immediately whenever the ownable is incompliant about being regarded as closer to nobody.) |

| | |
|---|---|
| There has been mutual respect and regard in negotiating and making all decisions that affect both you and your partner in the relationship, including sex. | There has been manipulation, coercion, duplicity, force, constraint, or any other style of one-sided, peremptory decision-making in the relationship. (The manhood "I" benefits greatly from all such transactions outside the bedroom, so normally in bed the resulting sexual identity confidence carries over.) |
| There has been affirmative and active consent, in every moment. | There has been a lack of consent. (When you decide to act peremptorily, you assume that your will is more important than the other person's, so they are closer to nobody than you. Sexually and situationally, that automatically tends to pump up your manhood "I.") |
| There has been a context of companionship, interest in each other's interests, interest in shared interests, emotional warmth and support available to each other. That context contains all sexual relating, and that context lasts after. | There has been emotional withdrawal, avoidance, anticompanionship. (This clue is especially telling when observed in the aftermath of a sexual encounter, when, for instance, there may be a recoil from the other person's flesh, emotional or physical denial that what was sensual between you both even happened, an assertion of autonomous physicality at the expense of the partner's feelings. If during sex you turned down your moral sonority to climax, to get off like the man there, your moral sonority will tend to stay tuned out for a while afterward as well.) |
| There has been enjoyment, joy, exhilaration, contact energy, shared fun—before, during, and after. | There has been harassing, teasing, jokes made at the partner's expense, laughter at the partner's discomfort, humiliation, some tiny sadism of mastery and alienation (some commonplace or ritualized reminder of who's the nobody there). |

| You and your partner have been profoundly present to each other, human self to human self, before, during, and after. | There has been fantasizing of the body of someone who is not there during the sexual encounter—a remembered stranger, a remembered picture. There has been fantasizing being with that other body, doing something to that other body instead, having that other body do something to yours. There has been fantasizing you're not with the person you're with. There has been fantasizing so as to evade the reality of the person you're with. There has been fantasizing so you can go off in your brain by yourself and get off on your own somehow. There has been fantasizing because equal reality with your partner is a turn-off. |
| --- | --- |
| *When you recognize clues in your relational life from Column A, you may expect to experience the eroticism of loving justice.* | *When you recognize clues in your relational life from Column B, you may expect to experience the eroticism of loving manhood.* |

THE END OF LOVING MANHOOD
IS THE BEGINNING OF SEXUAL SELFHOOD.

# ✧ 20 ✧

## LOOKING REALLY TURNS ME ON— SO WHAT'S THE MATTER WITH THAT?

Men are made, not born.

At any given decade in a man's life—whether in his teens, twenties, thirties, forties, fifties, or on up—he can look back and take stock of how effectively he has been trained so far to love manhood. This training has been etched as if first in sand, where errant tides may yet erase it, then later in mud, where it may be baked in the heat of sonship, then much later as if in the fossilized remains of what was once his human potential, now hardened to stone. How old he is, how long this training has gone on, how traumatic it was, how well the training got attached to his body and brain—all these factors together and separately determine the extent to which his learned love of manhood has eclipsed his desire to love justice.

Nobody was born with their sexuality already locked into the eroticism of possession, and nobody—no *body*—was born with any practical skill in the matter either. You can't just leave a penised human infant to grow up and figure out such stuff for themself. You can't just wait around patiently until the kid's first nocturnal emission, for instance, and then exclaim, upon examining the telltale bedsheets, "Congratulations! Now you're a man! Now you can own! Now your genital apparatus can fuck!" The kid won't have a clue what you're talking about. Owning someone else's body sexually would not even come to mind. If the kid thinks about doing anything, it might be hugging or rubbing and rolling around—and maybe laundering the sheets.

Learning to love manhood is arduous. Learning to feel love for manhood in your genitals is especially stressful. Your sexual anatomy had to be carefully taught, step by step, in order for you to come anywhere near feeling sexually aroused at the thought, or during an act, of sexual possession. You came into the world completely helpless, feeling hunger and discomforts of many sorts, but not gender anxiety waves. You had a long way to go before you became the star trainee who had learned the erotics of ownership so well that now you can do it in your sleep.

This book has charted some of the personal and social pressures on you to get good at the erotics of owning, starting early on in your life. You may or may not have gotten very good at it, and today your heart may or may not be in it. But if you were raised to be a man, you were strongly urged to hand over your sexual anatomy to possession, and you were strongly discouraged from discovering an eroticism that was consonant with human selfhood.

Of all the pressures pushing you to become skilled at sexual possession, the judgment of other men is the big one. Whether they will think you're a real-enough man—and what they will think of you or do to you if you're not—can induce gender anxiety waves that spur you on like crazy. If you have already got good at sex in manhood mode—or at least good enough to pass—you have largely the judgment of all those other men to thank.

You may even hear some of their voices now. You may still remember the ways they shamed you or cajoled you, the things they did and said to you to teach you the rules that separate boys from men. Recall how you felt when you were young, just starting out, just getting the hang of the manhood game. Remember the guy with the right stuff, the right ideas and info?—the guy who hustled you out onto the playing field with a bunch of other sweating, raw recruits (a new generation of frightened children, actually). He was always the guy's guy, and he proudly wore the colors for all the manhood teams of all time. In his imposing presence you may have felt a strange mixture of awe, nervousness, admiration, and alarm.

If boys were trained into the eroticism of loving manhood the way they get trained into contact sports, here's what the coach character would say ...

## Six Tips to Remember If You Are in Training to Have Sex Like a Man

OK, you guys, listen up! You think you wanna be a man? Lemme tell ya: that's not gonna cut it. You can't simply decide to get good at something and then automatically be good at it. You have to train—you have to start out with the right attitude and aptitude, but then you have to work out right, you have to learn from the right pros, you have to try out for the right team, and you have to practice, practice, practice.

### *Training Tip #1: Attitude and Aptitude*

Now, I'm gonna assume you got your early-childhood training over with, and I don't have to walk you through it again. You got some rewards and you got some punishments, and so you figured out the basic difference between a man and a nobody. I'll give you a chalk talk on this if I catch any of you wienies forgetting which end is up. Your job is to be the man there. Your job is to make sure there's someone underneath you who's closer to nobody. Got that?

Good.

Now, if you already got taught that lesson as a kid through severe punishment, you may have already learned from that experience how to detach certain feelings inside yourself, because to feel them was too painful. This trick can be adapted later in your life when you try out for the manhood team. So don't feel sorry for yourself because you once got beat up and bullied a lot, or some grownup humiliated you a lot. Just remember the trick of emotional detachment you learned when you were little. Then as you grow up, all you have to do is remember to detach emotionally whenever you need to feel turned on in manhood mode. It's a snap. Just select to feel the fight-or-flight feelings that helped save your ass, and lop off any lingering moral sonority, which gets in the way of your manhood "I." In terms of your potential as a player on a top-ranked team, your childhood experience of gender discipline and humiliation gave you a real leg up.

Those of you guys who were deprived of such a punishing childhood may feel out of the running. You may lack a certain knack for manhood acting, a certain penchant, a fire in the belly that you sense in other men around you. While it is true that certain childhood distress translates into high motivation for manhood—and prompts high aptitude as well—*everybody* has a chance. So don't quit yet, little fella. If your childhood did not adequately prepare you for emotional detachment, there are many *other* ways to get those gender anxiety waves charging through your genitals just as well as anybody's. The next five training tips can help you overcome whatever head start you may lack.

Hang in there, guy!


### *Training Tip #2: Working Out*

I hate to break this to you guys, but genitals are not like biceps or pecs or abs—you can't pump them up on machines. And you know those ads for clear-plastic suction tubes that promise a bigger penis in a vacuum? I'm afraid they don't work.

To become comfortable in manhood mode, you need to work out your whole body. You need regular workouts to develop your fight-or-flight reflex system. The problem, see, is your basic physiology: when it comes from the factory, it doesn't come wired for manhood mode. You're gonna need it to do something it doesn't really feel like doing. You're gonna need it to want to *own* somebody else—and your body's gonna think, "Are you kidding? Get outta here!" To trick your whole body into feeling that sexual owning is natural, you're gonna have to get your genitalia wired to your autonomic nervous system. That's the best the human body has to offer. It doesn't come with a "hot to own" button. It comes with the next best thing, though: fight or flight.

Those of you whose punishing childhoods left raw nerve endings in your fight-or-flight reflexes are already well on your way—you guys have already been pumping some serious sexualized survival stress. But even for you lucky guys, regular workouts will be beneficial.

The trick is to work out your fight-or-flight reflexes *outside* of sex as much as possible before attempting the sexuality of possession with a live human being. Get that wiring buzzing, get that heart pumping, get that chest heaving, get those muscles toned and ready to pop. Expose yourself to hazard, peril, risk, dread. Expose yourself to scary situations. Maybe getting into fights will do it for you, if they're violent and dangerous enough. Maybe getting into trouble with authorities who could punish you. Maybe starting fires or setting off firecrackers or bombs. Maybe watching slash-'n'-gash flicks. Maybe doing something where you put your life in danger. Maybe doing something where you put someone else's life in danger. *Feel* that autonomic nervous system kicking in, getting more fit, more alert, more conditioned. *Feel* your fight-or-flight reflexes kick in in ways that *you can control.*

Now, the point of these exploits is to work out your fight-or-flight reflex system so you can call upon it to kick in when you need it—when you decide to perform the erotics of owning someone's body. Nevertheless, during some of those adventures with the fellas, you may feel oddly excited. If you keep your clothes on, no one will know, dummy!—but you may feel there's something wrong with you if your genitals get tingly in the middle of a fight-or-flight reflexes workout.

Most guys try very hard to discipline their genitals, to keep them from going boing in the groin around other guys—like in a locker room or a gang shower. It's a useful exercise on top of exercise—a sort of mental jujitsu, advanced practice in emotional detachment, but not every body gets good at it.

Well before you're a teenager, you will feel sensation in your genitals just about anytime your fight-or-flight reflexes kick in, willy-nilly, whenever you feel on the spot, just because more blood and more sensory alertness flood all through your young body. As you age, though, if your sexual anatomy is getting

properly conditioned to be triggered by gender anxiety waves—
and as you effectively shut off one sensory feeling after another
in order to focus feelings on penile operationality—you will
have to find your own private tricks for shutting down feelings
in your genitals altogether whenever you must.

So don't become overly concerned if fight-or-flight workouts
turn you on. Just be careful in the nude, dude, and you'll turn
out OK.

Now, I know some of you guys may be feeling at a disadvan-
tage right now, because all this talk of scary workouts makes
you feel left out. You never had much taste for that sort of thing.
Fighting, getting your body smashed up in a game, getting into
trouble, getting into danger—it all seemed too stupid, too
lemminglike. Or you just felt too chicken. So your fight-or-flight
reflex system didn't get the same workout that other guys' did.
And you sense, perhaps, that this deficiency will somehow
show in your prowess as a sexual owner.

Hey, listen up, nookie rookie, don't feel so sorry for yourself.
The next four training tips will help you play catch-up—and in
the end you'll love manhood just like all the real guys.

### Training Tip #3: Learning From the Pros

Choose your role models carefully. Look for heavy-hitting paradigms who've really made it as a man because they've made
perfectly clear exactly which nobodies they're not. Watch how
these guys make decisions outside of sex—how they determine
who's a nobody and how they treat those nobodies. Watch very
closely how that gives these guys a competitive edge during sex.
(If you haven't been observing this crossover skill in your life
before now, that just goes to show how much you still have to
learn, young would-be man!)

Notice what a pro does to prop himself up outside of sex and
you'll have a darn good idea what props him up to have it.
(What did you think, human sexual anatomy acts out manhood
*without* propping up? Gimme a break. That merely human body
of yours could never hack it without help.) So watch closely
how the pros carve out the relational context in which it makes

sense to have sex in manhood mode: notice how they buy bodies for sex, which body types they buy, or which body types they'd like to take and use. Watch who they decide to do it to, then watch how they make their moves—play by play, choice by choice. This pep talk is way too short to review all you can learn from a professional personal trainer, so watch yours closely— and try to feel what it's like to *be* him. Try to feel what it's like to *feel like* him, try to feel what it's like to feel like doing *what he likes doing*, try to feel like *you're* doing what you see him do, try to feel like he feels when he *does* it. (Try to feel like him—not like the nobody he's doing it to, dummy!) That's how you get your body and brain in tip-top condition to get good at the manhood act yourself.

I realize some of you guys are feeling left out again. Much to your dismay, you never got close enough to a real pro to feel the vibes of his gender anxiety waves charging with hell-bent fury through his life choices and his genitals. So you not only feel left out; you feel uninitiated into manhood altogether. Or maybe your particular pro just passed you some of his playbooks, pictures of the body types he uses, and he told you to go to your room and figure out the moves in this game for yourself. And other than that, he never showed you the ropes a man uses to tangle and strangle his sexual reflexes. So now you sit there all tied up in knots of your own.

But buck, up, young broncaroo. The next three training tips will get you mounted and riding hard in the saddle in no time.

### *Training Tip #4: Team Work*

Your experience of punishment in childhood may have left you with a terrific aptitude for loving manhood, but it may have left you at loose ends about how to feel like an owner, not someone who feels like getting owned. The anxiety that was infused into your flesh-and-blood body may not have helped you draw the line, so you may have entered puberty still needing orientation. And since to own is closer to manhood and to be owned is closer to nobody—well, who *really* wants to come in second place, am I right?

So you may be wondering how you'll rank when you finally score. You may have excelled in various exploits that gave your fight-or-flight reflexes a humdinger of a workout. Your workout may have helped you disengage your sexual reflexes from your moral sonority. But your rod might not yet have divined its way to a watering hole.

Similarly, you may have been apprenticed to one of the all-star pros—and you may have identified intensely with his proximity to manhood—but you may not yourself feel reliably aroused at the prospect of owning someone's body all by your lonesome. That's a tall order. Complicating matters, you may have felt aroused in the company of a pro, whose companionable and protective treatment of you—although enormously instructive—may have stimulated sexual stirrings if he ever let you feel safe, sustained, and seen hanging out with him. And if you did not find the tingly feeling repugnant (for fear that this might be what *being owned* feels like), you may inadvertently have found it briefly pleasant. So your proximity to a pro, salutary in so many other respects, may have left you feeling urgently that you had better get your genitals in shape to join the team of owners before it's too late.

It's not really so simple to kill off your receptivity to moral sonority. And since moral sonority can stimulate you to feel sexual too, you've got a big problem on your hands, young would-be man. It takes many years and lots of effort before you can feel safely inured to the sexual feelings that sometimes arise from moral sonority. And in order to shut off those feelings toward other owners, you gotta learn to shut them off *completely*—toward ownables as well. Sorry 'bout that, fellas.

But the good news is, there's safety in numbers. And that's why it's important to make the right team.

There are top-ranked teams and there are bottom-ranked teams. We won't even discuss the bottom-ranked teams. They know who they are.

You can identify the top-ranked teams, in terms of getting your genitals in shape for loving manhood, by the following three characteristics:

- **Top-ranked manhood teams have a common "enemy."** This common enemy could be another team or other teams. Or it could be some authority or force that is also the enemy of other teams. Having an enemy in common is crucial, because it keeps those gender anxiety waves stirring to "fight" rather than "flight." This has an obviously beneficial training effect if you want your genitals to get a big charge out of owning instead of being owned.

- **Top-ranked manhood teams have a common "patsy."** This common patsy could be another team, another set of individuals, or another single human being. You will recall that when two manhood acts clash head-on—and they throw down the gauntlet in a challenge to each other's ranking on the vertical scale of manhood—there are Three and Only Three Things that can happen: the first makes mincemeat of the second, the second makes mincemeat of the first, or they both agree to make a scapegoat of a third party, to forge a truce. A common patsy is crucial to all top-ranked teams. It helps team members stay safe from being destroyed by one another. Plus, in terms of genitalia training, having a patsy in common helps you feel you belong. And feeling throughout your body that you really belong to a top-ranked team helps you feel like wanting to have someone else's body belong to you. A patsy perhaps. The point is to train your genitals to feel a body bond with teammates so that you can more reliably act out sexually as an owner toward a patsy. Exactly how your penis learns to perform this neat trick becomes clearer with the next characteristic that top-ranked teams have in common.

- **Top-ranked manhood teams have a traumatizing tryout.** You have to pass through some excruciating pain or humiliation in order to qualify. You have to go through some sadistic basic training or hazing. Or your body has to be scarred. Or you have to experience some other threat of damage to your bodily integrity or your emotional well-being. Perhaps *you* will be required to play "patsy," so you'll get a taste of what the team can do to its scapegoats in real life. Perhaps you will be tortured or excoriated, or threatened with torture. Perhaps you will be maimed or maligned, or threatened with maiming. Perhaps you will be treated to a replay of some abuse that you will recognize because it happened in your childhood. When it comes time for tryouts for the truly top-ranked teams, the best teams always save the worst for a surprise. Team tryouts all have as their intended effect that you break all your physical and emotional bonds to whatever human family you foolishly felt you came from—and then forge a new body bond with the team that now owns you: the owning team. When you come through the trauma, you get to belong. And the experience of belonging may be secretly sexual. That's OK. It's meant to be sexual, and it's meant to be your secret. The sexual belonging you feel is how you feel the body bond that was the point of joining up with the owning team to begin with. Then, when your body is privately sticking it to a patsy of your own, you'll feel the weight of the entire team bearing down along with you. If, for instance, your team is a police squad beating up someone with body blows, you will feel as if you are all bludgeoning that poor sucker as one, in pure physical harmony! Go for it! Or if your team is gang-raping someone, you will be able to take turns one by one—and *still* feel connected to all your buddies, because your penis goes into the exact same hole where theirs have been! Imagine! Any fist or any nightstick or any weapon will do. Once you've survived the traumatizing tryout for a top-ranked team, you too can experience the armed force of a body bond against a bloody scapegoat, and it'll prop you up for the erotics of owning like nothing else in all the world.

## Training Tip #5: Practice in Private

If your childhood didn't work, if your workouts didn't work, if your personal trainer didn't work, if you never made a top-ranked team, what then? You say you didn't make the squad, or frat, or secret society, or elite special forces, or shock troops, or neighborhood gang? You say nobody asked you in? You say you quailed and you cringed at how much such comradeship could cost you? *Yo, my man!*—you must feel hopelessly behind!

So what are you gonna do about it, wimp out?

Come on, little would-be dude, don't give up now! There's *still* a chance to train your genitals to love manhood. You can shape up your genitals all on your own. But you're gonna have to do some homework. You're gonna have to teach certain parts of your sexual anatomy that they're cut off from certain other parts of you. You're gonna have to train your penis, in particular, to prefer its operational potential to its transformer or transducer potential. You're gonna get it accustomed to want only hard friction—never to pulsate for the sheer ecstatic joy of it. You're gonna go on a Serious Home Course of Sensate Focus. That's a fancy-ass way of saying you gotta learn a specific way to jerk off.

How you learned that your human body can get off on your own is probably an interesting story. You may have discovered this surprising potential all by yourself. Or you may have been told about it first and then figured it out. Or you may have been taught, by someone who talked you through it or by someone who touched you.

But to learn to love manhood, sooner or later you have to learn to jerk off in one particular way, to the exclusion of some other possible ways. The way you jerk off has to teach your penis to feel like a piston of some sort. Now, as it happens, that's a fine and fun way for the penis to feel. The problem is, in order for your sexual anatomy to feel like a full-fledged, bona fide member of the manhood team, you have to teach your penis to shut off loads of other potential feelings, and you have to teach the rest of your body to shut off loads of other potential feelings, and you have to practice this sensate focus just as often as you possibly can, so you learn it absolutely diligently, and so when the time comes for you to have sex with someone, you will have properly attuned your penis to your own personal gender anxiety waves and you will have properly anesthetized your neurological receptors for moral sonority from the body of anyone else.

It's a big job—but you can handle it, right?

Practice makes perfect.

Conveniently, you don't need anyone around when you're practicing this sensate focus with your penis in private. And the more you practice jerking off this way, the easier it becomes to feel a boundary around your sexual feelings when you're *inside* someone.

Body bond with other owners. Boundary against the ownable.

Are you digging this or what?

### *Training Tip #6: Practice in Public*

OK, guys, I'm assuming that even if you failed miserably at Training Tips #1 through #4, you still managed to get some kind of a handle on Training Tip #5. And I'm assuming that even if you excelled at Training Tips #1 through #4, you don't eliminate Tip #5 from your training just to show off what hot stuff you are. So listen up. I've got some news for all you jerkoffs out there. To stay in peak condition for the eroticism of possession as an owner, you're going to have to go on a lifelong training regimen. This is not something you learn once and for all; you have to stay in shape for it; you have to keep practicing, day in and day out, until you die, or else your *manhood* dies. Get that? To sexually own someone is not like falling off a log. It's more like trying to stay standing erect on a slippery log that has been cast adrift in turbulent seas. To sexually own another human being's body like it's yours to have, to take, to possess, you need serious training, and serious practice, and even pros sometimes lose their touch.

So you guys gotta go on a daily maintenance program called Eyeball Target Practice.

Here's the tried-and-true routine: you gotta practice eyeball target-shooting in public every chance you get, every chance you think you can get away with it, especially every chance you think other rookies might be looking, especially every chance you spot a body that looks "ownable" and "fuckable."

The way you look at that body, you gotta imagine it's an ownable object—maybe you can *have* it, maybe you can *take* it, maybe *it* can be yours.

Think to yourself, "I own, therefore I am. I fuck, therefore I'm a man."

Note that your aptitude for hitting on ownable targets does not depend on being sighted; it depends on your loving manhood. Any would-be man without vision can become adept at Eyeball Target Practice. *Hoo-ah!*

If your penis props up when you practice a target shot at an ownable, it means your genitals are catching on. Good shot. Nice going.

To achieve maximum training effect, here are some Pointers from the Pros:

- If you are eyeballing an ownable's body in the company of other would-be men but your penis does not prop up as you do so, do not—I repeat, do not—let any of those other men *know*. Especially, do not remark on your flaccidity around other men who may be exclaiming how perky their own just felt. Be very careful, so they don't suspect that yours is hanging loose. Make something up. Say, "Get a loada that!" or "Hubba hubba, what a pair!" Use your anxiety in the situation to your advantage. The more nervous you feel about other men's judgment on your genital arousal, the more genitally aroused you may feel. Gender anxiety waves kick in with amazing grace. But whatever happens, don't let limpness deter you from Eyeball Target Practice. Do it. Just do it. Day in and day out. The more you shoot the more you improve your odds, and the more often your basket could score.

- If your penis does prop up when you eyeball an ownable's body, remember at which body part, which place, which protuberance, which patch of hair. Memorize these particulars in precise, objective detail, the way you would plays from a playbook. Mentally replay your memorized target parts whenever the game of manhood flags and your penis could use a hand.

- When you eyeball an ownable's body, beware of moral sonority. Do not—I repeat, do not—attempt Eyeball Target Practice with the volume on your moral sonority monitor turned up. Do not permit yourself to be aware of any ownable's feelings, life history, feelings in relation to you, mood at the moment, or anything remotely individual or personal. You are in training to own here, young would-be man; you are not looking for a human life. You are not looking for anyone *else's* human life and you are not looking for your *own*. You are looking—you are eyeballing—for your *manhood*. Got that? Wimp out on that one, fella, and if any other owners catch on, you will be dead meat on the playing field.

- When you have scoped out an ownable that you feel like fucking, do not—I repeat, do not—get to know it very well. This is crucial to Eyeball Target Practice, and this is critical to optimum genital operations as a sexual owner. You may be obliged to feign some interest in the ownable's personality—it all depends how much resistance you enjoy. But your goal is to fuck an ownable, an object. Everything since childhood has been prepping you to become excellent at this: your castigating childhood, your hazardous workouts, your humiliating mentor, your terrorizing teammates—now's your big moment, big guy, and you don't want to blow it. So the best advice from the pros is, First make sure you can functionally and reliably fuck an ownable. Then later, if the worst happens, if you become best friends or something, or if you fall deeply in love, and if the eroticism of possession begins to feel inappropriate, or some other eroticism begins to feel more appropriate, some other human-to-human, body-to-body sexual commitment, for instance, you can still make tracks for the playing field before it's too late, and you will have technically scored a knockout as an owner even though you had to duck out of the relationship in order to save your manhood.

- There are ownables out there who seem to want to play catch—they seem to want to catch your eyeballs. And there are ownables who are not good sports about this at all. But remember, since you're the one shooting targets, you always get to decide which ones you want to try to hit on. Some days you'll feel like more of a long shot. Some days you'll feel like an easy lay-up. Some pros say that pressure in your pants always lets you know the difference: do you feel like having an ownable that's easy or do you feel like having an ownable that's more of a challenge, "hard to get"? A few owners feel that pressure from other men is actually what determines your decision—it's always your peers, they say, not really your peter. Doesn't matter much, when you get right down to it.

- As you scope out possible ownables, you may hit on some and you may miss some. That's the breaks in this game, bud. If you don't like your cumulative average, fake it. But whatever you do, do not try to explain away a low box score by attributing "power" to ownables. Do not buy the fallacy that some pathetic schlubs have fallen into: they feel so sorry for themselves, they posit that ownables have some kind of "power" over our penises! Whatta laugh. True, there are ownables who devote their lives to cultivating such "power." That's the only power they can muster, so they go all out. They go on a training regimen too—they starve themselves, they vomit their meals, they go under the knife, they spend goo-gobs of money to refashion how they look. You may sometimes feel flimflammed that this gives them some sway over your genitalia, because they seem to have some say in whether or not you score. By all means, let them *believe* they have that illusory power—it's the only thing that keeps them going, keeps them eager players in the game, even if they don't especially want to play catch with your pitch in particular. The field of ownables must always be as populated and perfected as possible, for the sake of all potential owners, for the sake of all true lovers of manhood. But don't *you* believe that ownables have any such power. Deep down don't *you* believe it. When you finally fuck like a real owner, you know as well as the one you're fucking that you're the one there with the power to own, and you always decide *whom* to own and *when* to own. Just take a look at an ownable who's all gussied up and desperately trying to tempt an owner to fuck it, but the owner ain't interested—he tuned out moral sonority ages ago and his gender anxiety happens to be in a trough. Not a spike in sight. That's peter powerlessness, baby. That's in the pits of no power.

### Rules and Regulations

There are certain long-standing rules and regulations in the manhood game. If you are in training to love manhood as an owner, you must familiarize yourself with these rules and regulations *before you begin to play*. I cannot emphasize this strongly enough. If you go out there and play sexual owner but you don't follow the rules and regulations to the letter, you could get nailed or jailed or both.

There's gotta be some clear-cut rules about what constitutes a regulation "fuckable ownable." Otherwise, what's to stop a teammate from making a pass at *you*? Forget it! Game over! Foul ball! So these rules and regulations exist for your own protection. These rules and regulations have been passed down from generation to generation because without them there would be mayhem and chaos. Every manhood-loving dickhead would be running around sticking it to some other dickhead or poaching some piece that already *belonged* to a dickhead, who'd then blow the filcher away. It would be such a fucking mess you would not believe.

Trust me, guys, play by the rules. Make Deep Bob proud of you. Remember whom you *can* own. Remember whom you *can* fuck. Remember whom you *must not* own. Remember whom you *must not* fuck. And remember whom you *must* own. Remember whom you *must* fuck. These regulations are for your own good, the good of manhood, and the good of your manhood "I."

So here's a convenient clip-'n'-save chart I've prepared. Fold it up and carry it in your wallet, along with a thick-skinned condom.

### Who's Hot, Who's Not
An Owner's Guide to Sex Objects
By Coach "Irony" John

| Body Type | OK to Own? | OK to Fuck? | Legal Aid |
|---|---|---|---|
| Your wife | Yes | Yes | "Marital rape" laws vary by locality. "Consent" is sometimes legally required, but this technicality is easily surmounted, especially if she'd be homeless without your money. |
| Your unwed live-in | Yes | Yes | Laws vary. In some localities, "consent" of a live-in ownable has become no more required in practice than that of a wife. |
| Your date | Yes | Yes | "Acquaintance rape" charges are extremely difficult to prove, but proceed with caution. |
| Your child | Yes | No | Laws against "incest" or "child sexual abuse" are on the books in nearly every jurisdiction, yet they have no demonstrable deterrent effect. If you want to try your luck, be sure to intimidate the kid not to tell. |

| Someone else's wife or daughter | No | Yes | In many localities, you chance being prosecuted for "rape"—theft of a father's or husband's chattel property—but nowadays, customary courtship can keep you out of court. |
|---|---|---|---|
| Someone not your child but under age of "consent" | No | No | Laws against "statutory rape" don't have much deterrent effect either, but proceed with caution. |
| Your slave | Yes | Yes | Though legalized slavery has been out of fashion for some time, it still crops up now and then, off the books as it were. Whatever turns you on. |
| Someone penised, over age of "consent" | No | No | Laws prohibiting "sodomy" vary by locality. Even where technically legal, many penised targets will violently resist. Proceed with *extreme* caution. |
| Someone working in prostitution, any age, any genitalia | Yes | Yes | OK to rent or lease as well. |

This land is your land. This land is my land. This land is our fatherland. And always remember, men: honor the ground rules of thy forefathers that thy days and nights may be *long* in it.

### Bonus Training Tip: Training the Tip

As you become more and more advanced in loving manhood, you can gauge your progress by how successfully you have selected and isolated sensations in your penis. If you find that when you feel sexual you have almost no feelings left that would hint at moral sonority with someone else's body, you know that this training program has been a success. All the reflexes of your sexual anatomy have been fine-tuned for possession as an owner. If you further find that when you feel sexual what you primarily feel is self-contained sensation located in, and originating in, your penis—and solely in its sensory potential as a piston at that—accept such biofeedback as a commendation ("Well done, young would-be man") and a meritorious badge of honor that will stand you in good stead throughout your life.

And here's a little more fun. Practice this exercise when you're jacking off, for a dipstick check now and then.

Once you've got the shaft of your penis fairly full of blood—using your hand, stroking the shaft however you like it, fast or slow, brusquely or gently, but not touching yourself anywhere else, not letting your body feel pleasure anywhere else (very important!)—feel what happens when you put pressure against the very tip, the glans. Feel the reflex that happens when with the palm of your hand you butt pressure against the tip of your erect penis, perpendicular to the angle of the shaft. Feel what happens? Your penis stiffens a bit. Your penis, if it is already engorged, and if feelings are already isolated there, gets a little stiffer when you apply force against its tip. Practice this now and then when you're jerking off. Train the tip to enjoy whatever degree of pressure it enjoys the most.

Then, when you're about to fuck, time your point of entry so that there is some resistance left—some lack of relaxation in the ownable, some lack of explicit invitation, or some absence of a volitional, voluptuous embrace. You and only you know just how much resistance your penis would enjoy now. You and only you know, because you've trained the tip. So as your penis pokes in past that resistance—like a petite puncture—your disembodied shaft will feel a pleasurable, stiffening shock, and it will become all the harder the more forcefully you popped in. This can be your private pleasure. There need be no other hint of violence, no other signs of forced entry. Merely in this poke-in-past-resistance moment, when you feel flush with the pleasure of possession, like a homesteader staking a land claim. And perhaps, if your partner winces at that point of entry with an instant flash of pain, cringes slightly with the initial sting of being owned, you can, if you like, take some secret satisfaction in that pain too. It's up to you. You're the owner now. A lord with your own manners.

## A Personal Risk-Assessment Guarantee

This training is cumulative, it's comprehensive, and it's all of a piece (wink wink).

None of these training tips will threaten your manhood "I." Nor will anything in this training regimen give you any personal incentive or motivation for loving justice and becoming a man of conscience. No need to worry about that, you have my word. All this training does is take your raw material reflexes and retool them for the erotics of economics.

So play hard, stay hard—and go get 'em, guys.

*Coach "Irony" John*

WITHOUT SEXUAL OBJECTIFICATION,
THERE COULD BE NO MANHOOD—
AND HUMANS WOULD TRULY BEHOLD ONE ANOTHER
FOR A CHANGE.

# ✧ **21** ✧

## I LIKE HANGING OUT WITH JUST GUYS A LOT—IS THERE SOME KIND OF A PROBLEM WITH THAT TOO?

The voices we hear when other men judge us are in dead earnest. The pitch and timbre are familiar: do not step out of line, they warn us; do not discredit manhood. Our fear of their ominously gruff voices seems never to be stilled. As if beguiled by their menace, we abandon the courage of our own convictions; then we stand at attention and salute, afraid to dishonor men's power to command.

Like Coach "Irony" John of Chapter Twenty, such remembered mentors can seem quite proud, affable, cocksure, and sporting. But Coach "Irony" John is not a real human being. I made him up. We *all* make up such characters whenever we act as if we believe in them. We *all* make up such fictions whenever we act as if other men have any special power to judge our life decisions.

Whenever we hear and rehear the judgmental voices of other men in our minds, we reexperience pressure to conform to the manhood act. We also feel that pressure whenever we wish to "fit in" among men, whenever we hope to "pass" as a member of the men's club, whenever we want to "belong" within the exclusionary society of real, other men. That's when we hear the damning refrain yet again: do not step out of line or we shall not let you in; do not embarrass manhood or we shall shut you out and shun you.

Manners matter among men. You simply cannot be a real man among men without them. Whenever you are in the company of real other men, you must always do as they do, and you must always do as they expect you to do. That is the undergirding principle of all social decency and decorum among real men. But ofttimes you may find yourself in need of more detailed advice, or more specifics in politesse. That is precisely the subject to which our next expert shall politely speak:

## Proper Etiquette Among Real Men (Or, Mister Mann's Guide to Excruciatingly Correct Male Bonding)

### Forms of Address

DEAR MISTER MANN:

What is the proper way to address another human who, upon casual inspection, also appears to have been raised to be a man?

TO WHOM IT MAY CONCERN:

There is an amusing medley of suitable forms of address for such a one, ranging from "Yo, sucka, whassup?" to "Howzithangin?" You cannot go wrong, however, with the all-purpose honorific "Man." You cannot possibly call this person "Man" often enough. Liberally litter your conversation with the monosyllable ("Know what I mean, Man?"), and you will endear yourself and be fondly remembered for a long, long time.

## Terms of Endearment

DEAR MISTER MANN:

What is the proper way to express my affection for another human who was raised to be a man whom I have come to find pleasant company?

GOOD BUDDY:

What exactly do you mean by "affection" and what exactly do you mean by "pleasant"? Mister Mann trusts you are not insinuating that you have become sweet on this person, perhaps due to an overdose of fructose. Assuming you innocently meant otherwise, the following physical gestures are appropriate and warranted: (1) pound this person's body as hard as you can, somewhere below the neck or above the belt; (2) feign a fisticuff elsewhere (as to the face or the groin); (3) smack the naked butt with a wet towel in the shower or locker room; (4) smack the clothed butt with the palm of your bare hand when you are both in some uniform. Mister Mann affectionately recalls how, in quest of the perfect butt smack, his penised college classmates periodically held "grabass" tournaments in their underwear in the dormitory basement, thus turning this cheeky gesture into a sport all its own. (Properly speaking, it was always pronounced *gruh-BAHSS.*) If you are not abundantly comfortable with any such bun dance, Mister Mann advises that you simply shake hands like a vise.

## Vocational Guidance

DEAR MISTER MANN:

Can you suggest which line of work I should go into? I am much disconcerted by the results of a vocational aptitude test I was once given, because it ranked my score on a scale of "masculine" to "feminine" at a rather discomfiting point. Do jobs have a gender? Am I more likely to become a real man among men in some occupations or professions than in others?

TO THE APPLICANT:

Your delicate question raises the rather more pressing question, Which fashion statement do you wish to make?

To wit: An airline company was once faced with the problem of trying to induce a crew of recent immigrants to vacuum the cabins of its airplanes. The maintenance crew refused, believing vacuuming to be "women's work." So the airline equipped the recalcitrant crew with huge, battleship-gray, industrial-strength vacuum tanks, at which point the crew members obligingly did the work. The fact that the tanks were now more cumbersome made the work all the more agreeable.

Indeed, the costume and tools of the trade do make the man—or at least the real man among real men.

If you are fortunate in that you or your ancestors did not recently get off a boat of some sort, you would do well to elect a vocation in whose proper attire not overalls but rather a necktie figures prominently. This useful noose about your neck obviates the need, whenever you meet another penised human, to show this other person that you have one too. Having to unzip your fly at every encounter—to prove it's still there—would be awkward and unseemly. Moreover, wearing a cravat as a caveat, you need not address your colleagues as "Man" quite so insistently.

If you elect a vocation for which you must occasionally wear a dress (the clergy, for instance, or the judiciary), be certain that you do so only with a secure ideology of masculine supremacy over your head—a lawful or a divine one, but preferably both. Then make certain that you network only with supremacists in similar frocks, so as to discourage any rude speculation that you have any sympathies or tendencies in common with clits or flits.

## Jests and Whimsy

DEAR MISTER MANN:

What is the proper way to respond to humorous pleas-antries in the polite society of real men? I am especially perplexed about how to respond when the butt of the joke is some poor unfortunate who could not possibly qualify for admission to the polite society of real men. Ought I go "tsk-tsk" in feigned pity? Or ought I guffaw explosively, perhaps with gratitude that I am not so un-fortunate? Please advise quickly, as I expect soon to be re-galed with just such a jest.

CHUCKLES:

A knowing snigger is always appropriate. Even if you did not entirely comprehend the gist of the joke, you cannot go wrong with a knowing snigger. Furthermore, when the jester begins with "Hey, didja hear the one about . . . ?" you should always greet this cliché with bemused enthusiasm, as though it were already the cleverest bon mot you had heard in a long time. The jester will welcome this confident show of unconditional support, and perhaps reciprocate someday.

You are quite correct to be concerned about proper protocol in all matters of whimsy, as failure to show proper amusement may raise suspicions as to whether you yourself have the breeding to be a bona fide member of polite society. Ignore any sympathies you may inadver-tently feel for the butt of the humor. Pay all your attention to the humor*ists*. It is they who must be your guide in all things jocular, because it is they who can banish you from polite society.

## Social Climbing

DEAR MISTER MANN:

What is the proper way to behave in the company of

other men who have accumulated much more wealth than I, or who have much more access to institutional power than I?

UPSTART:

Obsequiously, if you know what is good for you. The honorific "Sir" may shield you from the disdain you so deserve. This point is summed up in a rather crude maxim, which Mister Mann, in respect of one of your more precious private parts, prefers to render thusly: Kiss *ss to save your *ss.

## Noblesse Oblige

DEAR MISTER MANN:

What is the proper way to behave in the company of other men who have accumulated far less wealth or institutional power than I?

LORD AND MASTER:

Superiorly and condescendingly, of course—but guardedly, if you know what is good for you. Make certain you are never alone; make certain you know who your social peers are; make certain that you all stand together, standing up to void your bladders in all the best men's rooms—the best hotels, the best government agencies, the best corporate headquarters, the best houses of worship, the best brothels. These days—at least among the penised—one never knows which peons may decide to pee on *you*. But when you're on a top-ranked team, there's safety in numbers. So if you and your cronies can get away with pissing on some peons, urine luck.

## *A Disruptive Controversy*

DEAR MISTER MANN:

I and my adoptive brethren have been having a series of serious disputes. Perhaps you can help us resolve them. We argue about homosexual "rights" (liberals) versus the "wrong" of homosexuality (conservatives); we argue about abortion "rights" (liberals) versus the "wrong" of abortion (conservatives); we argue about pornographers' and pimps' "rights" (liberals) versus the offensiveness of smut (conservatives). I fear the polite affairs of real men will be permanently disrupted if we cannot avert the social strife that such issues seem inevitably to precipitate.

POLITICAL NAIF:

You and your adoptive brethren have not yet found a way to agree to disagree, and in the polite society of real men that is *very bad form.* You are wise to ask Mister Mann to intervene. I shall explicate first the issues in all such controversies, then the execrable manners being displayed to dispute them.

Those of you who are "conservative" are correct when you cast all these issues as problems of ownership. You, leaning rightward, prefer *private* ownership—with each bona fide ownable being owned by only one bona fide owner at a time. Whatever might induce or permit disruptions in said status quo you would quite reasonably deplore.

Those of you who are "liberal" are also correct when you regard all these issues as problems of ownership. You, leaning leftward, prefer *collectivized* ownership— with each bona fide ownable being available to be owned by any number of bona fide owners, sequentially or simultaneously, even through modern means of mass production. You would, reasonably enough, place no particular cap on the number of owners by whom an ownable may be owned. And you would, reasonably enough, increase the field of available ownables as well—

including as many from the list of "Who's Hot, Who's Not" as might be feasible and fun. The more the merrier.

Viewed as problems of ownership, your messy debates take on formulaic clarity. Viz.:

*Conservatives would have it be resolved that:*
WHEREAS lesbianism rebuts the presumption that the penis is uniquely an instrument of sexual owning, and WHEREAS male homosexuality opens to regimented sexual owners the option of getting owned as well, thus enticing promiscuous preverts of all sorts to abandon the time-honored principle of private property in sex, THEREFORE lesbianism and homosexuality must be despised and denounced.

*Liberals would have it be resolved that:*
WHEREAS lesbianism and homosexuality open sexual options to be transacted irrespective of sexual anatomy, eliminating old obligatory forced choices and opening a panoply of new ones, and WHEREAS gay rights would actually diversify and democratize the eroticism of ownership, THEREFORE lesbianism and homosexuality must be extolled and announced.

*Conservatives would have it be resolved that:*
WHEREAS abortion eliminates one of the greatest rewards of owning capital, which is that you can use it to make more, thus eroding the traditional principle of private property in sexual reproduction, THEREFORE abortion must be reviled and impermissible.

*Liberals would have it be resolved that:*
WHEREAS abortion eliminates the economic onus on owners to pay for the harvest of crops that may, inadvertently, result from their sowing of wild oats, and WHEREAS the availability of abortion induces more tillables to be serially and nonmonogamously plowed, thus affirming the principle of collectivity in sexual ownership, THEREFORE abortion must be grudgingly permitted.

### Conservatives would have it be resolved that:

WHEREAS pornography and prostitution provide sexual owners with enjoyable outlets for sexual possession when one's personal ownable has (or is) a headache, but WHEREAS pornography and prostitution infringe on real estate property values, THEREFORE pornography and prostitution must be available but restricted—kept under the counter and in the less desirable neighborhoods.

### Liberals would have it be resolved that:

WHEREAS pornography mass-markets ownables for completely democratic sexual consumption, and WHEREAS prostitution is a viable career path for ownables with a feisty entrepreneurial spirit, THEREFORE commerce in pornography and prostitution should be completely unregulated, and TO THAT END pornographers should have unfettered freedom to profit from retailing documentation of sexual abuse, and sexual possession of prostitutes should pose no risk to consumers' health (by whatever governmental regulation may be required in an otherwise completely free market).

As you can see, the debate between private and collectivized sexual ownership is not without merit on both sides. What's crucially important to both viewpoints is consistent maintenance of one's position as sexual owner: the certain knowledge that when you want to get it up to f*ck, you can, without impediment. Mister Mann is appalled, however, at how often would-be real men forget this, whether in the polite society of men who lean right or in the polite society of men who lean left.

For instance, Mister Mann has heard both factions accuse the loyal opposition of being less favorable to the interests of ownables: liberals will say it's the conservatives who hate women, and conservatives will say it's the liberals who hate women. Puh-*leeze!* Gentlemen, that is no way to conduct this debate. It is beneath you. The ownables don't matter. Ownables *never* matter. That is at the crux of proper genital functioning as a proper sexual owner. Always remember, gentlemen, what these debates are fundamentally about: *private* sexual ownership versus *collectivized* sexual ownership. Is the ownable more interesting as a virgin or as a whore? Is your body bond with other ownables stronger if you own on your own or if you own with a gang? It's a matter of taste. You only find out for yourself which you like when you focus on the sexual possession, the f*ck done properly as an act of owning, the boundaried identity that only inheres in you when you own and f*ck like the man there. Mister Mann respectfully implores you to get at least that much straight.

There is more at stake here than tradition versus reform. There is more at stake here than capitalism versus socialism. There is manhood itself at stake, gentlemen: and the very grave risk, if you do not abide by the rules of etiquette appropriate to the polite society of real men—if you do not respectfully agree to disagree—that you will inadvertently invite the collapse of the vertical scale of manhood as we have *all* come to know it and as we have *all* come to it, cherishing it hard in our heart of hearts.

Gentlemen, I rest my case.

### *Avoiding Unpleasant Confrontations*

DEAR MISTER MANN:

I am dreadfully distraught. An acquaintance of mine, a certain human raised to be a man, has been making threatening gestures in my direction of late. It would appear that he wishes to bloody my nose. I am horrified at this prospect, but I fear I have no choice but to do worse than bloody his nose in reply. Then, supposing he replies to that, what then? Oh, woe betide me! Whatever shall I do to avoid such escalating untidiness?

GENTLE CHUMP:

You are quite correct to wish to circumvent the splatter of a spat. Have you considered a male bond?

## *A Query to Follow Up*

DEAR MISTER MANN:
  What's a male bond?

QUICK-WITTED ONE:
  How nimble of you to ask.
  Duels with pistols and foils went out of fashion long
ago, along with horses and buggies. The modern custom
is to avert such nonsense to begin with. Nip it before
there's blood.
  The male bond, though of ancient and estimable lineage, has only recently been perfected as an everyday social grace among humans raised to be a man. The proper
etiquette of the male bond has become more and more socially useful—and more and more sexually necessary—
especially as more and more slugs raised to be a woman
have been crawling out from under their rocks, and especially as this has given uppity ideas to poofters as well.
As a consequence of such disruptions to polite society, every would-be real man would do well to observe this custom with great care when among other would-be real
men.
  The male bond is essentially a very sudden and spon-
taneous four-act drama. Sometimes players enact it with
much flourish and gusto. Sometimes players follow the
basic script with mere pedestrian adequacy. Although it's
only a matter of manners—of make-believe and
playacting—you must pay close attention to each act, lest
you screw up and get screwed.

### *Cliff Notes, or*
### *A Male Bond in Four Acts*
  *Act I* occurs when another player—someone who
wishes to make you believe he is a real man—issues a
challenge to your ranking on the vertical scale of manhood. To make you believe his own ranking, this make-
believe man insinuates, for instance, that you are weak,
not strong. He hints you are vulnerable, not tough. He

implies you are soft, not hard; wimp, not butch; queer, not straight; powerless, not powerful; submissive, not dominant; empathetic, not callous; defenseless, not armed. He says so in so many words or gestures. He alleges you are loyal to someone you respect and love ("You are pussy-whipped, a nigger lover, a limp-wrist simp"). He impugns your sexual anatomy ("Whassa matter, girlie?—can't get it up?"). He throws down a gauntlet: he holds out a loyalty oath to the vertical scale of manhood—and he promises to hold you up to ridicule and contempt among real men if you do not sign it, by signing away your selfhood and whomever else's you may hold dear.

*Act II* occurs when you accept the challenge and you sign the loyalty oath, swearing your allegiance to manhood. You do this not by attacking your attacker back (that could get bloody unpleasant, remember). You do this by forswearing your connection to some other human life. You sell out or put down or deride or dismiss some other human life such that in your challenger's eyes, and in your own, that human life is nobody to you. You betray someone you love (you allow as to how they mean little or nothing to you). Or you insult someone who's physically or ethnically different. Or you mock the collective patsy. Somehow, thinking fast, you spit in the face of someone else's humanity. You lose your own in doing so, of course, but you spare yourself the inconvenience of a duel to the death with another make-believe man.

*Act III* occurs when you have successfully met the challenge—and your challenger accepts your personal signature on the loyalty oath. Your challenger has been persuaded that you feel more loyalty to the bond between you as make-believe men than you feel to some other connection you may have once felt to another human life. Your challenger believes that you are more loyal to the vertical scale of manhood than you are to some targeted patsy's selfhood. Your challenger and you now bond, in the blissful belief that you both truly love manhood.

(Perhaps you can appreciate what an improvement this social custom provides over duels and hand-to-hand combat. The male bond, done correctly, is perfectly blood-less. Of course, your personal incentive to obey the custom may be dictated by some residual fear of bloodlet-ting. But as you grow older and begin to move in the bet-ter social circles, where the well-made male bond is the smart thing to do, you merely need acquiesce to it gra-ciously, or you merely need proffer the occasional chal-lenge to some other would-be swell, and you'll be quite safe and real in the company of safely real men.)

*Act IV* occurs when you encounter—in the flesh, face to face—the human you recently disavowed or betrayed or put down or mocked in order to qualify as a real man during the challenge of the male bond. If you handled your emotions correctly during the drama of that bond, the memory of your recent gender success ought still be fresh in your body and your brain. Hence, you should have no difficulty conducting your affairs in Act IV, when you now must deal with this particular human as if they are indeed nobody to you. Treating such an actual human as a nobody is much the preferable course of action. For one thing, it is so much simpler than trying to resuscitate in your frame of mind either their humanity or yours. Such well-intentioned efforts are not recommended; in fact they can be disastrous, as they inevitably lead to much teeter-totter wobbling and a rent-asunder sense of who you are. Fortunately, most male bonds obviate any temptation you may feel to reconnect with anyone's self-hood, which is why the male bond is such a jolly good show—though always a hard act to follow.

(Eminently civilized as the male bond may be, your doleful loved ones and various other riffraff in your life may not share your appreciation for it—especially when your affection and loyalty for them has been sold out in lieu of your loyalty to manhood. But they do not belong to the polite society of real men, so their voices do not count.)

## *Becalmed Among Chums*

DEAR MISTER MANN:

I seem to be missing something. Help.

There are several humans of my close acquaintance, a fair number of them male, and occasionally some of us male friends are wont to gather with one another to share in a favorite diversion of some sort. Our companionship appears altogether consonant with our loyalties to all the humans we might love and honor, however. Even though those other humans be not immediately present, they are present in our hearts, and all my friends and I acknowledge and respect that fact. As an unfortunate consequence, we therefore appear to have no history among us of that "male bond" thing you speak of. We appear to enjoy being together as chums or soulmates, not as competitors as to our alleged manhood ranking, and certainly not as challengers to one another's. Meagerly, we seem merely to love one another even as we love all our loved ones and as we love our own selves. We share feelings as appropriate. We feel safe, sustained, seen, and not alone, as appropriate. We seem not to be desperately seeking manhood together so much as we are delighting in our mutual selfhood, with one another and in the rest of our lives, becoming all the while what would seem to be described best as an experience of our own best self.

So can you suggest ways in which my male friends and I might improve our social skills—along the lines you recommend? We are all most curious to experience for ourselves this polite society of real men of which you speak. And your intriguing advice has made us all the more eager to practice among ourselves the proper etiquette for conferring real manhood upon one another.

WIMPETTE:

Mister Mann has no patience for your wretched plight. You have utterly failed to grasp that to truly love manhood you must learn how to share *contempt*. Really! It is failures like you who disgrace the polite society of real men by trying to *pass* in it, when you are no more eligible for it than is a slug or a bugger.

But since you ask so *pathetically*, Mister Mann shall deign to give you the courtesy of a curt reply.

Mister Mann suggests you wait it out. Sooner or later, one of your inadequate cohort will experience the painful dissolution of a relationship, and he will want to take comfort in thinking it was all the fault of someone he once "loved." Sooner or later, one of you will feel an economic squeeze in the workplace, and he will want to take comfort in thinking it's all the fault of the uppity. Sooner or later, one of you will be humiliated by someone whose manhood ranks higher up the cliff, and be filled with impotent rage. Wait. Just wait. A generic Gender Danger is sure to come along. And when it does, sooner or later, all your much-touted "selfhood" will turn to self-pity; and the instant that happens, expect a *fury* of male bonding. One of you will appeal to another for sympathetic, unconditional support of his status on the vertical cliffside of gender. One of you will need you to agree with him that were it not for some *nobody*, his manhood would not now be endangered. One of you will be unable to trust your fellowship unless you assure him that you scorn the same enemies or scapegoats he does. And one of you will try to reach out to this pitiable cliffhanger. One of you will offer to cast him a lifeline. But you will not be able to save him from free-fall, nor save him from himself, until you both subtly swear your fealty to Deep Bob—by giving someone below you the boot.

## Choosing the Right Fork

DEAR MISTER MANN:
Which fork should I use?

DIM-WITTED ONE:

There's only one fork of any significance on life's path: the choice between loving justice and loving manhood. Mister Mann had of course hoped that you would have figured that one out by now.

WITHOUT MALE BONDING,
THERE COULD BE NO MANHOOD—
AND HUMANS WOULD TRULY BE LOYAL TO ONE ANOTHER
FOR A CHANGE.

# HOW CAN I BE CLOSE TO MEN AND NOT FEEL LIKE I'M QUEER?

Far from the rough-and-tumble practice fields where we first learned the manhood game, and far from the cushy clubhouses where some few of us may take our ease during time-outs—far, far, far away from all of that, sons are sometimes sent to war. On the fighting field—in actual battle—the rooting voice of Coach "Irony" John is no comfort at all. In the trenches, in the foxholes, in the cockpit, in the mobile hospital, the priggish voice of Mister Mann is useless. When a son is sent into combat to fight a war, he needs much more from boot camp than Eyeball Target Practice and Manly Manners. He needs to know why he's *there*. And he needs not to feel so damned *scared*.

Manhood and organized warfare have a close historical connection. Manhood, as an artifact of human consciousness, may even have begun about the same time as organized warfare. Alternately, organized warfare may have begun along with the delusional notion of manhood. History is iffy here. It's one of those chicken-and-egg problems.

There have been many sons in history who have hated war, who have hated having to fight wars, who have wanted wars to end. To many of these pacifistic individuals—all of whom in some sense share a reverence for selfhood—the complex interrelationship between manhood and war looks like a different problem entirely: how can conscientious objectors ever bring an end to militarism?—and how can chickens stop omelets?

What could conceivably induce a son to "want" to fight a war, after all? There are millennia of militarist history, for starters. But what makes a son *feel* like fighting a war? How does love of manhood so engage a son's body and brain such that waging war becomes tantamount to defending gender?

So far as I know, no popular understanding of the relationship between militarism and manhood has ever come to terms with the emotional and physical phenomena of inculcated gender anxiety.* The lesson of manhood—"Not to be a man is to be less than nobody"—not only prescribes the manhood act so that it is functionally suitable for war; the lesson of manhood makes war virtually inevitable. Without "real men," there could be no real war; without real war, there could be no "real men."

To understand more deeply how sonship and warfare are intimately linked—to cathect the terrors and passions in a penised human that make manhood and war not so much a tautology as a theology—we shall hear in this chapter yet another voice. This is the voice of one who speaks on behalf of all war machines of all time. His basso, metallic intonations are well known to policymakers and military strategists for all nations now on earth. This is the cavernous voice of a man who comprehends, as only an epic poet really can, what reasons the heart has—what cadences resound in one's viscera—when manhood and war are declared in the same breath.

## The Rime of the Ancient Armorer

As you begin your baby steps,
    As you become a lad,
As you climb up the manhood cliff,
    In armor you'll be clad.

*In "Disarmament and Masculinity," in *Refusing to Be a Man*, I analyzed conflicts between warring nations in terms of genderizing dynamics between men. Here, I extend that analysis to the personal experience of the penised soldier.

You dare not sally forth without it,
    You dare not take that chance;
But fear you not, there'll always be
    A wee hole for your lance.

Yanked from your mother's womb you were,
    Then ripped from her embrace,
Lest you still feel at one with her,
    Lest you be Dad's disgrace.

You had no language yet, poor babe,
    With which to utter fright,
But soon you toughened up so you'd
    Forget her with your might.

Yon armor's what you need, my boy,
    It comes in young men's sizes,
Remember what's at stake without it,
    Remember what the prize is.

Your mom will bid you sad adieu,
    As you try on your armor,
And as you don the breastplate too,
    She'll wonder if you'll harm her.

But no, you'll save a soft place,
    Somewhere deep inside you,
Somewhere in that tin you wear,
    Somewhere she can hide you.

No men you meet will ever know
    Your mother's life lives through you,
Who knows what they would think of that?
    Who knows what they'd do to you?

You'll wear your armor proudly, man,
    Your spear too, it is trusty;
But you may never take it off,
    And weeping makes it rusty.

You'll wear your armor safely, man,
    'Twill guard your precious life,
'Twill keep you self-containerized
    If e'er you take a wife.

Rude buggers too be all about,
    'Twould surely make you wince
To fancy what they'd love to do
    To *your* sweet innocence.

The rapist likes to rape the lassies,
    Because of course for him it's
butch—but armor worn by manly men
    Keeps male behinds off limits.

You'd be at risk without that armor,
    'Twould make thy dry eye soften:
A lass raped oh so frequently,
    A lad raped just as often!

With helmet shut you're sure to feel
    Your eyeballs scope correctly,
With iron on your backside too
    No one dares touch you rect'ly.

So thank your lucky stars at birth
    You came with your own dong,
And if you're hoist on someone's prick
    Declare you too can prong!

To armor, lads, to arms and war!
    Brute combat's not the hardest;
Your tank is built to last, except
    There's steel plate where your heart is.

Remember when your hand is full,
    Remember when you pull it,
Your uniform is muscled firm
    So you could stop a bullet.

Most soldiers' lives are short and sweet,
    Before they're shot and die,
But always keep in mind, young man,
    Old soldiers never lie.

Believe the tales they tell you true,
    Get comfy in your cage;
They locked you in, they keep you in,
    It shields them from sons' rage.

And when you bed a lass your own
    In boudoir well appointed,
Remember with your armor on
    You may feel stiffly jointed.

Indeed you both may feel it when
    Caresses turn to clanking,
You may not even know in fact
    If you are only wanking.

I never told you otherwise,
    I never promised roses;
The suit you wear works best when you're in
    War and other poses.

But keep your armor on, my lads,
    Not just to save your ass;
With armor on no man will e'er
    Mistake you for a lass.

The lassies do their best withal,
    They bump and grind their fannies,
They keep their pace ten steps behind
    To keep clear who the man is.

But don't depend on lassies, lad,
    They cannot do't alone,
You need your armor on so you can
    Throw the dogs a bone.

Disgust may rise up in your gorge
　　When you feel what you've done
To learn to loathe all lassies who've
　　But tried to save your bum.

A cry in need you may well feel
　　For comrades who are peers,
Alas, they too are armored shut
　　And may well cast you leers.

They may well call you pansy-ass,
　　They may well call you faggot,
They may well call you girlie, queer,
　　And treat you like a maggot.

Since boyhood you've been duly groomed
　　To never seem a Ms.
And now you sweat inside because
　　The touch you crave is *his*.

You're stuck, my lad, you're armored in,
　　That's what this fear's about,
So even in a man's embrace
　　There's no way you'll come out.

The fear that shut you in when you
　　Were shamed away from Mother
Will follow you where e'er you go
　　To keep all warriors brother—
　　To keep all lovers *other*.

WITHOUT HOMOPHOBIA,
THERE COULD BE NO MANHOOD—
AND HUMANS WOULD FEEL NO DESIRE
TO WAGE WAR
ANYMORE.

# ✧ **23** ✧

## IF THEY TAKE AWAY MY PORNO,
## WILL THEY TAKE AWAY MY
## MANHOOD NEXT?

No sooner had the Ancient Armorer ended his oracular decla-
mations than my attention was arrested by a mysterious "Psst!"

I looked around, startled. I saw no one.

"Psst!" it came again.

I had been browsing in a shop at a magazine rack, assuming
I was quite alone, casually researching for this book, in fact; and
as I looked around again I saw a gentleman dressed in a well-
cut gray suit. He had his eyes on me.

"Psst!" he said.

"Me?" I whispered.

"*Yo're* the fella who's writin' a book 'bout the ind of manhood," he announced.

"Yes, I am," I acknowledged, wondering how in the world he
knew.

"A terr'ble, terr'ble tragidy," he muttered, and I cocked my
ear to understand his elegant regional diction. "Glad yo're
gonna do somethin' 'bout it, son. This great nation needs mo'
fahn young men lahk you." As he ambled nearer I could make
him out more clearly. Age had not been kind. His body was
paunchy, his face full of bloat; broken capillaries in his pink
complexion had made his elder's nose a map of winding back-
country roads.

"Well, sir—" I began.

"I got somethin' you should see," he declared. "An impo'tant documint that b'longs in that book yo're writin'."

"I should perhaps explain," I interrupted. "It's true that my book is about the end of manhood, but perhaps not in the way you think. I mean to disarm the very notion. I mean to challenge its foundation as a myth system. I mean to explicate the ways it's enforced. I mean to point out how it preempts our life choices. I mean to—"

"Finished yet?" the old man demanded.

"Well, I could say more, I suppose," I stammered, "but—"

"Finished with the *book*?" he gruffed.

"No, actually, I have one more chapter to write."

"Ovahedjicated pansy," I thought I heard him say.

"Excuse me, sir?" I said.

"This ind of manhood—it's gotta *stop*."

"Oh, that's what I think too!" I offered brightly, before I realized I had perhaps misheard his point.

"Ah did not spend mah entahr careeah as a public servant only to see the ind of manhood come to pass. Befo' Ah die, Ah am determined to do everythin' within mah powah to prevint that terr'ble tragidy from occurrin'."

"Well, I guess I can understand why you might feel that way," I said, noting that now his passion had produced a sort of palsy in his dangling left arm, and his limp left hand jerked back and forth as if groping for something firm to hold on to. "I can only imagine how upset you must feel."

"Cut the crap," he said with finality; "here's yo' last chaptuh." As he said so his steadier right hand reached out to pass me what felt like a document wrapped in a plain brown paper bag. I recognized his accent then too; I'd heard it often on television, echoing through the halls of power, at the highest levels of government, in standing committees, on special commissions. I felt, for a moment, extremely touched, even honored. Perhaps this kindly government official had sought me out, followed me here, to entrust me with a sensitive state secret or a scandal or something. Just like in the movies. Wow.

"Whatcha waitin' for—the cows to come home?" he demanded. "Open it."

"Here?" I wondered.

"Where else," he said.

"I don't understand, sir," I said, as I slipped the important document from its wrapper. "This is a stroke book."

"Oh," the old man mumbled, slightly more red-faced than before. "Pahdon me." He fumbled in his attaché case, rummaging among several similar documents in plain brown wrappers, then handed me another. "Open it," he instructed. "And gimme back that other thang."

"OK," I said, unwrapping what he had leaked. It appeared to be a transcript on official-looking paper. On every page each neatly typed line was numbered, as if for future legal citation.

"Mark my word," said the elderly Southern gentleman. "The ind of manhood—it's gonna be a terr'ble terr'ble tragidy."

I stood staring at the document, marveling, lost in thought. When at last I looked up to thank him, the old man was gone.

✧

# TOP SECRET

## OFFICIAL GOVERNMENT TRANSCRIPT

### NATIONAL COMMISSION ON MANHOOD HEARINGS

Witnesses scheduled to testify in closed session:
Coach "Irony" John
Mister Mann
Colonel Armorer

Presiding: The Honorable Mr. Chairman

HONORABLE MR. CHAIRMAN: Welcome, gentlemen. My heart thanks you for your patience. I know the robing rooms you've been waiting in have lacked for certain creature comforts: no booze, no broads--no idle pleasures of any sort. Gentlemen, your stamina and fortitude are to be commended. Myself and my fellow Commissioners do thank you for coming here today to tes-

tify, to help us get to the bottom of the dilemma we are
charged with wrestling with, and what we can do about
it, so that this fine nation of ours can again prosper and
prevail. I therefore hereby gavel this session of the National Commission on Manhood to order. Long live Deep Bob!

VOICES FROM HEARINGS CHAMBERS: Long live Deep Bob!
Ho! Ho! Ho!

HONORABLE MR. CHAIRMAN: Order. We shall have order.
Thank you. Our first witness is Mr. "Irony" John from the
Great State of--of-- Can somebody please read this to me? The
Great State of Athletic Prowess--and you are a coach, is that cor-
rect?

COACH "IRONY" JOHN: That is correct, Your Honor.

HONORABLE MR. CHAIRMAN: And what exactly is it that you
coach?

COACH "IRONY" JOHN: I coach sex, sir.

[Laughter from the hearings chambers.]

HONORABLE MR. CHAIRMAN: I understand you are here to testify
before us as an expert, and you have a prepared statement, is
that correct?

COACH "IRONY" JOHN: That's correct.

HONORABLE MR. CHAIRMAN: You may begin.

COACH "IRONY" JOHN: Thank you, Honorable Mr. Chairman. I
come before you to tell you about an impending tragedy.
The men of this country are in trouble. Serious trouble.
Manhood itself is on the line, threatened at every turn. We have
ownables agitating for economic parity, Your Honor, and it is producing limp dicks across the land.
    Where I come from, the Great State of Athletic Prowess,
you learn there's a right way to fuck and a wrong way to fuck.
The right way is when you have somebody beneath you. The wrong
way is when you don't.

[Laughter.]

We've got dual-income couples out there today, and in a few cases the ownable even earns more than the owner. So when they hit the hay, and he's got an economic equal lying there beside him, how's he gonna get it up? An equal! How can anyone fuck an equal like a real man? What am I supposed to tell the rookies who are still in training? What am I supposed to say when they come back to me after a few seasons and tell me, "Coach, I got a problem playing the position of sexual owner. My ownable's income has turned my weenie to a marsh-mallow." It would break your heart to hear their sobs.

HONORABLE MR. CHAIRMAN: Can you please pass the witness a tissue there? Thank you.

COACH "IRONY" JOHN: Excuse me, Your Honor, excuse me for that emotional outburst, excuse me, please forgive me, sir, Your Honor, please--I'm so--ashamed.

HONORABLE MR. CHAIRMAN: You may continue, Coach--just soon as you can get a grip.

COACH "IRONY" JOHN: Thank you, Your Honor, thank you. We've got frustrated workers in offices across our land and frustrated students and professors too, 'cause now they're told to bite their tongues when that sweet 'n' saucy pretty young thing comes sashaying past their gaze, and all their lives they've been reading high-toned, glossy magazines featuring alluring photo lay-outs of bazoom babes in all the occupations, in all the acad-emies, in his job, in that school, and these men are getting horny and ornery, Your Honor, because they were led to expect higher education would be a pickup scene and the workplace would be a bunny hutch, and now the law says they got to cool it, and they are sick and tired and they are not going to take this--!

HONORABLE MR. CHAIRMAN: If I may interrupt, Coach?

COACH "IRONY" JOHN: Yes, please, of course, Your Honor, sir.

HONORABLE MR. CHAIRMAN: I understand the agitation in your voice. I do, believe me. I would, however, like to explain your un-happy reference there to our government's policy on sexual harassment. Please convey our government's sincere apologies to all trainees concerned. You see, our government had an eco-

nomic interest to protect, on behalf of some of our major bene-
factors: the corporations. They were having the most annoying
worker-turnover problem you can imagine. All the lowly
ownables doing scut work, you see--well, one by one they'd
get up and quit and go look for another job whenever any man
said something sweet and endearing or gave 'em an innocent pat
on the fanny. And rehiring and retraining costs money--it
was eating into company profits--so a policy against sexual
harassment looked like an economical solution. The big corporations liked it too, even if they did have to bear liability for em-
ployees who sexually harassed, because that was cheaper
in the long run than runaway job-hopping by desirable
ownables. But do be assured, Coach, that we are diligently working
on an economical solution to the sexual problem you describe,
which we all now recognize; we truly do. You may continue
with your prepared statement.

COACH "IRONY" JOHN: Thank you, Your Honor. We've got
would-be men out there, real would-be men, looking around the
workplace and seeing ownables doing every job that men
can do. Just as well and sometimes better! They're looking
at ownables flying airplanes, not just serving coffee or tea. They're
looking at ownables building ships, not just sitting under a parasol
while a man rows the boat. They're looking at ownables
in the armed forces, not just folding bandages. And in some
religions they're even looking at ownables wearing the cloth,
which you always needed a joystick for before! Every year, there
gets to be fewer and fewer jobs that only a real man can
perform, so there gets to be less and less chance he'll know
for sure he's a man because he does a man's job! This economic
crisis is going to come home to roost, Your Honor, and I am here
before you today to bring you fair warning.

HONORABLE MR. CHAIRMAN: Excuse me, Coach, for in-
terrupting once again. I just want to make sure I get your drift
there, in my own down-home style. Are you saying that the cock
isn't getting laid the way he likes; the hens aren't laying
because they're out crowing up the dawn; and all across
this country there are roosters who feel like capons?

COACH "IRONY" JOHN: That's the problem exactly, Your Honor.

HONORABLE MR. CHAIRMAN: I see. This is indeed very
grave. And do you know what would possibly prevent it?

Do you by any chance appear here today with any recommen-
dation in hand?

COACH "IRONY" JOHN: Yes, I do, Your Honor, sir. I most certainly
do.

HONORABLE MR. CHAIRMAN: And what is the solution
you propose, Coach?

COACH "IRONY" JOHN: Based on my expert knowledge of the
way my trainees respond to homework in private and eyeball
target practice in public, and based on my own personal
observations, which are all firsthand--

HONORABLE MR. CHAIRMAN: Excuse me again, Coach. I wish
to modestly remind you that though these hearings are closed,
you are speaking on the official record.

COACH "IRONY" JOHN: I realize that, Your Honor; thank you for
your concern for modesty, which I share. But I feel this crisis
is so crucial that I must go public with my very own story:
I masturbate to pornography.

[Gasps, murmurs, wheezing.]

HONORABLE MR. CHAIRMAN: Order. Order. I demand order in
my chambers.

COACH "IRONY" JOHN: I am proud to say that I masturbate
to pornography, as a manly citizen of this great nation of great
men. I believe that masturbating to pornography helps me be a
real man too. I believe it helps restore me to my rightful
dignity and pride as a real man, as a real sexual owner,
whenever my confidence flags, whenever my ownable gets uppity,
whenever I'm in doubt as to whether Deep Bob loves me, whenever
I'm in doubt about my bond with other men. I believe that
masturbating to pornography combines the best of both
worlds--the private and the public--even as it combines, in my
imagination, my private parts with the pubes of whomever I might
desire to own. It's easy, and it gets me hard. It is an effective
pick-me-up. No ownable need be any the wiser. My collection
is my own private business. And I can remember the pornography
I masturbate to whenever I like, even when I'm inside her.
    So my recommendation to this National Commission on
Manhood is that you act fast before it's too late to make

pornography more readily available to all would-be real men. And be careful to lay out the pornography so that when a man looks at it he knows exactly who's the sexual owner and who is definitely not, by which I mean it's fine with me personally if the sexual owner is sometimes off-camera--that way I can pretend it's me. In terms of the sex technique I teach, it would be a great social service to all my trainees, if you could help keep clear the distinction between sexual owner and sexual ownable. It would be a great comfort, as well, for all the would-be real men out there whose ownables have begun to earn more than pin money.

HONORABLE MR. CHAIRMAN: This troubles me greatly, Coach. I had thought we had the matter of uppity women under control. I thought we had figured how to throw the sows some sops and keep 'em hogtied behind their back. Do you mean to say that without porno all our lashing back will come to naught?

COACH "IRONY" JOHN: That is correct, Your Honor. Without pornography, us men have nothing to come to.

HONORABLE MR. CHAIRMAN: I see. This is more grave than I had thought. Thank you for your expert testimony, Coach. Next witness, please.

MISTER MANN: Please allow me to introduce myself. My name is Mister Mann.

HONORABLE MR. CHAIRMAN: How do you do?

MISTER MANN: I've never been better, Your Honor. And how's the wife and kids?

HONORABLE MR. CHAIRMAN: They're fine. Very fine. Thank you for asking.

MISTER MANN: Thank you kindly for the cordial invitation to appear before your august body this afternoon, which I was honored to accept.

HONORABLE MR. CHAIRMAN: Not at all.

MISTER MANN: I'm much obliged.

HONORABLE MR. CHAIRMAN: You're too kind.

MISTER MANN: No, you're too kind.

HONORABLE MR. CHAIRMAN: Unless I miss my guess, Mister Mann, you are an expert on proper manners among the well-bred.

MISTER MANN: That is quite correct. Protocol. Social relations. That sort of thing.

HONORABLE MR. CHAIRMAN: I understand that you too have prepared a statement for the members of this manhood inquiry.

MISTER MANN: I have, Your Astuteness. Ahem.

[Here follows Mister Mann's statement, reproduced exactly, as per his express wishes, from an engraved document he submitted into evidence.]

## To the Esteemed Members
### of the National Commission on Manhood:

If it please the Commissioners, I wish to call your attention to a serious crisis that threatens to rend the very fabric of social life among real men as we know it. I speak, of course, of the intractable economic diversity among manhood's aspirants. You may be more familiar with the term "class differences," though I prefer to speak of unfortunate disparities of wherewithal. Noble though all their aspirations to manhood be—each and every one, praise Bob!—some, it must be acknowledged, have deeper pockets than do others. And we simply cannot have so many poor wretches reaching into their pockets only to find so little there! In a great country such as ours—founded as it was by slaveowners, religious fanatics, guerrillas and mercenaries of all stripes—surely we can do better than that. Surely we can find some charity in our

hearts toward the more lowly manhood aspirants. It is but
the polite thing to do.

There are always going to be genteel circles of real men at
the highest echelons of this great nation of ours, and they
will always be able to buy, rent, or lease whichever sexual
ownable tickles their fancy. It is not they for whom I
appeal. Rather, I petition on behalf of the more piteous
sorts, the hoi polloi, the downtrodden, the economically
challenged. How are they to hold their heads high as real
men knowing only too well the lifestyles of the rich and
infamous—knowing only too well how much wealth the
top-ranked sexual owners have to fool around with?

Gentlemen of the Commission, there could be mass class
uprising from the have-nots and get-it-nots if we are not
prudent.

I recommend, therefore, the following plan: I urge upon
this government that it permit immediately the
mass-production and distribution of p*rn*gr*phy as widely
though discreetly as possible. P*rn*gr*phy offers even a
poor would-be man a cheap shot at sexual ownership. The
luckless lout can possess the ownable whenever he likes, at
a price anyone can afford. In the time-honored tradition of
bread and circuses, p*rn*gr*phy gives all the appearance
of populist "freedom" and "democracy." It offers the
muddled masses of manhood aspirants something to busy
themselves with. It will keep their minds off their poverty
of opportunity to possess ownables with all the savoir-faire
of the truly rich. It may also do something remedial for the
poor souls' poverty of imagination.

I beg your indulgence to hear me out on one further point,
Gentlemen: the trickle-down economics of such a plan.
The more available p*rn*gr*phy, the more ownables will
be needed to produce it, hence the more opportunity for

owners to specify with greater and greater exactitude
which qualities of ownability are optimal for manhood.

There then devolves, you see—among producers,
distributors, small-time capitalists, and consumers—a sort
of free-market sexual economy in which ownability in
p\*rn\*gr\*phy sets the standard for ownability in bed. This
delightful development will keep ownables on their toes,
as you can imagine.

The ownable in the p\*rn\*gr\*phy must be shown to be
there because she *desires* to be, because she got *paid*. This
mercantile conceit is absolutely central to the plan. Every
time a man *buys* her, or a mass-produced documentation
of her body being sexually owned, he may then feel that
he too has put something of *his* into the kitty. Even at
five bucks a throw, this will enhance his self-esteem
as a sexual buyer. And when he ejaculates onto the
pages of the p\*rn\*gr\*phy that was manufactured
from her body and that he bought and paid for, he will
feel like a real man again, a real member of the
owning class.

Respectfully submitted,
with praise and honor to Deep Bob,
from whom all good manners flow,
I remain,
your obedient servant,

Mister Mann

HONORABLE MR. CHAIRMAN: Thank you, Mister Mann, for your
stirring--your most enlightening--for your expertise and grace.
Next witness, please. Is this one gonna be another porno
freak too? Er, excuse me, Colonel, I did not realize my mi-
crophone was--er--please be seated. Welcome to this hearing on
a subject you must know well: our nation's manhood.

COLONEL ARMORER:

"The man should be trained for war,
and the broad for the recreation of the warrior,"
    Said my great hero, Nietzsche.
Men should be trained to whore,
and broads should be made all the sorrier;
    So I think porn is peachy.

HONORABLE MR. CHAIRMAN: What is this? I don't understand.
Can we get a translator in here or something? Am I to understand
that you are telling me as a military man that pornography
and prostitution are essential in order to conduct your far-
flung exploits in the name of our great nation's manhood?

COLONEL ARMORER: Aye, aye.

HONORABLE MR. CHAIRMAN: I don't believe I follow your
reasoning, Colonel.

COLONEL ARMORER:

To forge combat units between us
Across race and class strife het'rogen'ous,
There's nothing that beats
The lure of a piece;
It's like jerking around the same penis.

To teach troops to kill off our enemy,
To make them see foes as "no friend o' me,"
We train them to rape--
It's sexy! It's hate!--
Then their guns could as soon give an enema.

When Johnny comes marching back home again,
You'll know for a fact just where he has been:
He's fought at the front,
He's shot at some cunt,
The grunt has closed ranks with real military men.

HONORABLE MR. CHAIRMAN: Our Commission has heard previous testimony from witnesses arguing vociferously in favor of
more and more porno, and many say porno's only measurable
effect is that it produces a pleasant sensation in one's genitals
now and then. Coach "Irony" John has testified to that point, on

his own authority, which I have no reason to doubt. And that was
the gist of Mister Mann's tasteful remarks as well. But you, Colonel Armorer, say that you stock the stuff in your PXs and
you set up military-run brothels all about our bases abroad
because porno and whoring have some further intended effect
as part of your overall military goal, which is to produce warriors
with unit cohesion despite race and class enmity, and cadres
of killers who can stick it to the enemy on any command
from above. Am I correct in my reckoning?

COLONEL ARMORER: Aye, aye.

HONORABLE MR. CHAIRMAN: And what might such a command from above <u>be</u>?

COLONEL ARMORER:

The judgment comes down inside a man's head:
"Defend your manhood or you'll be dead;
Unless you fuck
You're out of luck,
And you will be mincemeat on the bed."

Pornography's what we use to spell out
The chain of command during every bout,
So they'll follow our orders,
Invade any borders,
And learn to have sex like a very good kraut.

HONORABLE MR. CHAIRMAN: I see. And you say porno
is essential to official military strategy--so there will always be
enough properly trained soldiers always ready to spring into action, always ready to obey our Commander-in-Chief, Bob,
and always willing to protect and defend our great nation's
manhood?

COLONEL ARMORER:

My job is to help men lay waste for their worth.
Without porn and war there would be a great dearth
Of lads who can kill
Just for the thrill;
They wouldn't know their warheads from holes in the earth.

The lore is passed down to son from father:
"You're not a real man until you've bought her."
That's why sons whore;
There's even more:
That's why sons serve as cannon fodder.

Without a war every generation
There'd be complete humiliation:
No fatherland,
No manhood, and
No boys marching loyally into cremation.

HONORABLE MR. CHAIRMAN: I do myself recall a little ditty I
learned from boot camp before I got my own marching orders:

"This is my weapon, this is my gun"

> [Here the Honorable Mr. Chairman gestures, pointing
> first to his shoulder--]

"This one's for killing,

> [--then under the table toward his lap.]

this one's for fun."

> [Laughter from hearings chambers.]

My memory has been refreshed. I believe I can now appreciate
better for myself, sir, why you speak as poetically as you
do. Therefore, Colonel, I am especially eager to hear your
thoughts on one further line of questioning, if I may with your
permission pursue it. I am speaking not of the porno problem in
general but of the homo problem in particular. I realize that
as a military man you have given serious consideration
to the homo problem. I respectfully recognize that you are already
on the record expressing your utter animadversion at the prospect
of having homos in the military--not so much because homos
cannot physically become the sort of warriors you require,
but rather because you cannot recruit normal warriors if you've
got known homos running around bareass in the barracks. The
homo warrior would make the normal warriors feel somewhat
insecure in such close quarters, is that a fair statement?

COLONEL ARMORER:

All's fair in war,
and war's what I'm in love with.
All's bare in war--
But soldiers I just hug with.

HONORABLE MR. CHAIRMAN: So may I ask you, Colonel, to
search your military mind for a moment, ransack it if you please,
and ask yourself whether you find any socially redeeming
value in all the homos who seem to keep coming out of the
woodwork--or whatever it is they come out of? Would you give
me your considered opinion, sir, before we decide finally what
to do with them--before we decide to quarantine them, for
instance, or somehow, discreetly, send them to an early
grave? Before we do anything rash, I would like to know how you
would handle homos in terms of the military interests of our great
nation's manhood.

COLONEL ARMORER:

The laws against sodomy must be obeyed:
Keep sphincters shut, all labia splayed;
So boyz n real manhood
Will target girlz maid'nhood
And never forget how the man gang gets laid.

The problem with homos is not that they score;
In principle peckers are merrier the more.
But when lads dodge lasses
In quest of male asses,
They violate space that a nobody's for.

This peril to manhood is militar'ly clear;
We must not concede it's OK to be queer.
Yet I have discerned
There is much to be learned
From watching what happens when men fuck a peer.

Manhood is nothing if not vive la différence,
And person to person you might lack that inference.
If women get equal,
The logical sequel
Might need to resemble same-sex sexual violence.

If a homo's been trained to love manhood enough,
You can learn from the ways that he stuffs his stuff--
For instance, fist-fucking
And deep-throated thrusting
Are tools you can use when a slut needs it rough.

Just because manhood must always be proved
Does not mean that manhood cannot be improved.
So don't go ballistic
At gay sex sadistic;
It offers new ways that the earth can be moved.

Of course we could make the pink army lose;
We could send them to death just like the Jews.
But don't rush to gas 'em--
Watch homos do S-M:
Their self-hate can spin off hot options to choose!

THE HONORABLE MR. CHAIRMAN: I see, Colonel. I had
not myself previously contemplated that socially redeeming
value, but I shall certainly have to take a look now that you mention it. I trust I do not have to go far out of my way to take such
a look. And I assume you are recommending--purely in the
military interests of our nation's manhood--that homo porno
of the sadomasochistic sort be allowed to proliferate alongside
normal bondage and discipline. You are a credit to your military
training, Colonel, and your stealthy devotion to our nation's
manhood is impressive and inspiring. I shall keep your fine
words in mind should my beloved dear wife ever become too
tempted by sexual equality, heh-heh.

[Laughter.]

COLONEL ARMORER:

The stigma on queers calls for celebration;
It's truly a boon for the sake of our nation.
It keeps men in dread
Of being equal in bed,
So they'll work out their terror through copulation.

From my point of view, the best motivation
For hetero sex is the realization
That though we're all queer

Men can always steer clear
By banging vaginas in desperation.

HONORABLE MR. CHAIRMAN: I see. Very interesting. I had not
considered my intimate relations with my dear wife in quite
such a light before. Very interesting, indeed. I hope she
does not get it into her pretty little head to read your remarks
here today, heh-heh.

     [No laughter.]

But may I continue in my line of questioning, Colonel? I
was asking you about the homo problem, not the heterosexual
problem. And the question that occurs to me next is this: What
about homos who are so far from warrior material that
they have no sexual preference for sexual torture? I am
speaking of homos who are so queer, they cannot physically get
it up to cause anyone any pain. I realize such a defect is unthink-
able to you, Colonel, in your noble line of work. Such a per-
version insults the very foundation of manhood everywhere.
Nevertheless, I have it on good authority that there are some very
pathetic perverts out there, and violence does not turn them on
any more than does a nice pair of tits and a gash. So have
you given any thought, Colonel, as to what we should do
with them? Can these sexual oddities make any contribution to
manhood whatsoever?

COLONEL ARMORER:

To really love manhood if one is a fairy,
One has to get over whatever is scary--
Work out that soft bod,
And pump up that rod,
And joke about tits so you won't be called Mary.

When growing up homo a boy sure feels weird;
The manhood he lacks won't grow in with his beard.
He fears it's his hormones,
Until he finds porno
That shows being gay's not as sick as he feared.

Gay porno can help him have manhood his own:
Those pecs in the pics, firm buns, a long bone;
True manhood though various

Is <u>always</u> vicarious,
So stroking to photos he's never alone.


Homos need porno because it can heal ya;
Now more than ever because they might feel a
Panic come on--
Their buddies are gone!--
But porno is handy, like necrophilia.


HONORABLE MR. CHAIRMAN: Thank you, Colonel, for your
most charitable comments on homo self-acceptance, but
that is not the subject of our inquiry. I realize that homos need
porno in order to experience their own pathetic rendition of manhood, especially during these dispiriting plague years--when
only homos on video can play on and on anymore. But you
have not convinced me that these softhearted, limp-fisted homo
types can be of any use to our nation's <u>manhood</u>.


COLONEL ARMORER:


'Tis true that some homos may feel isolation;
'Tis true that some homos may feel alienation
From selfhood abandoned
When manhood commanded
To hate their femme flesh for the sake of our nation.


Although they are sissies of boybods quite fond,
They're certainly more than entitled to bond:
The tension they work off
Whenever they jerk off
Could be of some use to keep women well conned.


Whenever men's manhood just seems to be hanging,
Or when women's anger might need some defanging,
The joint chiefs and I
Have a strategy sly:
Promulgation of porn--it's as good as gang-banging.


We never intended to leave gay guys out
Of the loyal estrangement that manhood's about.
Gays have certain know-how;
Their porno can show how
To take turns playing stud, with fair turnabout.

Although now and then they get fucked in the end,
Their manners confirm that they'll bond like real men,
'Cause deep in their trenches
They prove they're not wenches
Like the bitches for sale in the porn they defend.

Though fags do not fancy to punt through the hoop
That men have traditionally used when we schtup,
We've learned that we love it
When fairies say "Shove it"
To all of the women that porn helps us dupe.

For manhood to prosper from top to the bottom
Our nation requires that we honor Deep Bob an'
Give thanks one and all for
The lies we must fall for--
Especially porno, which shows that we've bought 'em.

In fairness the fairies make their contribution
Whenever they dance in their doomed revolution
And sell out their sisters
who're porno resisters,
In order to bond in men's next evolution.

So to arms, straight and gay, to armaments brave!
To war and sure victory over the grave!
With porno to guide us
And Bob deep inside us
No man will go gentle to any dark cave!

HONORABLE MR. CHAIRMAN: I see, Colonel. Well, speaking
for myself, I must say I have found this hearing very, very interesting. Coach "Irony" John has testified that the very sexual
functioning of our nation's manhood depends upon more
and more porno. Mister Mann, likewise, has argued that
harmonious relations among various social strata of our nation's
manhood depend upon more and more porno. Your own vivid testimony, Colonel, persuades me that not only our military
posture, but our underlying hold on heterosexual manhood
itself, depends upon more and more porno. And you go so far
as to predict that some team-player homos might like to cooperate
with us normal men--to expand our sexual horizons and
help us lash back more effectively. I realize we have not
been lashing back like we should. And I appreciate your novel
idea, Colonel, that maybe in cahoots with homos, we can keep

ownables in line once and for all by jointly expanding the
porno trade. Where I come from, we take a more conservative
approach, of course; we don't talk so down-to-earth in front
of our ownables; the very notion of buying sex is one we don't
even care to whisper. Although I know what you fellows are talking about, don't get me wrong--I myself know the location
of just about every cathouse in my home state. But I sure
as heck don't tell my press secretary when I'm about to make
a call! Perhaps times have changed. Perhaps manhood is not as
simple as once it was. Perhaps I and my fellow commissioners
need to reconsider some of our outmoded positions, for the
security of our blessed nation, for the virility of our invincible
manhood. I am much obliged, gentlemen, for your expertise and
wisdom and for all the light you have shed. My eyes, I feel,
have truly been opened--and now this hearing on the state
of our nation's manhood is temporarily adjourned, so that I may
relieve myself. Would you please pass me my attaché case over
there? Thank you kindly. Long live Deep Bob!

VOICES FROM HEARINGS CHAMBERS: Long live Deep Bob!

WITHOUT PORNOGRAPHY,
THERE COULD BE NO MANHOOD--
AND HUMANS WOULD DESIRE
TO EMBRACE SEXUAL SELFHOOD
INSTEAD.

# EPILOG: THE END OF MEN

In 1923—the year of Hitler's first putsch in Munich—Martin Buber, then a forty-five-year-old German Jew teaching religion in Frankfurt, published a book of philosophy called *Ich und Du* ("I and You"). In this profound and prophetic work, Buber enunciates what he calls "man's twofold attitude": the difference between saying "I" to "You" and saying "I" to "It." "The basic word I-You can only be spoken with one's whole being," Buber explains. "The basic word I-It can never be spoken with one's whole being." Buber characterizes this latter relational act as "experiencing and using." But in beholding one's encounter with "You," and in speaking one's "I" to that "You," one's whole being becomes transformed:

> The You encounters me by grace—it cannot be found by seeking. But that I speak the basic word to it [I-You] is a deed of my whole being, is my essential deed.
>
> The You encounters me. But I enter into a direct relationship to it. Thus the relationship is election and electing, passive and active at once....
>
> The basic word I-You can be spoken only with one's whole being. The concentration and fusion into a whole being can never be accomplished by me, can never be

accomplished without me. I require a You to become; becoming I, I say You.

All actual life is encounter.*

Unlike Dr. Jekyll, the fictional physician who believed his "profound duplicity of life" to be metaphysical, or in men's nature, Buber sees "man's twofold attitude" as a matter of interpersonal ethics.

A close reading of Buber's text today reveals that, here and there, he tried to include in his pellucid insight the nitty-gritty of genderizing human relations. "When He or She takes the place of It," he writes for instance, one's "I" nevertheless speaks the basic word "I-It."† Further, "As long as love is 'blind'—that is, as long as it does not see a whole being—it does not yet truly stand under the basic word of relation [I-You]."‡ Buber even refers to the ruse of the prototypical roué, who says "You" but means "It": "After all, producing the sound 'You' with one's vocal cords does not by any means entail speaking the uncanny basic word [I-You]. Even whispering an amorous You with one's soul is hardly dangerous as long as in all seriousness one means nothing but experiencing and using."§

Buber's unremittingly humane vision escaped with him in 1938, when, targeted as the Nazis' "It," Buber departed to Jerusalem, where he taught social philosophy at Hebrew University until 1951.

✧

I first read *Ich und Du* more than twenty years ago, but it did not much come to mind again until I was very near the end of writing *The End of Manhood*, when I realized I had unconsciously borrowed Buber's concept of "I-You." I had renamed it the two-way truth of selfhood: your sense of yourself as a real human self that can only come from recognizing and regarding some-

---

*Martin Buber, *I and Thou*, translated by Walter Kaufmann (New York: Charles Scribner's Sons, 1970), p. 62. (*Du* in German is the familiar second-person pronoun one speaks informally. There is no such distinctively intimate "you" in English, although "thou" still has this everyday meaning among a few religious sects—where, for instance, "Thee I love" means "I love you.")

†Buber, p. 53.
‡Buber, pp. 67–68.
§Buber, p. 85.

one else as a real human self also; your sense of yourself as a real human self that can only come from being recognized and regarded by someone else as a real human self also.

Or, as I had inadvertently restated Buber yet again: you are never more real than when someone else is real to you.

Manhood is a lie—the biggest myth of all. You can meaningfully inhabit the manhood "I" only in the act of addressing someone as "You who are less than me"—or only by saying to someone, somehow, "To me, you are closer to nobody. To me you are an it." Whenever anyone born with a penis asks himself, "What does this manhood sham mean for *me*?" he reaches a far more personally useful answer than when he asks, "But what must this mean for *other men*?" Asking the question to include "other men" merely holds out false hope for cohesion with true believers of the lie.

The radical feminist critique of gender has made possible an epochal insight into sexuality and personal identity. Today humans have the opportunity and challenge to begin to live life free of the manhood sham. Instead of feeling ashamed of the difference between oneself and the specifications of this fictitious "sex," someone born penised can now begin to *honor* that difference. Instead of a lifetime indentured to gender, we now may freely find ourselves relationally with *a sexual selfhood that is worth having.*

"The male sex" is a political and ethical construction. We construct it socially and personally through our decisions, our institutions, our public policies, our theologies. There is no mythic deep masculinity. There is in nature no absolute division of the human species into two sexes. The male sex is an abstract fiction. Penises exist. The male sex does not. Our subjective experience of "the male sex" originates in our acts, not our anatomy. Belonging to "the male sex" means a birthright entitlement to treat other humans as if they are "It"—not as real as one's manhood "I." Behavioral *dominance* creates the difference that we assume exists between "the sexes." But there are *not* "two and only two sexes." There are as many "sexes" as there are people, and each one can be what Buber calls "the innate

You"—an "I" who, in "the current of reciprocity," can speak the basic word "I-You."

The cutting-edge question for the next millennium is this: Why must human experience be "gendered" at all? Why must *any human* continue feeling the urgency to keep manhood feeling "real"—to distinguish themself from various "Its" and "nobodies" by perpetuating injustice? Why must we tolerate any longer the injustice that is intrinsically required in order to shore up the manhood "I"?

Answering this question privately and publicly will become the most radically liberatory project in human history. It promises to deconstruct injustice at its very root and reveal a unified theory of all oppression.

How you choose to have a personal self ultimately has political consequences. One cannot possibly and positively be "the man there" without somebody underneath. Nor can one be "white" or "Aryan" without personally helping to keep the category "real" by helping to keep selected others outside it or put down. Any personal identity that is premised on identification with a dominant social category is also premised on inequality and disidentification. And "biological superiority" truly is, in Andrea Dworkin's words, "the world's most dangerous and deadly idea."*

Manhood is a personal and social hoax that exists only through interpersonal and social injustice. Manhood is the *paradigm* of injustice. *Refusing to believe* in manhood is the personal and ethical stance of resistance to all injustice done in its name. And refusing to accept the manhood imperative—the lie that there *must* be a "male sex" to "belong" to—is a personal and political principle of revolutionary liberation beyond any amplitude we can now possibly imagine.

Refusing to believe in manhood is the hot big bang of human freedom.

✧

Many people earnestly believe that manhood can be redefined, reformed, revitalized, some essence salvaged, some archetype

---

*The phrase is from the title of an essay collected in Dworkin's *Letters from a War Zone* (Chicago: Lawrence Hill Books, 1993).

accessed, some fairy tale retold, some divinity embodied, some ether inhaled. It cannot.

Some people caution that men as a group won't clean up their act, or alter their egocentric behavior, or take any responsibility for fundamental social change, because manhood offers men too many creature comforts and perks. "Guilt-tripping" and "man-blaming" will not inspire meaningful change, some people argue, because there's no motivation for men as men to act differently. There's no carrot, there's only stick. And this is true. "For men as men" *there can never be any other incentive than to try with all their might to experience themselves "as men."*

I realize I am only one individual, only one human being on earth right now, and I cannot presume to speak for what all "men as a group" will say or do or think. Good. I don't *have* to. And most important, I know I don't *want* to.

By some lucky fluke I live in the era begun by the radical feminist critique of gender,* and I can now try to articulate what I know personally—from the inside of my own life—about what it has meant to try to accommodate to manhood's demands. And I can now begin to realize the difference—in my own life— between "acting in one's self-interest" and "acting in the interest of *one's own best self.*"

"Acting in one's self-interest" means exactly what it says: you make your choices based on your calculation of whatever personal payoff you expect to get. Acting "self-interestedly" implies *selfishness* or *one-upmanship,* acting in ways that *dis*advantage someone else in order to advantage *oneself.* Acting in one's self-interest implies a kind of ruthless individualism, being out only for oneself, being capable of any manipulation or derogation to make someone else look bad—so as to be rewarded with a boost to one's sense of "self."

In conventional wisdom, the alternative to such individualism is "altruism" or "collectivism." Both imply *selflessness*— "altruism" because it entails rather thoroughgoing deference to the needs of someone else, and "collectivism" because it entails anonymously serving, and blending into, some group identity. Anthropologists have studied a variety of human societies to try

*Which encountered me by grace when I read Andrea Dworkin's first book, *Woman Hating* (New York: Dutton, 1974).

to understand both altruism and collectivism, in hopes of finding feasible alternatives to war, rape, imperialism, and other no-
toriously "self-interested" behaviors.

Either you can be all out "for yourself" (selfishly)—they
say—or else you can be all out "for someone else" or "for some
identifiable group" (selflessly). This conventional view is very
flawed. It remains locked into transactions that are both gendered and genderizing.

Ruthless individualism not only names a *quality* that is cul-
turally "masculine"; it describes *the set of transactions* that
construct manhood—behavioral choices through which one ac-
cumulates a history in which it makes sense to speak a
manhood "I." The personal identity that results—the sense of
so-called self as a so-called man—depends structurally on discounting the reality of *other selves*. "I-It" is the only word in
manhood's relational vocabulary.

"Acting in the interest of one's own best self" expresses a
truth about the personal moral identity that is *selfhood*: "Acting
in the interest of one's own best self" is acting in conscience
with a complete and passionate commitment to the selfhood of
others. Selfhood does not depend on discounting the reality of
others in order to be real; selfhood experiences its own reality
only through acts that affirm the reality of other people, irrespective of social gender or any *other* hierarchical category. Selfhood can speak the basic word "I-You."

The difference between "self-interest" and "the interest of
one's own best self" is a subtle shift in language but a seismic
shift in the map of human possibility.

This shift has profound implications, particularly for someone raised to be a man: It means that the way to feel better
about oneself is not to try to feel better about oneself "as a
man." It means, Don't try to redeem manhood. It means, Don't
let manhood—and other men's judgment on you—determine
your life. Instead, the way to feel better about yourself as a *self*
is to live conscientiously as an ally of everyone's selfhood including your own. It means becoming personally and politically
committed to ending all interpersonal injustice and all social
policies enacted to make manhood seem true.

You cannot really have a self without taking such responsibility. This means taking responsibility both for what you do and for what needs to be done.

Understanding what "manhood" really is—what sorts of interpersonal behaviors make the fiction seem fact—is essential for living a life not shamed by it, for choosing a life that does not buy into it, for living a life alert to moral sonority through connection, caring, companionship, intimacy, trust. One cannot *have* those experiences charging with hell-bent fury to assert and prove an identity that only exists in battle—that battles only exist for—and that only feels real when one regards someone else as less real. Nor can one live such a life in denial about one's own misogyny. The subjective sense of manhood—belonging as a real man among real men—has a fundamental, structural source in misogyny that is both cultural and individual. Decoding and deconstructing manhood thus means acknowledging—in conscience—that one is a recovering misogynist. For anyone raised to be a man, the life of loving justice does not begin before this point.

The loyalty oath we swear to manhood exacts a staggering price. For many humans born penised, the constant quest to be the man there, to be a man among real men, means being cut off from the most significant source of selfhood. Authentic, passionate, and integrated selfhood is centered in the possibility of acting as a moral agent, as a choice-maker, as someone who owns responsibility both for what one has done wrong and for what one has done right. This means taking responsibility for one's acts of *in*justice—acts of inequality, disidentification, dismissal, violence—as well one's acts of *justice*—*relocating* one's "I," paying attention to (and accumulating a history of) acts that express loving justice, not gender anxiety. You become such a selfhood "I" whenever you act out of your deep conviction that "You" and "We" are equally real. Only through acts whose consequences we stand behind do we ever stand side by side one another. Only then does the Revolution from Between stand a chance. And only then are any of us on this planet ever truly connected.

Selfhood is utterly contradicted by the demands of trying to stand as a man, trying to withstand manhood enough to pass, measured against a standard held out by other men. One cannot stay tuned to moral sonority—one cannot make ethical choices based on the reality of oneself and others—and at the same time acquiesce to the imperatives of manhood. Logically, therefore, the beginning of selfhood means the end of all one's deference to other men's judgment on one's "manhood," the end of one's compulsion to try to be "a real man," and the end of one's believing that "other men as men" have anything to say that is at all *relevant* to one's potential selfhood. The beginning of selfhood thus means the complete end of factoring the category "manhood" into any of one's personal decision-making: The beginning of selfhood means no longer paying obeisance to other men's judgment on your beholding your beloved (and so it means the end of sexual objectification). The beginning of selfhood means no longer allying with men as men on terms that disallow loyalty to other life (and so it means the end of male bonding). The beginning of selfhood means the full acceptance of all feelings between us consonant with moral sonority (and so it means the end of homophobia). And the beginning of selfhood means the mutual self-possession of our human sexuality (and so it means the flat-out rejection of commoditized sex).

For all practical purposes and in everyday, practical effect—in how one deliberates, in what one cares about, in the values one bases all one's relational choices upon—the beginning of selfhood means the end of men.

# ACKNOWLEDGMENTS

I have been remiss in not citing my intellectual forebears and personal mentors. Careful readers will note that my not referencing these sources within my text is at odds with this book's moral premise. My choice of this book's unconventional form allowed me freedom to dislodge conventional ways of thinking about gender and personal identity, but my essentially dramatic method would not allow me to disclose the thinkers whose lives and works had most inspired me and informed me. To find the conceptual underpinnings of this book (indeed, to find loving justice in my life and my own capacity for it), I had a lot of help. Here, specifically, are some of the teachers and teachings to whom my own personal moral and intellectual history—and consequently this book—is indebted.

**From my mid-teens to my early twenties:** Dietrich Bonhoeffer *(Life Together)*, the works of Bertolt Brecht, Vernon Faillettaz, Joseph Fletcher *(Situation Ethics)*, Erich Fromm *(The Art of Loving)*, the ancient Greek dramatists, Howard and Edna Hong, the works of Henrik Ibsen, the life and words of the historical Jesus, the life and works of Søren Kierkegaard, John A. Robinson *(Honest to God)*, the life and words of Socrates, Margaret and Vincent Stoltenberg, Paul Tillich *(The Courage to Be)*.

**From my early to late twenties:** Martin Buber *(I and Thou)*,

The Open Theatre (1971–74) and Joseph Chaikin *(The Presence of the Actor)*, Tom Driver, the works of Luigi Pirandello, the Prophets and the Writings, Bernard Steinzor *(The Healing Partnership)*, the Union Theological Seminary Black Students Caucus (1968–69).

**From my thirties to now:** Near the end of my twenties I came out, and I turned from playwriting (my passion till then) to writing nonfiction about issues of sexuality and politics. I did not yet know the word "feminism." I began by writing a book-length manuscript intended as a personal guide for boys about sex and fairness. In the process—thanks to considerate friends who knew me then—I realized how much of my own life and behavior contradicted my aspirations, and how much I had yet to learn. So in 1974, about to turn thirty, I abandoned that manuscript and began a new phase of my life. This next list mentions influences from this period that—to my mind—are especially evident in *The End of Manhood*. I know I have not remembered them all.

Ti-Grace Atkinson *(Amazon Odyssey)*, the life and works of James Baldwin, Kathleen Barry *(Female Sexual Slavery)*, Susan Brownmiller *(Against Our Will: Men, Women and Rape)*, the life and works of Barbara Deming, Phyllis Chesler *(About Men)*, Caryl Churchill *(Cloud Nine)*, Mary Daly *(Beyond God the Father)*, the life and works of Frederick Douglass, Andrea Dworkin *(Intercourse; Letters From a War Zone; Our Blood: Prophecies and Discourses on Sexual Politics; Pornography and Civil Rights: A New Day for Women's Equality* [coauthored with Catharine A. MacKinnon]; *Pornography: Men Possessing Women; Right-wing Women; Woman Hating)*, Shulamith Firestone *(The Dialectic of Sex)*, David Gilmore *(The Making of Manhood)*, Judith Lewis Herman *(Trauma and Recovery)*, Shere Hite *(The Hite Report: A Nationwide Study of Female Sexuality; Women and Love: A Cultural Revolution in Progress)*, Audre Lorde ("Black Women's Anger"; "Uses of the Erotic: The Erotic as Power"), Catharine A. MacKinnon *(Sexual Harassment of Working Women; Feminism Unmodified)*, John Stuart Mill and Harriet Taylor Mill (writings collected as *Essays on Sex Equality)*, Kate Millett *(Sexual Politics)*, Gloria Naylor ("Letter to Winston"), Joseph Pleck *(The Myths of Masculinity)*, Janice G. Raymond *(The Transsexual Empire: The Making of the She-Male)*, Emmanuel Reynaud *(Holy Virility: The Social Construction of Mas-*

*culinity)*, Diana E. H. Russell *(International Tribunal on Crimes Against Women)*, Peggy Reeves Sanday *(Fraternity Gang Rape: Sex, Brotherhood, and Privilege on Campus)*, Frederick Schauer ("Slippery Slopes"), Ntozake Shange *(Some Men; For Colored Girls Who Have Considered Suicide When the Rainbow Is Enuf)*, Gloria Steinem *(Revolution From Within)*, Anne Fausto-Sterling *(Myths of Gender)*, Susan L. Taylor ("In the Spirit"), Laurence Thomas *(Living Morally: A Psychology of Moral Character)*, Alice Walker ("Coming Apart," "Embracing the Dark and the Light"), Andrew Tolson *(The Limits of Masculinity: Male Identity and Women's Liberation)*, Monique Wittig *(The Straight Mind)*, Virginia Woolf *(Three Guineas)*, the life and works of Mary Wollstonecraft.

I thank Twiss and Pat Butler for their generosity as I wrote, and I thank those many friends and colleagues whose readings in draft have enriched this book as well.

My editor, Rachel Klayman, and her assistant, Jeremy Rosenholtz, have rescued me from misspeaking myself in ways both great and small, and I am deeply grateful to them.

My literary agent, Elaine Markson, has been a rock of strength and support.

The central philosophical project of both *Refusing to Be a Man* and *The End of Manhood*—to clarify that gender is an ethical category, not a metaphysical one—could not have been imagined apart from Andrea Dworkin's brave, blazingly brilliant, and compassionate intellection. The love and collaboration that she and I began to share in 1974 (when she had just published *Woman Hating)* have both sustained and challenged me.   —J.S.

## ABOUT THE AUTHOR

John Stoltenberg is the radical feminist author of *Refusing to Be a Man: Essays on Sex and Justice* (rev. edn, London and New York: UCL Press, 2000), *The End of Manhood: Parables on Sex and Selfhood* (rev. edn, London and New York: UCL Press, 2000), and *What Makes Pornography "Sexy"?* (Minneapolis, Minnesota: Milkweed Editions, 1994). He is cofounder of Men Against Pornography (www.geocities.com/CapitolHill/1139) and a frequent speaker and workshop leader at colleges and conferences (www.speakerspca.com). Born in Minneapolis, Minnesota, he graduated cum laude from St Olaf College majoring in philosophy and English, then received a master of divinity degree in theology and literature from Union Theological Seminary and an M.F.A. in theater arts from Columbia University School of the Arts. From 1981 to 1991 he was managing editor of three U.S. women's magazines—*Essence*, *Working Woman*, and *Lear's*. He has completed a young adult novel, *Goners*, and is at work on a book about the culture of sexual orientation. In collaboration with the composer Adam Sherburne, of the band Consolidated, he has written book and lyrics for a rock/hip-hop opera titled *Cocklash*. He has lived with the writer Andrea Dworkin since 1974. Their home is in New York City.

## ABOUT A RELATED VIDEO SERIES

*Sex and Selfhood: New Issues for Men of Conscience* is a series of frank, provocative video talks by John Stoltenberg, designed to open four issues of sexuality and personal identity for group discussion: sexual objectification, male bonding, homophobia, and pornography. The set of four 20-minute VHS videotapes comes with a *Facilitator's Guidebook* containing poster designs for outreach, interactive discussion guides, and reproducible worksheets. For purchase information contact Kundschier Video Design, 5305 Woodlawn Boulevard, Minneapolis, Minnesota 55417, tel. 888–558–6823 (toll-free in North America), fax 612–728–1028.